Modeling
Reactive Systems
with Statecharts

Other McGraw-Hill Books in the Software Development Series

HERKOMMER • *Number Theory: A Programmer's Guide*   00-07-913074-7

JONES • *Applied Software Measurement*   0-07-032826-9

JONES • *Estimating Software Costs*   0-07-913094-1

JONES • *Handbook of Team Design*   0-07-032880-3

LOSHIN • *Efficient Memory Programming*   0-07-038868-7

MUSA • *Software Reliability Engineering*   0-07-913271-5

SODHI/SODHI • *Software Reuse: Domain Analysis and Design Processes* 0-07-057923-7

To order or receive additional information on these or any other McGraw-Hill titles, in the United States call 1-800-722-4726, or visit us at www.computing.mcgraw-hill.com. In other countries, contact your local McGraw-Hill representative.

Modeling Reactive Systems with Statecharts

The STATEMATE Approach

David Harel and Michal Politi

McGraw-Hill

New York   San Francisco   Washington, D.C.   Auckland   Bogotá
Caracas   Lisbon   London   Madrid   Mexico City   Milan
Montreal   New Delhi   San Juan   Singapore
Sydney   Tokyo   Toronto

Library of Congress Cataloging-in-Publication Data

Harel, David, 1950–
    Modeling reactive systems with statecharts : the statemate approach
    David Harel, Michal Politi.
        p.   cm.
    Includes index.
    ISBN 0-07-026205-5
    1. System design. 2. Computer software—Development.
    3. Statecharts (Computer science) 4. Object-oriented programming
    (Computer science) I. Politi, Michal. II. Title.
    QA76.9.S88H3677 1998
    005.1'2—dc21   98-17831
                                                                     CIP

McGraw-Hill

*A Division of The **McGraw·Hill** Companies*

1 2 3 4 5 6 7 8 9 0 DOC/DOC 9 0 3 2 1 0 9 8

ISBN 0-07-026205-5

The sponsoring editor of this book was Simon Yates. The editing supervisor was Ruth Mannino, and the production supervisor was Clare Stanley. It was set in New Century Schoolbook by Kim Sheran and Paul Scozzari of McGraw-Hill's Professional Book Group Hightstown composition unit.

Printed and bound by R. R. Donnelley & Sons Company.

McGraw-Hill books are available at special quantity discounts to use as premiums and sales promotions, or for use in corporate training programs. For more information, please write to the Director of Special Sales, McGraw-Hill, 11 West 19th Street, New York, NY 10011. Or contact your local bookstore.

 This book is printed on recycled, acid-free paper containing a minimum of 50% recycled, de-inked fiber.

For our dear parents,

*Joyce and Harold Fisch
and the late Zvi and Lena Frenkel*

With love and respect

Contents

Preface

This book provides a detailed description of a comprehensive set of languages for modeling reactive systems. The approach is dominated by the language of Statecharts, which is used to describe behavior, combined with Activity-charts, which are used for describing the system's activities (i.e., its functional building blocks, capabilities, and objects) and the data that flows between them. These two languages are used to develop a conceptual model of the system, which can be combined with the system's physical, or structural, model described in our third language, Module-charts. These three languages are highly diagrammatic in nature, constituting full-fledged visual formalisms, complete with rigorous semantics. They are accompanied by a Data Dictionary for specifying additional parts of the model that are textual in nature.

The approach described here lies at the heart of the STATEMATE system, which the authors have helped design and build at I-Logix, Inc. since 1984. STATEMATE is most beneficial in requirements analysis, specification, and high-level design. In addition to supporting the modeling effort using the aforementioned language set, STATEMATE provides powerful tools for inspecting and analyzing the resulting models, via model execution, dynamic testing, and code synthesis.

This book discusses the modeling languages in detail, with an emphasis on the language of Statecharts, because it is the most important and intricate language in the set and the most novel. Statecharts are used to specify the behavior of activities, whether they represent functions in a functional decomposition or objects in an object decomposition. We describe the syntax in a precise and complete manner and discuss the semantics in a way that is intended to render the model's behavior clear and intuitive. Our presentation is illustrated extensively with examples, most of which come from a single sample model of an early warning system (EWS). Appendix B provides a summarized description of this model.

Whenever possible, we have tried to explain our motivation in including the various features of the languages. We also provide hints and guidelines on such methodological issues as decomposition criteria and the order in which charts are to be developed.

While we do provide a brief description of the STATEMATE system in Sec. 1.4, this book is not intended to be a user manual for it but, rather, a definitive description of its languages and a guide to their use. For more on STATEMATE's capabilities, we refer the reader to the documentation supplied by I-Logix, Inc.

This book should be of interest to a wide variety of systems developers (both in software and hardware) and to teachers and students of software and hardware engineering.

Acknowledgments

Thanks are due to Jonah Lavi for initiating David Harel's interest in this area in 1983, an interest that led to the invention of the Statecharts language. The other two languages, Activity-charts and Module-charts, and the ways they are integrated with Statecharts, were developed by the authors together with several people, predominantly Rivi Sherman and Amir Pnueli. We would also like to express our deep gratitude to the many other extremely talented and dedicated people at I-Logix Israel, Ltd., led with insight, wisdom, and sensitivity by Ido and Hagi Lachover, for conceptualizing, designing, and building the STATEMATE tool.

Introduction

This chapter describes the role of models in a system development life cycle and characterizes reactive systems, the ones for which the languages of this book are particularly suited. It then introduces the early warning system (EWS), a reactive system that we shall use as a running example throughout the book. It also presents an overview of the modeling languages and a brief description of the STATEMATE toolset, which was built around the language of Statecharts and which supports the modeling process and provides means for executing and analyzing the models, synthesizing code from them, and more.

1.1 System Development and Methodologies

We first describe the background for our work and the context in which our modeling languages fit.

1.1.1 Specification in a system life cycle

It is common practice to identify several phases in the development life cycle of a system, each of which involves certain processes and tasks that have to be carried out by the development team. The main phases of the classic waterfall model (Royce 1970) are *requirements analysis, and specification, design, implementation, testing,* and *maintenance.* Over the past 20 years, many variations of this model were proposed, as well as quite different approaches to the life cycle (Dorfman and Thayer 1990b). Some center around prototyping, incremental development, reusable software, or automated synthesis.

Most proposals for system development life cycle patterns contain a requirements analysis phase. Correcting specification errors and misconceptions that are discovered during later stages of the system's life cycle is extremely expensive, so it is commonly agreed that thorough comprehension of the system and its behavior should be carried out as early as possible. Special languages are therefore used in the requirements analysis phase to specify a model of the system, and special techniques are used to analyze it extensively. As described later, we advocate various kinds of analyses, including model execution and code synthesis. In this book, we shall use the terms *model* and *specification* interchangeably.

The availability of a good model is important for all participants in the system's development. If a clear and executable model is constructed early on, customers and subcontractors, for example, can become acquainted with it, and can approve of the functionality and behavior of the system before investing heavily in the implementation stages. Creating precise and detailed models is also in the best interest of the system's designers and testers. Clearly, the specification team itself uses modeling as the main medium for expressing ideas and exploits the resulting models in analyzing the feasibility of the specification. Chapter 16 contains more about the ways our models can be used for later stages of development.

1.1.2 Development methodologies and supporting tools

A term commonly used in connection with the development process is *methodology*. A methodology provides guidelines for performing the processes that comprise the various phases. Concentrating on the modeling and analysis phase, we may say that a methodology consists of the following components:

- The methodology's *underlying approach* and the *concepts* it uses, that is, the terms and notions used to capture the conceptual construct of the system and to analyze it.

- The *notation* used, that is, the modeling languages with their syntax and semantics. Sometimes these contain constructs that are sufficiently generic to be relevant to several different concepts of the underlying approach.

- The *process* prescribed by the methodology, that is, which activities have to be carried out to apply the methodology and in what order, how does the work progress from one activity to the next, and what are the intermediate outputs or products of each. The methodology usually also provides heuristics for making the process more beneficial.

- The computerized *tools* that can be used to help in the process.

This book is mainly about notation, in that it describes a set of modeling languages and illustrates their use. However, it also describes several concepts and notions that underly a number of development methodologies. Thus, while our approach to modeling and analysis is not necessarily connected to any particular methodology, it is more compatible with some methodologies than with others (just as flexible programming languages can be used with very different program design and implementation methods but might be more fitting for some specific ones). In particular, our approach can be used smoothly with variants of Structured Analysis (DeMarco 1978; Military Standard 1988) as well as with other methodologies, such as object-oriented analysis. Moreover, although the book does not get into the details of any particular methodological process, we do describe the STATEMATE set of tools (from I-Logix, Inc.) later in the chapter. STATEMATE can be used in conjunction with several relevant methodologies to apply our modeling and analysis approach, and implements all features of the languages described in the book.

1.2 Modeling Reactive Systems

As explained above, the heart of the specification stage is the construction of the system model. In this section we discuss the overall nature and structure of models, thus preparing for the subject matter of the book, which involves the modeling languages themselves. However, we should first say something about the kinds of systems we are interested in.

1.2.1 The nature of reactive systems

Our modeling approach, particularly the Statecharts language, is especially effective for reactive systems (Harel and Pnueli 1985; Manna and Pnueli 1992), the behavior of which can be very complex, causing the specification problem to be notoriously elusive and error-prone. Most real-time systems, for example, are reactive in nature.

A typical reactive system exhibits the following distinctive characteristics:

- It continuously interacts with its environment, using inputs and outputs that are either continuous in time or discrete. The inputs and outputs are often asynchronous, meaning that they may arrive or change values unpredictably at any point in time.[1]

---

[1]This should be contrasted with *transformational systems,* in which the timing of the inputs and outputs is much more predictable. A transformational system repeatedly waits for all its inputs to arrive, carries out some processing, and outputs the results when the processing is done.

- It must be able to respond to interrupts, that is, high-priority events, even when it is busy doing something else.

- Its operation and reaction to inputs often reflects stringent time requirements.

- It has many possible operational scenarios, depending on the current mode of operation and the current values of its data as well as its past behavior.

- It is very often based on interacting processes that operate in parallel.

Examples of reactive systems include on-line interactive systems, such as automatic teller machines (ATMs) and flight reservation systems; computer-embedded systems, such as avionics, automotive, and telecommunication systems; and control systems, such as chemical and manufacturing systems.

1.2.2   An example: The early warning system

Many of the characteristics mentioned earlier are present in the simple early warning system (EWS) that we use as an example throughout this book to illustrate the ideas and features of the languages. The EWS monitors a signal arriving from outside, checks whether its value is in some predefined range, and if not, notifies the operator by an alarm and appropriate messages. This is a general kind of system, the likes of which can be found in a variety of applications. Here is a brief informal description of the EWS that will become useful for understanding the details later on:

> The EWS receives a signal from an external sensor. When the sensor is connected, the EWS processes the signal and checks if the resulting value is within a specified range. If the value of the processed signal is out of range, the system issues a warning message on the operator display and posts an alarm. If the operator does not respond to this warning within a given time interval, the system prints a fault message on a printing facility and stops monitoring the signal. The range limits are set by the operator. The system becomes ready to start monitoring the signal only after the range limits are set. The limits can be redefined after an out-of-range situation has been detected or after the operator has deliberately stopped the monitoring.

See Fig. 1.1 for the schematic structure of the EWS.

1.2.3   Characteristics of models

A system model constitutes a tangible representation of the system's conceptual and physical properties and serves as a vehicle for the specifier and designer to capture their thoughts. In some ways, it is like the set of plans drawn by an architect to describe a house. It is used mainly

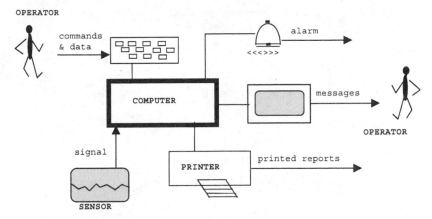

Figure 1.1 The early warning system (EWS).

for communication, but it should also facilitate inspection and analysis. The modeling process involves conceiving the elements relevant to the system and the relationships between them and representing them using specific, well-defined languages. When the model reflects some preexisting descriptions, such as requirements written in natural language, it is useful to keep track of how the components of the developing model are derived from the earlier descriptions.

To achieve the goal of enabling systems developers to model a system, our modeling languages have been designed with several important properties in mind: to be intuitive and clear, to be precise, to be comprehensive, and to be fully executable. To achieve clarity, elements of the model are represented graphically wherever possible; for example, nested box shapes are used to depict hierarchies of elements, and arrows are used for flow of data and control. For precision, all languages features have rigorous mathematical semantics, which is a prerequisite for carrying out meaningful analysis. Comprehension comes from the fact that the languages have the full expressive power needed to model all relevant issues, including the what, the when, and the how. As for executabilty, the behavioral semantics is detailed and rigorous enough to enable the model to be both executed directly, like a computer program, and to be translated into running code for prototyping and even for implementation purposes.

1.2.4 Modeling views of reactive systems

Building a model can be considered as a transition from ideas and informal descriptions to concrete descriptions that use concepts and predefined terminology. In our approach, the descriptions used to capture the system specification are organized into three views, or projections, of the system: the *functional,* the *behavioral,* and the *structural.* See Fig. 1.2.

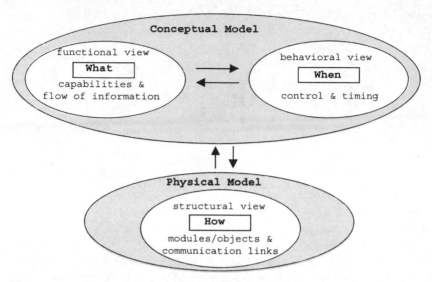

Figure 1.2 The three specification views.

The *functional view* captures the "what." It describes the system's functions, processes, or objects, also called activities, thus pinning down its capabilities. This view also includes the inputs and outputs of the activities, that is, the flow of information to and from the external environment of the system as well as the information flowing among the internal activities. For example, the activities of the EWS include sampling the input signal, comparing the read signal value with the predefined limits, and generating an alarm. The information flows in the EWS include the signal that flows from the external sensor, the operator commands that are input from the operator console, and the message and alarm notification that are output to the operator.

The *behavioral view* captures the "when." It describes the system's behavior over time, including the dynamics of activities, their control and timing behavior, the states and modes of the system, and the conditions and events that cause modes to change and other occurrences to take place. It also provides answers to questions about causality, concurrency, and synchronization. In the EWS example, the behavioral view might identify those states in which the system is waiting for commands, processing the signal, generating an alarm, or setting up new limit values. The behavioral view would also identify the events that cause transitions between these states. For example, it would specify what causes the system to generate an alarm or when the processing stops and the set-up procedure starts. Hence, it specifies precisely when the activities described in the functional view are active, and when the information actually flows between them.

There is a tight connection between the functional and behavioral views. Activities and data-flow need dynamic control to come to life, but the behavioral aspects are all but worthless if they have nothing to control. Technically, each activity in the functional view can be provided with a behavioral description given in the behavioral view, whose role it is to control the activity's internal parts, that is, its subactivities and their flow of information.

The *structural view* captures the "how." It describes the subsystems, modules, or objects constituting the real system and the communication between them. The EWS could be specified in the structural view to consist of an operator monitor, a control and computation unit, a signal processor, an alarm generator, and so on.

While the two former views provide the *conceptual model* of the system, the structural view is considered to be its *physical model,* because it concerns itself with the various aspects of the system's implementation. As a consequence, the conceptual model usually involves terms and notions borrowed from the problem domain, whereas the physical model draws more upon the solution domain.

The main connection between the conceptual and physical models is captured by specifying the modules of the structural view that are responsible for implementing the activities in the functional view. For example, the EWS activity that compares the input signal with the predefined limit values is implemented in the control and computation unit.

1.2.5 Modeling heuristics

Modeling heuristics are guidelines for how the notation should be used to model the system. This involves several issues, such as:

- The mapping between the methodology's concepts and the elements allowed in the notation. If the notation is flexible and its constructs can be used to depict several different concepts, this mapping has to be defined carefully.

- The type of decomposition to be used. Some possibilities are decompositions that are function based, object based, mode based, module based, or scenario based. The type chosen depends, in general, on the conceptual base of the methodology, although within a given methodology there is often some flexibility, according to the nature of the system and the role the model will play in the overall development effort. In the context of our notation, this issue is mainly relevant to the functional view and will be discussed further in Chap. 2.

- The step-by-step order of the modeling process. Which view are we to start with? Should we be working in a bottom-up or top-down fashion? Again, this is an issue that mostly depends on the methodology, but it is also affected by what is already known about the system.

```
    Activity: PROCESS_SIGNAL
    Defined in Chart: EWS_ACTIVITIES

    Termination Type: Reactive Controlled
    Mini-spec: st/TICK;;
    TICK/ $SIGNAL_VALUE:=SIGNAL;
          SAMPLE:=COMPUTE($SIGNAL_VALUE);
          sc!(TICK,SAMPLE_INTERVAL)
```

Figure 1.5   An activity entry in the Data Dictionary.

1.3.2   Statecharts

Statecharts (Harel 1987b) constitute an extensive generalization of state-transition diagrams. They allow for multilevel states decomposed in an and/or fashion, and thus support economical specification of concurrency and encapsulation. They incorporate a broadcast communication mechanism, timeout and delay operators for specifying synchronization and timing information, and a means for specifying transitions that depend on the history of the system's behavior.

Figure 1.6 contains a statechart taken from the EWS model. It consists of a top-level state EWS_CONTROL, which is decomposed into two substates. One of the substates, ON, is decomposed into two parallel behavioral components, MONITORING and PROCESSING; each of these is further decomposed into exclusive states. This means that the system must be in two states simultaneously, each from a different component. For example, when the statechart starts, the system is in WAITING_FOR_COMMAND and in DISCONNECTED. The chart also depicts events that cause transitions, such as ALARM_TIME_PASSED, which causes the system to go from the GENERATING_ALARM state to WAITING_FOR_COMMAND, and RESET, which causes the system to leave both COMPARING and GENERATING_ALARM and enter WAITING _FOR_COMMAND. Some transitions are guarded by conditions, such as the one from WAITING_FOR_COMMAND to COMPARING, which is taken when the event EXECUTE occurs but only if the condition in(CONNECTED) is true, namely, the system is in the CONNECTED state of the SAMPLING component. Some transition labels contain actions, which are to be carried out when the transitions are taken. For example, when moving from COMPARING to GENERATING_ALARM the system sends a HALT signal to the PROCESSING component.

Here, too, each element in the statechart has an entry in the Data Dictionary, which may contain additional information. For example, an event entity can be used to define a compound event by an expression involving other events and conditions. Statecharts are discussed in Chaps. 4, 5, and 6.

1.3.3 Module-charts

A module-chart can also be regarded as a certain kind of data-flow diagram or block diagram. Module-charts are used to describe the modules that constitute the implementation of the system, its division into hardware and software blocks and their inner components, and the communication between them.

Figure 1.7 shows a module-chart for the EWS. It contains internal modules, such as the control and computation unit (CCU), the SIGNAL_PROCESSOR, and the OPERATOR_MONITOR. The latter module contains the submodules KEYBOARD and SCREEN. (Here, too, the hierarchy of modules is depicted by encapsulation.) The module-chart also contains environment modules, such as OPERATOR and SENSOR, and it is noteworthy that these are similar to the external activities depicted in the functional view. The communication signals between modules include KEY_PRESSING from the OPERATOR to the KEYBOARD, the ALARM_SIGNAL from the CCU to the ALARM_SYSTEM, and so on.

Elements of the module-charts also have entries in the Data Dictionary, in which additional information can be specified.

Module-charts are described in Chap. 9.

1.3.4 Relationships between the languages

The relationships between the concepts of the three views are reflected in corresponding connections between the three modeling languages.

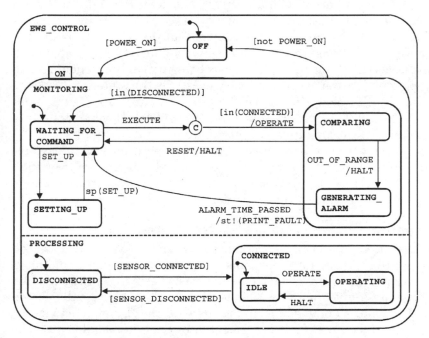

Figure 1.6 A statechart.

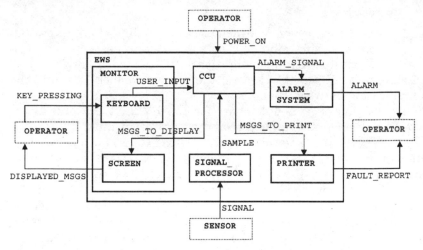

Figure 1.7 A module-chart.

Most of these connections are provided in the Data Dictionary, and they tie the pieces together, thus yielding a complete model of the system under development.

The main relationship between the functional and behavioral views is captured by the fact that statecharts describe the behavior and control of activities in an activity-chart. We thus associate a statechart with each control activity in an activity-chart. In Fig. 1.4, the @ symbol denotes that the statechart named EWS_CONTROL (which appears in Fig. 1.6) is to be taken as the "contents" of the control activity.

Another relationship between activity-charts and statecharts involves activities that are specified as being active throughout states. For example, in the Data Dictionary entry for the state COMPARING, we can specify that the activity COMPARE is active throughout (see Fig. 1.8). This means that COMPARE will start when the state COMPARING is entered and will terminate when it is exited.

There are ways to directly refer to activities from within a statechart. For example, the event sp(SET_UP), which labels a transition in Fig. 1.6, occurs when the activity SET_UP terminates (the sp stands for stopped). It causes the transition from the SETTING_UP state to WAITING_FOR_COMMAND. Chapters 7 and 8 are devoted to the connections between activity-charts and statecharts.

The relationships between the conceptual and physical models of the system are reflected in connections between activity-charts and module-charts. One such connection involves specifying which module implements a given activity. This is done in the activity entry of the Data Dictionary. For example, in the entry for the COMPARE activity we might say that COMPARE is implemented in the CCU module.

Another connection involves associating an activity-chart with a specific module in the module-chart, thus describing the module's functionality in detail. This kind of association is specified in the Data Dictionary entry for the module. For example, the activity-chart EWS_ACTIVITIES (which was shown in Fig. 1.4) describes the functionality of the EWS module. See Fig. 1.9.

Chapter 10 is devoted to describing these relationships.

1.3.5   Handling large-scale systems

Methodological approaches, particularly the models that they recommend constructing, are essential for developing large systems. Our own approach is thus intended primarily for such systems. These involve vast quantities of information and numerous components and levels of detail, as well as portions that may appear repeatedly in many parts of the model. Such systems are usually developed by several separate teams. Our languages support features designed specifically to ease in this work.

Although a single chart can describe a multilevel hierarchy of elements, it is not advisable to overuse this capability when the model grows beyond a certain size. Accordingly, our languages allow splitting large hierarchical charts into separate ones. See Fig. 1.10, in which a separate chart is used to describe the contents of activity A.

Chapter 11 is devoted to this subject.

A related issue involves coping with visibility and information hiding by setting scoping rules of elements in the model. It is also possible to introduce global shared information in a model component called a

State: **COMPARING**
Defined in Chart: **EWS_CONTROL**

Activities in State:
       COMPARE (Throughout)

Figure 1.8 Specifying an activity throughout a state.

Module: **EWS**
Defined in Chart: **EWS**

Described by Activity-Chart: **EWS_ACTIVITIES**

Figure 1.9 An activity-chart describing a module.

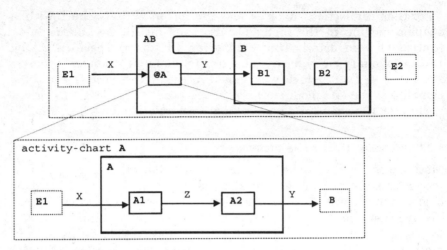

Figure 1.10 Splitting up charts.

global definition set. This is analogous to the scoping issue in programming languages.

Scoping is discussed in Chap. 13.

A very important feature of our languages is that of *generic charts,* which allow reusing parts of the specification. A generic chart makes it possible to represent common portions of the model as a single chart that can be instantiated in many places, and in this it is similar to a procedure in a conventional programming language.

Generic charts are described in Chap. 14.

Another feature that contributes to reusability is that of *user-defined types,* which are described in Chap. 3. This feature makes it possible to define a data type that will be used for many data elements in the model.

1.4   The STATEMATE Toolset

We now provide a very brief description of the STATEMATE toolset (Harel et al. 1990), which supports the languages and approach presented here. STATEMATE was intended primarily to help address the goals of the specification stage, although it supports some of the activities carried out in other stages, too. See Fig. 1.11 for a schematic overview of the STATEMATE toolset.

We should note that the modeling approach and languages presented here have a life of their own, whether they are used in conjunction with a computerized tool or not. Moreover, there are other tools, both commercial and of research nature, that support Statecharts and other aspects of the approach. We describe STATEMATE here both because we have been part of the team that designed it and because it still seems to be the most powerful tool of its kind available.

For entering the information contained in the model, STATEMATE has graphic editors for the three graphical languages, as well as a Data Dictionary. It carries out syntax checking and tests for consistency and completeness of the various parts of the model. While constructing the model, the specifier can link original textual requirements to elements of the model. These links can be used later in requirement traceability reports. STATEMATE also provides extensive means for querying the model's repository and retrieving information from it. A number of fixed-format reports can be requested, and there are document generation facilities with which users can tailor their own documents from the information constituting the model.

Our view of system development emphasizes "good" modeling, but it also regards as absolutely crucial the need to enable a user to run, debug, and analyze the resulting models and to translate them into working code for software and/or hardware. Accordingly, STATEMATE has been constructed to "understand" the model and its dynamics. The user can then execute the specification by emulating the environment of the system under development and letting the model make dynamic progress in response.

Using STATEMATE the model can be executed in a step-by-step interactive fashion or by batch execution. In both cases, the currently active states and activities are highlighted with special coloring, resulting in an (often quite appealing) animation of the diagrams. It is also possible to execute the model under random conditions and in both typical

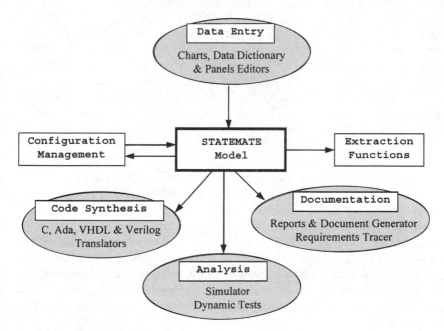

Figure 1.11 The STATEMATE toolset.

and less typical situations. A variety of possible results of the executions can be accumulated to be inspected and analyzed later.

We should note that it is possible to execute only part of the model (in any of the execution modes), as long as the portion executed is syntactically intact. This implies that there is no need to wait until the entire model is specified to carry out executions, and even an incomplete model can be executed and analyzed. Moreover, it is possible to attach external code to the model, to complete unspecified processing portions, to produce input stimuli, or to process execution results on-line. This openness enables STATEMATE to be linked to other tools.

STATEMATE also supports several dynamic tests, which are intended to detect crucial dynamic properties, such as whether a particular situation can be reached starting in a given state. These tests are carried out by the tool using a form of exhaustive execution of scenarios. We shall not get into a discussion of the feasibility of such exhaustive executions here; the reader is referred to Harel (1992b) for some comments on the matter.

Once a model has been constructed, and has been executed and analyzed to the satisfaction of the specifiers, STATEMATE can be instructed to translate it automatically into code in a high-level programming language. This is analogous to the compilation of a conventional program into assembly language, whereas model execution is analogous to its direct interpretation. Currently, translations into Ada and C are supported, and a variant of STATEMATE enables translation into hardware description languages VHDL and Verilog. Code supplied by the user for bottom-level basic activities can be appropriately linked to the generated code, resulting in a complete running version of the system. The resulting code is sometimes termed *prototype code,* because it is generated automatically and reflects only those design decisions made in the process of preparing the conceptual model. It may not always be as efficient as final code, although it runs much faster than the executions of the model itself, just as compiled code runs faster than interpreted code. For some kinds of systems, however, this code is quite satisfactory.

One of the main uses of the synthesized code is in observing the model performing in circumstances that are close to its final environment. The code can be ported and executed in the actual target environment, or as is more realistic in most cases, in a simulated version of the target environment. To this end, STATEMATE makes it possible to construct a "soft" version of the user interface of the final system, which can then be activated, driven by the synthesized code. The resulting setup can be used to debug the model by subcontractors and customers, for example. Again, Chap. 16 contains a discussion of how such code can be beneficial in the design phase of system development.

Associated with the code synthesis facility is a debugging mechanism with which the user can trace the executing parts of the code
back up to the model using back animation. The requirements traceability feature makes it possible to trace problems back up to the (textual) requirements.

For more on these topics, we refer the reader to the STATEMATE documentation supplied by I-Logix, Inc.

2

The Functional View
Activity-Charts

This chapter deals with the language of Activity-charts, which is used to depict the functional view of the system under development. We describe how the functionality of a system is specified by a hierarchy of functional components, called *activities,* what kind of information is exchanged between these activities and manipulated by them, how this information flows, how it is stored, and so on.

Many of the concepts and notions represented in this view are quite well known, and are not specific to our approach. They are used in other notations and methods, perhaps with small variations. In fact, activity-charts can be viewed as a variant of hierarchical data flow diagrams, but they embody many enhancements and use some special terms and notations.

2.1 Functional Description of a System

The functional description of a system specifies the system's capabilities. It details the functional components, or activities, that the system is capable of carrying out and how these components communicate through the flow of information among them. It does so in the context of the system's environment, that is, it defines the environment with which the system interacts and the interface between the two.

The functional view does not address the physical and implementational aspects of the system. As for the dynamic and behavioral issues, it attempts to separate them from the functional description whenever possible, but, as we shall see, there is a close relationship between functionality and behavior. For example, the functional view is appropriate for telling whether a medical diagnosis system can monitor a patient's blood pressure and, if so, where it would get its input data and which functions would have access to the output data.

However, to deal with such issues as the conditions under which the monitoring is started and the question of whether it can be carried out parallel to temperature monitoring, the behavioral view must be considered as well as its connections with the functional view. These crucial parts of modeling the system are described in Chaps. 4 to 8.

The structural view, which deals with sensors, processors, monitors, software modules, and so on, is described in Chaps. 9 and 10.

2.1.1 Functional decomposition

The main method for describing the functionality of a system in our approach is that of functional decomposition, by which the system is viewed as a collection of interconnected functional components (or *activities,* as they are called in our terminology), organized into a hierarchy. Thus, each of the activities may be decomposed into its subactivities repeatedly until the system has been specified in terms of *basic activities,* which are those that the specifiers have decided require no further decomposition. Basic activities are specified using alternative means, such as textual description, formal or informal, or code in a programming language. The intended meaning of the functional decomposition is that the capabilities of the parent activity are distributed between its subactivities. The order in which these subactivities are performed and the conditions that cause their activation or deactivation are not explicitly represented in the functional view and are usually specified in the behavioral view, as discussed in later chapters.

Note that the term *functional decomposition* is usually identified with the Structured Analysis methodology (DeMarco 1978), in which the functional components of a system are functions in the mathematical sense of the word. Here, we use this term in a broader meaning, where the main idea is to decompose the functionality of the entire system into activities, the functional components, which may very well be reactive in nature and which together capture the whole picture.

The activities themselves can represent different concepts used in conventional modeling techniques. They can be objects, processes, functions, use cases, logical machines, or any other kind of functionally distinct entity.

Which one is selected depends on the modeler's preference, but it is recommended to try to stick with a common type of functional component, based on a single conceptual approach or methodology. To some extent, this selection dictates the nature of the interface and communication between the activities as well as some of the behavioral aspects.

In the following subsections we discuss two types of decomposition: *function-based decomposition,* in which the activities are system functions and *object-based decomposition,* in which they are objects. Both styles are illustrated by the EWS example of Chap. 1.

2.1.2 Function-based decomposition

In function-based decomposition, the activities are (possibly reactive) functions. To illustrate it, we consider the EWS example. We start with a narrative that describes its functionality and reorganize it into the following list of requirements:

- The EWS receives a signal from an external sensor.

- It samples and processes the signal continuously, producing some result.

- It checks whether the value of the result is within a specified range that is set by the operator.

- If the value is out of range, the system issues a warning message on the operator display and posts an alarm.

- If the operator does not respond within a given time interval, the system prints a fault message on a printing facility and stops monitoring the signal.

As the first step of our functional description of the EWS, we identify the various functions that are called for by these textual requirements:

SET_UP	Receives the range limits from the operator.
PROCESS_SIGNAL	Reads the "raw" signal from the sensor and performs some processing to yield a value that is to be compared to the range limits.
COMPARE	Compares the value of the processed signal with the range limits.
DISPLAY_FAULT	Issues a warning message on the operator display and posts an alarm.
PRINT_FAULT	Prints a fault message on the printing facility.

Notice that the description of the activities also contains information about the data they handle. An activity may transform its input information into output information to be consumed by other functions that can be either internal or external to the system. For example, the activity PROCESS_SIGNAL transforms its input, the raw signal, into a value that is checked by the COMPARE function. (The signal processing can be a simple conversion of an analog signal into a digital representation at a fixed rate. Of course, it could also be a more complex transformation, such as computing the average value over some time interval.)

In the function-based decomposition approach the interface of an activity is described in terms of input and output signals, both data and control. Also, the model will usually present the source activity of input information and the target activity of output information.

2.1.3 Object-based decomposition

In an object-based approach, the decomposition is defined by the entities on which operations are performed or, alternatively, is based on the active agents, or the active components, of the system (these are called *logical machines* in the ROOM methodology; see Selic et al. 1994). In our approach, the interface between objects consists of the events and messages that cause the internal operations to take place and sometimes the data that is used in these operations, just as in function-based decomposition. This is somewhat different from object-oriented design (OOD) paradigms, in which an object's interface consists of its operations.

To illustrate, we decompose the functionality of the EWS system into the following components, using encapsulation guidelines that are often presented in object-oriented methods. When applicable, a component is characterized by its subject and associated operations:

SIGNAL_PROCESSOR   Handles the signal from the sensor. It reads the signal, processes the read value, and checks the processed signal against the legal range.

FAULT_HANDLER   Consists of all functionality related to fault situations. It handles a fault occurrence by issuing the alarm, printing the fault report, and resetting the fault situation.

RANGE   Handles the range limits against which the processed signal is compared. It reads the range limits provided by the operator, validates the read values, stores the current legal range, and makes its values and status available to the other objects.

MMI_HANDLER   Takes care of all interaction with the operator (i.e., the human-machine interface). It accepts commands and data from the operator and displays messages and other information.

CONTROLLER   Controls the behavior of the entire system.

This decomposition is not overly detailed, and some of the components can be further decomposed into lower-level objects that help them accomplish their goals.

2.1.4 System context

One of the first decisions that should be made when developing a system involves its boundaries, or *context*. We must determine which entities are part of the system's environment—these can be other systems, functions, or objects (depending on the decomposition approach)—and how they communicate with the system itself.

In both approaches to the preceding EWS description some of the inputs come from outside the system and some of the outputs are sent outside. For example, in the function-based decomposition, the raw signal consumed by PROCESS_SIGNAL comes from the SENSOR, which is not part of the specified system but belongs to the environment. Similarly, the printed message produced by PRINT_FAULT is sent to the OPERATOR, which is also external to the EWS. In the object-based decomposition, the interaction with the environment is handled by the `MMI_HANDLER` that interfaces with the `OPERATOR`, and by the `SIGNAL_PROCESSOR` that reads the signal from the `SENSOR`.

As a result, we may now decide that the EWS's environment consists of two external entities, or systems: the (presumably human) `OPERATOR` and the `SENSOR` (see Fig. 2.1).

The system context is sometimes given as part of the requirements, before the beginning of the specification process. However, it is often the responsibility of whoever carries out the functional description to determine the best way to set up the system boundaries.

For example, we could have defined the specification boundaries of the EWS differently because they were not given as part of the textual description, removing the printing facility from the system itself and turning it into an external entity.

2.1.5 The decomposition process

Some specification methodologies that are based on functional decomposition provide guidelines for how the subfunctions ought to be defined and the order in which the functional description should be prepared. According to one of these methodologies, the analyst should start by describing the system's context, that is, the environment entities and the information flowing between them and the system itself. The process is then continued in a top-down manner, proceeding from the description of the entire system, to the description of its subfunctions, to their subfunctions, etc. Alternatively, a bottom-up approach may be adopted, whereby the basic, lowest-level functions are specified first and used as building blocks to construct higher-level functions. We shall not address such methodological issues of order and process here but concentrate on the way the concepts relevant to the functional view of specification can be expressed in our languages.

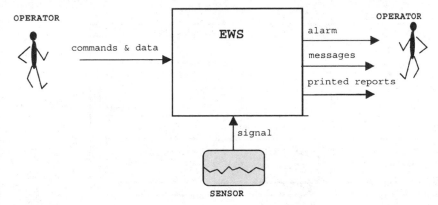

Figure 2.1 The context of the EWS.

The functional view is specified in our approach by *Activity-charts,* together with a *Data Dictionary* that may contain additional information about the elements appearing in the charts. The following sections describe the details of the Activity-charts language. Almost all our examples will use function-based decomposition, although the same language constructs can be used for other approaches, such as the object-based one.

2.2   Activities and Their Representation

2.2.1   The hierarchy of activities

The activities in an activity-chart are depicted as rectangular or rectilinear solid-line boxes, and the subactivity relationship is depicted by box encapsulation. An activity's name appears inside its box. Figure 2.2 shows one level of the decomposition of the EWS system.

The overall activity of the system has been named EWS_ACTIVITIES. In function-based decomposition, it is useful to use verbs for names of activities, with or without a qualifying noun, as we have done for the subactivities in Fig. 2.2. This helps convey the purpose of the functions the activities perform. In other decomposition approaches, some other naming policy may be more appropriate. In any case, names must follow the rules of legal element name, that is, they start with an alphabetic character, and consist of alphanumeric characters and underscores. See App. A.1.

We may further decompose subactivities into subsubactivities on lower levels, and the new activities may be drawn inside their *parent activities* in the same chart. See Fig. 2.3, in which SET_UP is decomposed into three subsubactivities. We use the terms *descendants* and *ancestors* to denote subactivities and parent activities, respectively, on any level of nesting. Activities that have no descendants are termed *basic,* while those that do are called *nonbasic.* Two activities with a common parent may not have the same name, but subactivities of different parents may be named identically.

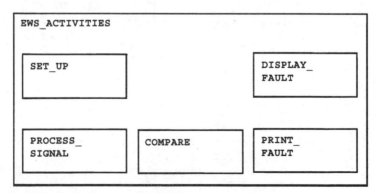

Figure 2.2   First-level decomposition of an activity.

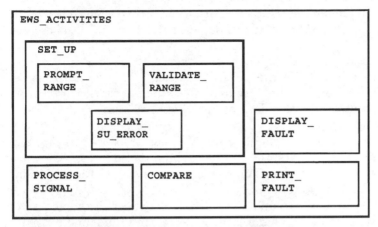

Figure 2.3   Multi-level decomposition of an activity.

All the activities appearing in the preceding examples are referred to as *internal regular activities,* to distinguish them from other types of activities participating in the functional description, which are discussed later.

Like many of the elements in our languages, some of the information related to activities is represented nongraphically. Each activity has a corresponding item in the Data Dictionary, which may contain additional information about it, such as textual descriptions, attributes, and relationships with other elements. Parts of the activity's Data Dictionary item are used to complete the description of its functionality, as discussed in Sec. 2.4.

2.2.2   The context of an activity

The functional description of a system may consist of multiple activity-charts linked together. Each such chart focuses on a portion of the system's functionality. It may describe the functionality of the entire system or that of some of its subsystems, or it may concentrate on some specific capability, object, or process being defined as a functional component in the higher-level decomposition. In each case, it is important to delineate the borders of the described portion, separating it from its environment, and to represent the flow of information between the two.

Each activity-chart contains one top-level box, with solid-line edges. This box represents the *top-level activity* of the chart, and its border-line separates this activity (and its internal description) from its environment. The components that constitute the environment are always referred to as *external activities* of the considered chart, although they may correspond to physical modules, humans, or activities or data-stores that are internal to other activity-charts in the overall model. Of course, they may also be real environment entities, external to the entire system under description. This issue will become clearer in later chapters, where the relations between charts in a full model are described.

External activities are depicted as boxes with dashed-line edges, which are located outside the top-level activity. They have the same names as the modules, the humans, the other activities (external, internal or control), or the data-stores that they represent in other parts of the specification.

For example, the environment of the EWS, as presented in Fig. 2.1, consists of two components, the OPERATOR and the SENSOR. They are drawn as external activities in the activity-chart of Fig. 2.5 that describes the overall functionality of the EWS.

Several external boxes in an activity-chart may bear the same name, in which case they are considered as representing the same external activity and are merely duplicated to help keep the chart uncluttered. Thus, for example, a flow-line (see Sec. 2.3.1) that represents the flow of information between an internal activity and an external one can be drawn to connect to the closest occurrence of the latter activity. When the identity of a particular external component is unknown or is irrelevant, it may be represented by an unnamed external activity box.

External activities are beyond the scope of the chart and are therefore not decomposed further into subactivities. Later we shall see that representing information flow between them is not allowed either.

2.3   Flow of Information between Activities

2.3.1   Flow-lines

To complete the functional view of the system, we complement the description of the activities themselves with the identification of inputs and outputs and the *flow of information* among subactivities.

We use the word *flow* to capture the communication and the transfer of information between activities. This flow of information can serve as a means not only to transfer data but to post commands and to synchronize by exchanging control signals. As in data-flow diagrams, we use labeled arrows for the visual representation of this flow. We refer to these connections as *a-flow-lines* (for *activity-chart flow-lines*), or just *flow-lines* for short.

The *label* on a flow-line denotes either a single information element that flows along the line (i.e., a *data-item,* a *condition,* or an *event*) or a group of such elements. We call a grouping of several information elements an *information-flow.* The flowing elements are used to specify communication according to the general specification approach that is adopted by the modeler. In particular, in the functional decomposition method they correspond to data and control flow.

A flow-line originates from its *source activity,* which is the activity that produces the information elements described in the flow-line's label, and it leads to its *target activity,* which is the one that consumes those elements. The communicating activities may belong to different levels in a multilevel activity-chart (see Fig. 2.4), but both cannot be external.

Referring to Fig. 2.4, we say that Y flows from A1 to B1, and U flows from A1 to A2. We also say that Y is an output of A and an input of B because the flow-line labeled with Y exits A and enters B, crossing their respective borderlines.

One of the graphical features present in all of our languages is that an arrow can be connected to a nonbasic box. In general, this means that the arrow is relevant to all the subboxes contained within the box in question. (See the discussion of this feature in the general setting of *higraphs* in Harel 1988.) In Activity-charts, this feature can take the form of a flow-line that leads to the edge of a nonbasic activity A but does not cross it. The arrow is taken to represent flow of information to all A's descendants. For example, the signal Z in Fig. 2.4 is accessible to both A1 and A2. Similarly, an arrow departing from the borderline of a nonbasic activity denotes the possibility that the corresponding information is produced by any of the descendant activities. For example, the arrow on the right-hand side of Fig. 2.4, emanating from B and labeled by V, can represent a global variable that is modified by the two activities B1 and B2, but it is used only by B2. Note that this convention enables us to replace several flow-lines from or to subactivities by one arrow from or to the parent, thus better representing the modeled flow. We also use this convention in cases where most of the subactivities consume or produce the information, but we do not want to specify exactly which ones they are.

Two types of flow-lines are allowed in Activity-charts: *data flow-lines,* drawn as solid arrows, and *control flow-lines,* drawn as dashed arrows. Typically, control flow-lines carry information or signals that are used in making control decisions (e.g., commands or synchronization messages) while data flow-lines carry information that is used in computations and data-processing operations. The different line types

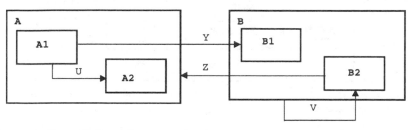

Figure 2.4   Flow of information among levels.

component of an array V, and produces a corresponding component of an array W. Similarly, a flow-line can be labeled by a portion of an array, such as $V(1..8)$, or by a record or a union component, such as $R.X$.

Information elements do not just appear along flow-lines. Their main use is in behavioral description. Using the Data Dictionary, one can define an information element that depends on the status or values of other elements. For example, we may define an event whose occurrence depends on the occurrence of other events, or a data-item whose value is expressed by values of other data-items. Information elements that have been defined in such a way cannot be used as labels on flow-lines.

We shall discuss the information elements in more detail in Chaps. 3 and 5.

2.3.3 Information-flows

The number of flow-lines in an activity-chart can be reduced by grouping information elements into an *information-flow,* which is used to label a common flow-line, thus helping a viewer to better comprehend the specification. The contents of the information-flow are defined in the Data Dictionary, associated with the name of the information-flow, as illustrated in Fig. 2.7. In the figure, the information-flow COM-MANDS, labeling a flow-line from OPERATOR to the control activity, is a compact representation of three separate flow-lines, each of which is labeled by an individual component event. Using the three commands, SET_UP, EXECUTE, and RESET., the OPERATOR controls the operation of the EWS.

We should emphasize that because an information-flow is merely an abbreviation of several flow-lines, the elements it contains do not necessarily flow together. Also, an information-flow may be further decomposed into other information-flows or into concrete information elements (data-items, conditions, events, or array or record components).

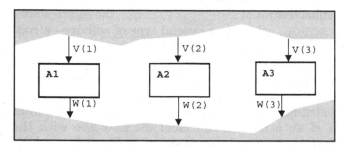

Figure 2.6 Array components labeling flow-lines.

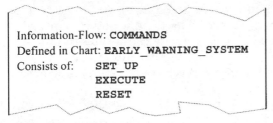

Information-Flow: COMMANDS
Defined in Chart: EARLY_WARNING_SYSTEM
Consists of: SET_UP
                 EXECUTE
                 RESET

Figure 2.7 Information-flow COMMANDS in Data Dictionary.

Another way of using the information-flow feature is to consider it as the name of a link (or interface) between activities. This idea may be used as follows: at an initial stage, before getting into more detail, we can connect activity A1 to activity A2 by a flow-line labeled with some noncommitting information-flow, such as A1_TO_A2. The contents of this line may then become increasingly more concrete, by filling in more of its contents in the corresponding information-flow item in the Data Dictionary. Clearly, this can be carried out repeatedly for nested information-flows. In any case, we expect the contents of all information-flows to be eventually specified in full.

2.3.4 Data-stores

As mentioned earlier, there are no restrictions on the time that data reside on a flow-line. Data produced by the source activity are available to the target activity even when the source activity is no longer active. In this sense, a flow-line may be viewed as a kind of storage unit. Nevertheless, it is often more natural to incorporate an explicit *data-store* in the chart, which serves to represent information that is stored for later use. In addition, a data-store may be used to specify the aggregation of large volumes of data that accumulate continuously over time. Data-stores can be used to describe a buffer in computer memory, a message queue, a file on a disk, a database, or even a single variable. In object-based decomposition, a data-store can be used to encapsulate the object data.

Information is written into the data-store by one or more activities and can be read by other (possibly the same) activities. Thus, the data-store can be viewed as a "passive" activity, that is, one that does not change or produce information.

Data-stores are drawn as rectangular boxes with dashed vertical edges. The name of a data-store may be any legal name (see App. A.1), but it must be unique among its sibling activities and data-stores.

Data-stores are always basic; they cannot contain other data-stores or activities. The internal structure of a data-store may be defined by associating it with a data-item. To do this, a data-item is defined in the

Data Dictionary with the same name as the data-store. Any structure then given to this data-item is inherited by the data-store. For example, to specify that the data-store Q is a queue containing records of a certain type, say, MESSAGE, one defines the data-item Q in the Data Dictionary as a queue of the user-defined type MESSAGE, the structure of which is described separately.

In the EWS example, we might want to show that the record LEGAL_RANGE, composed of HIGH_LIMIT and LOW_LIMIT, is stored in a data-store by the SET_UP activity and consumed by COMPARE. To represent this, the flow-line labeled LEGAL_RANGE in Fig. 2.5 is replaced by a data-store LEGAL_RANGE that contains the appropriate record, and it is then connected to the source and target activities. The appropriate part of the resulting diagram is presented in Fig. 2.8. LEGAL_RANGE is defined as a record data-item in the Data Dictionary, as shown in Sec. 3.4.2.

Notice that the lines flowing to and from the data-store LEGAL_RANGE are not labeled. This is because we can name the data-store with the same name as the data-item flowing to or from it, in which case the labels on the corresponding flow-lines can be omitted. However, in general, a data-store's inputs and outputs can be any information elements, even when there is a data-item matched (by name) to this data-store. Data-stores can also store control elements to be used for control decisions, so control flow-lines can flow to and from data-stores, too. Nevertheless, it is meaningless to have an event, which is of transient nature, stored in or flowing to or from a data-store.

Data-stores cannot be drawn as part of the activity-chart's environment. The components of the environment are always drawn as external activities even when their functionality is that of storage.

Textual descriptions of data-stores, and the relationships they may have with other elements, are entered in the Data Dictionary.

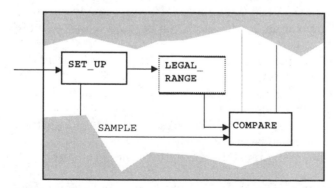

Figure 2.8 Data-store containing LEGAL_RANGE data.

2.4   Describing the Behavioral Functionality of Activities

We have seen that the functionality of the system is described by decomposing activities into subactivities and data-stores, and identifying the information that flows between them. This can be done repeatedly, until basic activities are reached, but it is not enough to present the full picture.

For *nonbasic* activities, which are decomposed into subactivities, we must provide information about the behavioral dynamics of the decomposition. In the methodology of Hatley and Pirbhai (1987) this issue is covered by what they call process activation tables. Other approaches deal with this differently. In our approach, we use the control activities for this (and more), as will be seen shortly. *Basic* activities are described by other means, which are specified via the Data Dictionary entry associated with the activity.

Describing the behavior of activities in our approach is a broad subject, and it is discussed in many of the later chapters. The present section should be viewed as an introduction.

2.4.1   Control activities

In many systems, the activities at each level of the functional decomposition perform their functions in a simple fashion. Some are continuously active, consuming their inputs and producing their outputs periodically. Others become active when their inputs arrive and stop when they have produced the outputs corresponding to these inputs. Sometimes, the behavior of activities follows more intricate patterns.

We address these aspects by introducing special *control activities,* which are drawn as subactivities of regular internal activities and whose function is to control their sibling activities. For example, as we shall see in Chap. 7, a control activity may explicitly start and stop its sibling activities. In the EWS model, EWS_CONTROL is responsible for determining the activation and deactivation of all the activities on the same level, that is, SET_UP, PROCESS_SIGNAL, COMPARE, and so on. (See Fig. 2.9.)

The control activity will typically receive signals from the siblings it controls or from other sources, make decisions based on them, and then, in turn, start and stop the activities it controls and produce signals that are consumed by its environment. In our example, the control activity EWS_CONTROL receives and reacts to the commands of the OPERATOR and to the OUT_OF_RANGE event generated by the COMPARE activity. (See Fig. 2.5.)

The control activity is depicted as a rectangle with rounded corners, and it cannot have subactivities. Rather, its specification is described in the language of *Statecharts,* the graphical language for

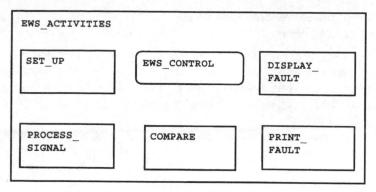

Figure 2.9 A control activity in an activity-chart.

modeling behavior. The control activity points to the statechart describing its behavior through its name, as explained in Chap. 7. The Statecharts language is described in Chap. 4, and the way a statechart controls the behavior of activities is discussed in Chap. 7.

Each activity may have at most one control activity. When an activity requires no further decomposition and its behavior can be conveniently described by a statechart alone, the control activity is its only subactivity. This situation is common in certain highly reactive systems. Like other elements, the control activity has an associated item in the Data Dictionary.

2.4.2   Activities in the Data Dictionary

As mentioned earlier, almost every element in our models has a corresponding entry in the Data Dictionary, in which various kinds of textual information about the element can be specified. Such additional information can be formal (i.e., possessing some semantics that is relevant to the model and its behavior) or informal. Some kinds of textual information are relevant to all types of elements, such as a one-line *short description* and an unlimited textual *long description*. These narrative additions, especially the long description, can be used to provide information about the element in an informal language, for the record. In addition, the general mechanism of an *attribute pair,* name and value, can be used to associate special characteristics with the element, as we shall see later on. The Data Dictionary can also used to associate a *synonym* with the element, usually a shorter name that is easier to incorporate into a detailed chart.

In the case of activities, the long description is very often used to add functional specification in a textual language that is not an integral part of our approach, such as an unstructured natural language. This additional information can be attached to basic or nonbasic activities alike.

On the other hand, for basic activities, our approach supports a number of formal executable textual descriptions that specify particular patterns of behavior. These are also associated with the activity in its Data Dictionary entry. The patterns are:

- A *reactive event-driven activity* is continuously "active" in an idle state and constantly waits for an event to occur and to cause it to perform some action. It then becomes idle again until the next event happens. An example of such an activity is a simple keyboard driver that accepts key press events and locally performs a very simple operation and/or transfers a command to some other activity. A reactive event-driven activity can be described by a *reactive minispec,* which is a list of reactions, each consisting of a trigger event and its implied action; see Fig. 2.10a. More complex reactive activities are described by statecharts, as we shall see, but simple event/action activities do not require a statechart, and they can be described by a reactive minispec.

- A *procedure-like activity,* when invoked, performs a sequence of operational statements and then stops. An example of such an activity is the VALIDATE_RANGE subactivity of the range SET_UP activity of the

```
Activity: PROCESS_SIGNAL
Defined in Chart: EWS_ACTIVITIES

Mini-spec: st/TICK;;
TICK/ $SIGNAL_VALUE:=SIGNAL;
       SAMPLE:=COMPUTE($SIGNAL_VALUE)
```

(a) Event-driven activity described by a mini-spec

```
Activity: VALIDATE_RANGE
Defined in Chart: SET_UP

Mini-spec: if (LOW_LIMIT < HIGH_LIMIT)
           then SUCCESS
           else FAILURE end if
```

(b) Procedure-like activity described by a mini-spec

```
Activity: COMPUTE_IN_RANGE
Defined in Chart: COMPARE

Combinational Assignments:
IN_RANGE:=(SAMPLE>LEGAL_RANGE.LOW_LIMIT)
       and (SAMPLE>LEGAL_RANGE.HIGH_LIMIT)
```

(c) Data-driven activity described by combinational assignments

Figure 2.10 Data Dictionary entries describing activities.

EWS. It is invoked when the user has inserted the range limits, and it checks the validity of the values, returning the check results. A procedure-like activity can be described by a *procedure-like minispec,* which is simply a list of actions; see Fig. 2.10*b.*

- A *data-driven activity* is also continuously "active," checking to detect any changes in the values of its inputs. When any of them changes value, the activity computes new output values and resumes its waiting. A logical gate in an integrated circuit is an example of a simple data-driven activity. In the EWS example, the COMPARE function has a subactivity COMPUTE_IN_RANGE, which is data-driven; it continuously monitors the processed signal and compares it to the legal range limits to calculate an IN_RANGE condition. (When this condition becomes false, the COMPARE function issues the OUT_OF_RANGE event.) A data-driven activity can be described by a collection of *combinational assignments,* which are ordinary-looking assignment statements that continuously compute the activity's outputs based on its inputs; see Fig. 2.10*c.*

Minispecs and combinational assignments are described in detail in Chap. 7.

2.5 Connectors and Compound Flow-Lines

Let us return to the technical mechanisms we provide for representing the flow of information between activities. Flow-lines in activity-charts can be combined using various types of connectors. The main motivation for this is to economize in the number of arrows, to reduce clutter, and to provide a clearer and more intuitive graphical representation. We refer to the resulting connected object, consisting of a number of flow-lines and connectors, as a *compound flow-line.* We now discuss the various types of connectors.

2.5.1 Joint connectors (fork and merge constructs)

A *fork* construct allows us to represent a single information element as flowing from one source to several targets. Instead of drawing separate lines departing from the source, we can draw a single departing line, which then splits up into separate arrows at a convenient place in the chart. For example, instead of drawing two separate lines emanating from COMPARE and labeled with OUT_OF_RANGE_DATA, as we did in Fig. 2.5, we can abbreviate as shown in Fig. 2.11.

Similarly, we can represent common information flowing from several sources to a single target by joining them at some convenient point before they reach their target. This is called a *merge construct,* and it

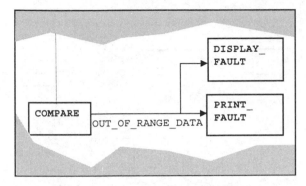

Figure 2.11 A joint connector (a fork construct).

indicates that the target may receive the information from either of several sources.

In both constructs, fork and merge, we refer to the connection point as a *joint connector.* The compound flow-line, consisting of the connected segments, may have several sources and several targets but only a single associated flowing element (which may actually be an information-flow consisting of several data elements). As for location, the flow element common to the entire construct can label any of the compound flow-line's segments.

2.5.2 Junction connectors

Another way of reducing the number of lengthy flow-lines in an activity-chart is to use a *junction connector.* Several flow-lines conveying different information elements may be connected using a junction connector to form a single flow-line that emanates from or enters a common box or connector.

Figure 2.12 illustrates several uses of junction connectors. Figure 2.12*a* contains three actual flows: X flows from A1 to B, Y flows from A2 to B, and Z flows from A3 to B. Notice that the line segment from the junction connector to B is unlabeled because it is used only to connect the different flowing elements to the common target.

The case of a common source is similar. In Fig. 2.12*b*, the flow-line that carries the three flow elements from A to the junction connector is labeled XYZ. In the Data Dictionary we define the element XYZ to be an information-flow containing X, Y, and Z as components. Clustering flowing elements in this way and using the combined information-flow to label the common arrow is usually done when there is some logical relationship between the flowing elements; the additional name helps to clarify this relationship.

Figure 2.12*c* illustrates how a number of junction connectors may be combined. Nine potential routes exist from the activities on the left to

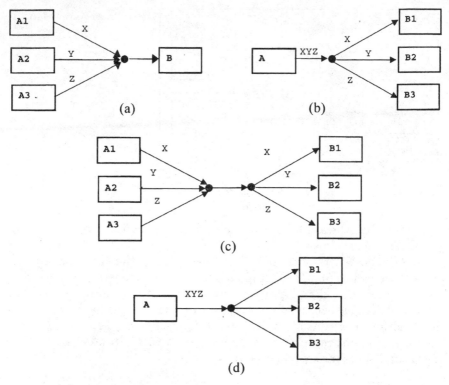

Figure 2.12 Junction connectors.

those on the right. However, the labeling used excludes six. The only three that represent actual flows are: X from A1 to B1, Y from A2 to B2, and Z from A3 to B3. A compound line with contradicting flow labels (such as the one composed of the segments labeled X and Y) is not considered a viable compound flow-line.

If we want to show more than one element flowing along a single line, the elements can be combined using an information-flow. Consider the example in Fig. 2.12d. It represents three compound flow-lines, each of which carries XYZ and has a single source and a single target. Notice that the same diagram drawn with a joint connector instead of a junction connector represents a single compound flow-line with one source and three targets. In this case the two are semantically equivalent, and although we used a junction connector, a joint connector might be preferred because it emphasizes that the same information is available to all three targets.

The junction connector is sometimes used with a record data-item and its components. In the EWS example, the COMPARE activity can be decomposed into two subactivities: one compares the processed signal SAMPLE with the HIGH_LIMIT field of LEGAL_RANGE, and the other compares it with the `LOW_LIMIT` field, as shown in Fig. 2.13. The junction connector is used here to direct the fields of the record to two different target activities.

2.5.3 Diagram connectors

When the source of a flow-line is far from its target, we can avoid drawing a lengthy arrow by using a *diagram connector*. The arrow emanating from the source ends in a named connector, and its continuation emanates from a second connector with the same name, which is positioned closer to the target. The pair of identically named connectors are identified as the same logical entity, and the result has the same meaning as a junction connector connecting the two arrows. It is important to emphasize that the arrow segments are matched according to the names of the connectors and not according to the labels along the segments. As a consequence, the label can be omitted from one of the segments.

Any legal name (see App. A.1) may be used to label the diagram connectors, as can any integer number. Thus one can use names that indicate the identity of the target (as in Fig. 2.14), flowing signal names, or simply serial numbers.

To make life even easier, we allow more than two diagram connectors to have the same name and thus denote the same logical junction. Several arrows can then emanate from or enter a common diagram connector, but all arrows connected to the same occurrence of the connector must flow in the same direction.

2.5.4 Compound flow-lines

The various types of connectors presented earlier can be used to construct a variety of *compound flow-lines*. The compound flow-lines are really the logical flow-lines that depict the actual flow between activities

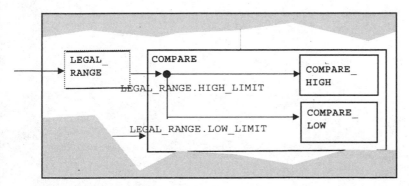

Figure 2.13 A junction connector with record fields.

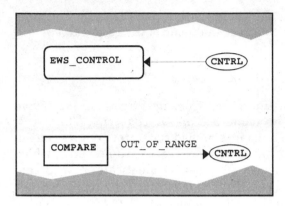

Figure 2.14   A diagram connector.

(or the other box-like entities in our other languages). When connectors are not used, a simple arrow that flows directly from one box to another depicts the actual flow, the logical flow-line consisting of a single segment. In Fig. 2.5, for example, no connectors are used, and all logical flow-lines are actually *simple flow-lines* (ones consisting of a single segment).

We have seen that a joint connector yields a single compound flow-line with multiple sources or multiple targets, while a junction connector produces multiple compound flow-lines. Diagram connectors are interpreted as junctions, and as such they can represent multiple compound flow-lines, although they can also be used in a way that results in a single flow-line.

The segments constituting a compound flow-line can be data flow-lines or control flow-lines. When both types appear in a single compound flow-line, the entire combination will be considered to be a control flow-line if the final segment that leads to the target is a control flow-line. This is because the type of flow is determined by the way the target uses the flowing information.

Information Elements

This chapter deals with the information elements of our languages: events, conditions, and data-items. The data-items can be of simple *predefined types* or compound *user-defined types*. All information elements are defined in the Data Dictionary, and they can be used in both graphical charts and textual constructs. Each is defined as belonging to a particular chart of a global definition set, that is, to one of the specification components that make up the entire model. Information elements obey certain scoping rules that are described in Chap. 13.

3.1 Information Elements in the Model

The interface of the entire system, as well as that of each component, is an essential part of the specification and design, capturing the way it communicates with its environment. In many methodologies (with the exception of object-oriented design methods), a major part of the interface consists of a set of information elements that flow to and from the system or component. Very often the system development starts with the interface already given, and the specifier has to construct the model accordingly.

The interface specification must fit the nature of the system under description and its environment. For example, if the system communicates with a hardware environment, the interface may be specified in terms of bits in a connector structure. In communication systems, the interface description may consist of a message structure, sometimes adhering to an industrial standard or a predefined protocol. The information modeling can be on a very concrete level—listing the bits of the connector or computer word—or on a higher level—involving abstract events, conditions, and data-items. While the modeler in our approach is encouraged to use abstractions, a *bit* is supplied as one of the predefined types.

For example, assume that one of the functional components of the EWS is the operator panel driver, through which the OPERATOR inserts the commands and the range limits. The driver interprets the OPERATOR input and conveys it to the appropriate activity. The operator panel consists of the following components:

- Three command buttons:

  Set-up   For starting the setup procedure

  Execute   For starting the execution mode

  Reset   For transforming the system into an idle mode

- Ten digit keys, *0* to *9,* for entering the range limits
- An *Enter* key for indicating the entry end of a range-limit value
- A *Sensor Connected* switch for indicating that the sensor is connected

These elements can be represented on various levels of abstraction. The three commands can be referred to as events, or, alternatively, they can be three-bit data-items. The range limits can be modeled by a bit-array of ten bits presenting the ten digits sent one at a time or by whole numeric values and so on. To some extent, the choices depend on whether such decisions have already been made (i.e., whether the interface is given or is awaiting the design or implementation phase).

As another example, the fault report of the EWS is basically a textual report consisting of the following information components:

- The *time* when the fault occurred
- The *out-of-range value,* which is the computed value after the processing
- The *legal range limits*

Again, different levels of abstraction can be used here, depending on where the borders of the specification are placed. The fault report can be modeled as a string of limited length, as an array of strings—one for each line in the report—or as a record of the numeric values that specify the report contents without being too precise about the implementation details.

Information elements are used not only in specifying interfaces but in the detailed behavioral and functional specification. It is natural to use them to describe the logic and control of algorithms and to specify computations, just as variables are used in programming languages.

It is only natural to translate the requirement that the system checks if the value of the result of the processing is within the specified range to a construct that contains a condition expression such as:

```
(SAMPLE > LEGAL_RANGE.LOW_LIMIT) and
(SAMPLE < LEGAL_RANGE.HIGH_LIMIT)
```

Here, SAMPLE denotes the processed value, and the allowed limits of the range are captured by the two fields of the record LEGAL_RANGE. All these elements are conventional real values, and they can be compared using standard relation symbols such as < and >.

In our notation, information elements can appear along the flow-lines of activity-charts and module charts, and in the textual constructs used in behavioral and detailed functional descriptions. Information elements appear in reactions, triggers, and actions, and in other expressions in statecharts, mini-specs, and combinational assignments, as well as in the parameters of generic charts. We will see examples in the coming chapters.

Information elements and user-defined types are defined in the Data Dictionary, where their type and structure are specified. The names follow the naming rules of App. A.1. As for all kinds of elements appearing in the Data Dictionary, we may attach additional information to these elements, such as synonyms, textual description and user-defined attributes, using the standard mechanisms of the Data Dictionary. Some examples are given in the more detailed sections that follow. We can also use information elements whose values depend on other elements. Actually, these are named expressions, like macros and aliases in conventional programming, and they are also defined using the Data Dictionary.

The following sections describe the particular types of information elements and the user-defined types. The way these elements are used in behavioral descriptions will be discussed in Chaps. 4–8, particularly Chap. 5.

3.2 Events

Events are communication signals that indicate that something has happened. Very often they are used for synchronization purposes. When they flow they do not convey any content or value, only the very fact that they have occurred. They are thus instantaneous, and if not immediately sensed, they are lost.

In the EWS example, the activity COMPARE sends the event OUT_OF_RANGE to the control activity (through a control flow-line) to indicate that the tested value is not in the expected range. This event is an indication to the control activity that it should start its response to a fault occurrence, that is, posting an alarm and issuing a fault message.

Events are used extensively in the modeling of real-time systems to indicate interrupts, clock ticks, timing, and synchronization signals and to model cause/effect connections between different parts of the system. In communication protocol modeling they mark message sending and acknowledge arrival. Events are also used in the modeling and implementation of interactive systems. Graphical user interface systems (GUIs) are based on user-generated occurrences and their subsequent responses and attached callbacks, all of which can be mapped naturally into events and corresponding reactions in our languages. This can be accomplished in a low-level fashion, referring to mouse button clicks and motions and keyboard manipulations or on a higher level, by abstracting them into menu selection and command activation.

In the EWS example, the OPERATOR's commands, EXECUTE, SET_UP, and RESET, are defined as events that control the system's operation. Here we chose the names to be imperative verbs, but it is also useful to use short phrases in the past tense for event names, such as OPERATION_COMPLETED or BUTTON_PRESSED.

In object-based decomposition, where the functional components consist of entities (or actors) and their associated operations, events can implement the request for individual operations. For example, we may model the request from the FAULT_HANDLER to DISPLAY_FAULT (i.e., post an alarm and issue a fault message) by an event bearing the same name; similarly, the event PRINT_FAULT will invoke the PRINT_FAULT operation.

A set of similar events can be organized in an array structure. For example, the EWS operator keyboard contains ten keys for digits, which are used to enter the range limits. The events of pressing these keys can be grouped in an array DIGIT_PRESSED consisting of ten event components. The individual component is accessed by its index in the array, just like in conventional programming languages, DIGIT_PRESSED(1) through DIGIT_PRESSED(10), where 10 stands for the digit 0. Chapter 5 shows how to detect that one of these ten events has occurred, without referring to each one explicitly. Figure 3.1 shows the Data Dictionary entry defining the event array. It shows that in addition to the array size designation we can also incorporate a short description and a long description, as in other Data Dictionary entries.

Other aspects of events, namely, event expressions and named event expressions, are discussed in Chap. 5, where our expression language is described in full.

3.3 Conditions

As with events, conditions are also used for control purposes. Conditions are persistent signals, that is, ones that hold for continuous time spans. They can be either true or false.

An example of a condition in the EWS is the signal SENSOR_CONNECTED, which is generated by the OPERATOR and is sensed by

```
Event: DIGIT_PRESSED
Defined in Chart: EWS
Structure: array 1 to 10

Short Description: Events of the digit keys being pressed
Long Description: An array of events depicting the
pressing of the digit keys on the operator keyboard.
The i'th component stands for the digit i, where
10 stands for the digit 0.
```

Figure 3.1   An event array in the Data Dictionary.

the control activity. This condition is self-explanatory, and it indicates whether the SENSOR is connected to the system—an essential prerequisite to activating the signal processing. Here, it is beneficial to use short phrases in the present tense as names of conditions to describe a situation that holds currently and for some continuous period of time.

Conditions are often used to describe the status of two-state entities, as in the preceding example. For example, a switch can be modeled by a condition SWITCH_ON that is either true or false. Conditions are also used to "remember" that some event has occurred until the required response is given.

Conditions, like events, can be organized in arrays to model the status of several similar elements. The information on the array index range is specified in the Data Dictionary.

Conditions, like other information elements, participate in detailed behavioral and functional descriptions. In subsequent chapters we shall see how they are manipulated, how they change values, and how they can influence the flow of control.

3.4   Data-Items

A data-item is a unit of information that may assume values of various types and structures. Data-items are very similar to the data elements in conventional programming languages: variables, constants, and so on. They maintain their values until they are explicitly changed and assigned new values.

Data-items are defined via the Data Dictionary, where their type and structure are specified, and other descriptive information can be added (e.g., attributes such as units, resolution, or distribution). Data-items can be of predefined types (integer, real, string, etc.), or records and unions composed of fields of various types. They can also be structured in arrays or queues. The modeler can also construct user-defined types that are based on predefined types and structures. These concepts are described in the following sections.

3.4.1   Data-items of predefined types

The basic types of data-items are similar to those existing in programming languages. A data-item can be *numeric,* either *integer* or *real.* For example, in the EWS, the data-item SAMPLE, which is the result of the processing performed by the PROCESS_SIGNAL activity, has a numeric value and can be specified as real or integer. The value of an integer data-item is usually limited by 2^{31}. It is also possible to limit the values of an individual integer data-item by restricting its range, or by shortening its actual length (in bits). For example, if the EWS is extended to deal with five sensors, the identification number of a sensor will be an integer whose value will be restricted to the range 1 to 5. There is no limitation on real values.

When dealing with hardware systems, such as integrated circuits, it is natural to speak in terms of bits and bit-arrays. For this purpose, it is possible to define a *bit* data-item that can take on the values 0 and 1 or a *bit-array* data-item that consists of a sequence of bits. The definition of a bit-array data-item specifies its index range (which determines the number of bits) and direction, to or downto, which determines the most significant bit in its value. The index range limits are nonnegative integers.

In the EWS example, the sensor is a hardware component whose output, the SIGNAL, is described as a bit-array data-item. See Fig. 3.2. The signal consists of 24 bits, with bit 23 being the most significant. The syntax for such data-type expressions is described in App. A2.5.

Both bit and bit-array data-items are considered numeric, in the sense that they can participate in numeric expressions with no need of any explicit conversion, as discussed in Chap. 5. Values of bit-arrays are usually displayed in binary (e.g., 0B00101111), octal (00057), or hexadecimal (0X2F), with the most significant bit being the leftmost one. A particular bit in the bit-array can be referred to explicitly. For example, SIGNAL(23) is the most significant bit of the sensor's output. Similarly, one can refer to a bit-array slice, such as SIGNAL(2..0), which are the three bits of least significance. Note

Data-Item: **SIGNAL**
Defined in Chart: **EWS**
Data-Type: **bit-array 23 downto 0**

Short Description: **System's input; comes from the sensor.**

Figure 3.2   A bit-array data-item in the Data Dictionary.

that if a bit-array is defined in the `to` (respectively, the `downto`) direction, the index range of its slices must be in ascending (respectively, descending) order.

A data-item can also be of type *string,* denoting a string of characters. String data-items are used when alphanumeric characters are involved, as in the EWS's `FAULT_REPORT`.

A string data-item can be used to introduce enumerated values. For example, we may define a string data-item `COMMAND` with one of three possible values, `'execute'`, `'set-up'`, or `'reset'`, that can be issued by the operator. Notice that the string value is written between single quotation marks. If needed, it is possible to specify the string length. For example, a data-item denoting an identifier name limited to 32 characters will be specified in the Data Dictionary with "Data-type: `string length=32`".

3.4.2 Records and unions

In addition to the basic types, a data-item can be a composition of named components, referred to as *fields,* each of which may be a data-item of any type or a condition. We support two kinds of compositions: *records* and *unions.* In a record, all components are present at any time, while a union contains, in any given time, exactly one of the components. Thus, a record can be viewed as an AND cluster of data, and a union as an OR cluster. The entire construct, record or union, is referenced by its name (e.g., on a flow-line), while a particular field is referenced using the dot notation:

```
record/union reference.field reference.
```

We mentioned that the `LEGAL_RANGE` data-item in the EWS is a record composed of two real fields: `LOW_LIMIT` and `HIGH_LIMIT`. The definition of this data-item in the Data Dictionary is shown in Fig. 3.3. The fields of `LEGAL_RANGE` are referenced by `LEGAL_RANGE.LOW_LIMIT` and `LEGAL_RANGE.HIGH_LIMIT`. The array notations and dot notation can be combined, so that if, for example, one of the fields of a record R is the bit-array `BA`, we may refer to the particular bit `R.BA(2)` or to the slice `R.BA(1..3)`.

A union construct is used when different types of values are relevant to different situations. For example, a union is useful when specifying a communication protocol that involves several kinds of messages, each carrying a different type of data.

Assume that the operator's input in the EWS example arrives via a single communication line that transfer two types of messages, commands and data (e.g., the range limits). Assume also that there is a channel along which the system is told the type of the arriving message. The data-item `MESSAGE_DATA` that carries the data can be

```
Data-Item: LEGAL_RANGE
Defined in Chart: EWS_ACTIVITIES
Data-Type: record
        Field Name: LOW_LIMIT        Field Type: real
        Field Name: HIGH_LIMIT       Field Type: real
```

Figure 3.3 A record in the Data Dictionary.

defined to be a union of two possible fields: COMMAND of type *string* (see Sec. 3.4.1) and LIMIT_VALUE of type *real*. The system will refer to MESSAGE_DATA.COMMAND when it expects a string denoting the command, and to MESSAGE_DATA.LIMIT_VALUE when it expects the numeric range limit value. As explained before, at any given moment only one field of the union "exists," and it is illegal to refer to any other.

The field type attached to every field of the record or the union in the Data Dictionary can be of the following data-types: basic predefined types (e.g., integer, real, etc.; see the preceding section); condition, array, or queue (see the following section); or a user-defined type. The field cannot be defined to be another record or union; this kind of construction must be done with an intermediate definition of a user-defined type. See App. A2.5 for the syntax of data-type expressions.

3.4.3 Data-item structure

Data-items can be organized in structures—*arrays* or *queues*—with each component of the structure having one of the data-types described earlier or a user-defined type, as will be discussed shortly.

An array is a sequence consisting of a fixed predefined number of components. Assume, for example, that the EWS is enhanced to deal with five sensors. It is then natural to talk about an array of the sensor's signals: SIGNALS, defined as an array of five components, each of which is a bit-array, 23 downto 0. See Fig. 3.4.

Each array component can be of any of the basic predefined types, a record/union construct, or a user-defined type. Each component is accessed by its index (e.g., SIGNALS(2)), and double indexing is used to refer to components of components (e.g., SIGNALS(1)(23)). If the array component is a record, the dot notation can be combined with indexing. For example, if AR is an array of records that have two fields, X and Y, then we may use AR(2).X to access the X field of AR(2).

The index range of the array is defined from *left index* to *right index*. There is no limitation on the array size. The index range limits are nonnegative integers, and the left index must be smaller or equal to the right index. (It might be more appropriate to call them "lower index" and "upper index," but the names came from the range limits in bit-arrays.) It is very common to define an array going from 1 to some named integer constant (these are described in Chap. 5). Assume that we have a constant definition NUMBER_OF_SENSORS = 5. Then SIGNALS can be defined as array 1 to NUMBER_OF_SENSORS, to emphasize the fact that the size of the array depends on some other value.

Sometimes the size of one array depends on the size or index range of another. For example, we might want to set things up so that if the system allocates memory for an array, then any copy of it must be of the same size. In this case it is possible to use three predefined operators that apply to an array V: length_of(V), lindex(V), and rindex(V). The operators are evaluated to constant integer values.

A *queue,* as opposed to the fixed size arrays, is a dynamic list of components. Queues are described in detail in Chap. 8, where communication mechanisms are discussed. As in the case of arrays, the components of a queue can be of one of the predefined data types described earlier or a user-defined type. The components cannot be directly defined as records or unions; a queue of such components can be defined with an intermediate user-defined type. Queues are defined in the Data Dictionary just like the other data-items.

3.5   User-Defined Types

It is often the case that several data-items in the model have the same characteristics, such as their data-type. It can be useful to define a named data-type, called a *user-defined type,* that will be used to define them all. In addition to providing clarity, this reusability is also efficient because the full data-type definition appears in only one location in the Data Dictionary.

In the EWS example, the range construct, with the low and high limits, appears at least twice: in the current LEGAL_RANGE and in the FAULT_REPORT that contains the values against which the faulty processed signal was compared. We can have the Data Dictionary contain the definition of a user-defined type RANGE, which will be used later in the definition of these two data-items. This is shown in Fig. 3.5.

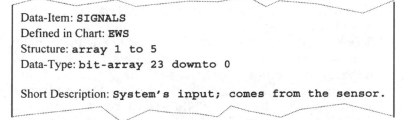

Data-Item: **SIGNALS**
Defined in Chart: **EWS**
Structure: **array 1 to 5**
Data-Type: **bit-array 23 downto 0**

Short Description: **System's input; comes from the sensor.**

Figure 3.4   An array data-item in the Data Dictionary.

```
User-Defined Type: RANGE
Defined in Chart: EWS
Data-Type: record
        Field Name: LOW_LIMIT        Field Type: real
        Field Name: HIGH_LIMIT       Field Type: real

Data-Item: LEGAL_RANGE
Defined in Chart: EWS
Data-Type: RANGE


Data-Item: FAULT_REPORT
Defined in Chart: EWS
Data-Type: record
        Field Name: FAULT_TIME       Field Type: TIME
        Field Name: FAULT_VALUE      Field Type: real
        Field Name: FAULT_RANGE      Field Type: RANGE
```

Figure 3.5   User-defined type RANGE in the Data Dictionary.

```
Data-Item: SCREEN
Data-Type: array 1 to 300 of ROW

User-Defined Type: ROW
Data-Type: array 1 to 200 of PIXEL

User-Defined Type: PIXEL
Data-Type: bit-array 7 downto 0
```

Figure 3.6   A definition of multidimensional array.

User-defined types are specified in terms of predefined types, record/union constructs, or data structures (arrays and queues). It is also possible to define them as other user-defined types or as conditions or arrays of conditions.

The user-defined type mechanism can also be used to define complex types, with multiple-level structure. The data-item FAULT_REPORT presented in Fig. 3.5 is a record, two of whose fields, FAULT_TIME and FAULT_RANGE, are themselves records. To achieve this multilevel structure, we must use the intermediate data-types, TIME and RANGE. We do not allow the definition of a record with an explicit record field.

There are no limitations on the multilevel usage of user-defined types. We can define multidimensional arrays, arrays of records, records with array fields, queues of records, etc., with any number of nesting levels.

For example, to specify a display screen whose size is 200 × 300 pixels, each of 8 bits, we use the data-item SCREEN and the user-defined types ROW and PIXEL, as shown in Fig. 3.6. A particular bit can be accessed by indexing. For example, SCREEN(7)(2)(0) is bit 0 in position (7,2) on the screen (i.e., pixel number 2 in row number 7).

In Chap. 13 we discuss the scope of elements (e.g., how their visibility depends on the chart in which they are defined). User-defined types are often required to be visible throughout the entire model, so they are usually defined in a global definition set, as discussed in Sec. 13.5.

The Behavioral View

Statecharts

This chapter describes the language of Statecharts (Harel 1987b),[1] which is used to describe the control activities in activity-charts. As explained in Chap. 2, these activities constitute the behavioral view of a model.

In this chapter and the two that follow, we concentrate on the pure features of Statecharts and their semantics, leaving those parts that pertain to the connection with Activity-charts to Chap. 7. Thus we do not concern ourselves here with the way activities are controlled by statecharts or with how statecharts are affected by activities, but only with the internal features of the statecharts themselves.

This chapter describes how states are organized into an *and / or hierarchy* and how they may represent levels of behavior and concurrency. We also show how transitions are used (with the various connectors) to describe changes in the states. In Chap. 5 we describe the textual expression language used in Statecharts to specify triggers and actions, and how it supports timing considerations. Chapter 6 describes the dynamic semantics of Statecharts. Throughout, the reader will observe that Statecharts constitute a powerful extension of conventional state-transition diagrams.

4.1 Behavioral Description of a System

A behavioral description of a system specifies dynamic aspects of the entire system or of a particular function, including control and timing.

---

[1]Parts of our description here follow Harel (1987b), although our version reflects some modifications and enhancements that were incorporated to make it better fit the STATEMATE modeling approach.

It specifies the states and modes that the system might reside in and the transitions between them. It also describes what causes activities to start and stop, and the way the system reacts to various events. The functional and behavioral views complete each other, as explained in later chapters.

A natural technique for describing the dynamic of a system is to use a *finite-state machine*. The described system or function is always in one of a finite set of *states*. When an event occurs, the system reacts by performing *actions,* such as generating a signal, changing a variable value, and/or taking a *transition* to another state. The events causing the reaction are called *triggers.* For example, a simple mechanism that controls a light bulb may be in one of two states, OFF and ON. The event BUTTON_PRESSED might trigger the transitions from one of these states to the other. On moving from OFF to ON, the mechanism sends a signal TURN_ON to the light bulb, and similarly, the bulb is turned off on the other transition (see Fig. 4.1).

Let us analyze the behavior of the EWS in terms of states or modes. From the informal description of the EWS presented in Chap. 1 we can identify several main states of the system:

WAITING_FOR_COMMAND	The system is idle, waiting for an operator command o start executing or to set up the range values.
SETTING_UP:	The range values are being set by the operator.
COMPARING:	The signal processing is being performed, and the processed signal is being checked.
GENERATING_ALARM:	The system is generating the alarm to indicate that the value of the processed signal is out of range and is awaiting the operator's reset.

These states are exclusive, that is, when the system is accepting new range limits, it is not performing signal processing or value comparisons. Similarly, the comparisons are not carried out when the alarm is generated. Regarding the transitions between states, when in WAITING_FOR_COMMAND, the EXECUTE command from the operator causes the system to move to the COMPARING state, and the SET_UP command causes a transition to SETTING_UP. This description implies that the system moves to the GENERATING_ALARM state in the event that

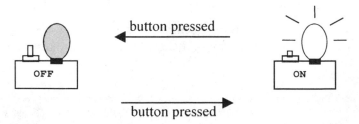

Figure 4.1 A finite-state machine that controls a light bulb.

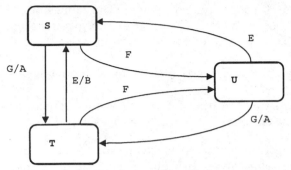

Figure 4.2   A simple state-transition diagram.

the tested signal is out of range. More details about the transitions between these states are given in the following sections.

In some of the states, certain functions from the functional description are performed (on the assumption that we are carrying out a function-based decomposition; see Chap. 2). For example, the SET_UP activity is performed in the SETTING_UP mode. In general, the functional and behavioral views are combined to yield the entire conceptual description of the system under description. This subject is discussed in Chap. 7.

Finite-state machines have an appealing visual representation in the form of *state-transition diagrams*. These are directed graphs in which nodes denote states and arrows denote transitions. The transitions are labeled with the triggering events and caused actions, using the following general syntax for a reaction: *trigger / action*. Figure 4.2 shows a simple three-state diagram that describes a system.

If, for example, the system is in state S and event F occurs, the system is transformed into state U. If, in the same state, G occurs, the system performs the action A and ends up in state T.

In our approach we use the Statecharts language to describe the behavioral view. This language is similar to state-transition diagrams, but includes many enhancements, such as hierarchy, orthogonality, expressions, and connectors. As in Activity-charts, the elements appearing in the charts have associated entities in the Data Dictionary. In the following sections and in the two subsequent chapters, we describe the details of the Statecharts language. The way in which statecharts relate to activity-charts is dealt with in Chaps. 7 and 8.

4.2   Basic Features of Statecharts

As in conventional state-transition diagrams, statecharts are constructed basically from states and transitions. The states in a statechart are depicted as rectilinear boxes with rounded corners. The names of the states appear inside their boxes and obey the name syntax given in App. A.1. The transitions are drawn as splined arrows, with the triggers serving as labels.

The main states of the EWS and the transitions and their triggers are shown in Fig. 4.3.

The triggers of the transitions in Fig. 4.3 are all events, which are regarded as instantaneous occurrences. There are two kinds:

- *External* events coming from external sources (such as the commands coming from the operator via the control panel: SET_UP, EXECUTE, and RESET).

- *Internal* events coming from internal sources (such as OUT_OF_RANGE, which is output from the COMPARE activity; ALARM_TIME_PASSED, which is the output of some invisible clock; and SET_UP_COMPLETED, which signifies that the SET_UP activity has terminated).

We shall see later that the event ALARM_TIME_PASSED can be defined to be more specific about the alarm duration, using the timing facilities provided by our languages. Note that we do not show the source of the triggering events in the statechart itself. We shall return to this issue in Chap. 8.

The trigger of a transition may be an expression that combines some events. It may also include a condition, enclosed in square brackets, or it may consist of the condition only. Thus if a transition is labeled E[C], the condition C is tested at the instant the event E occurs, guarding the transition from being taken if it is not true at that time. If the transition is labeled [C], the condition C is tested at each instant of time when the system is in the transition's source state, and the transition is taken if it is true.

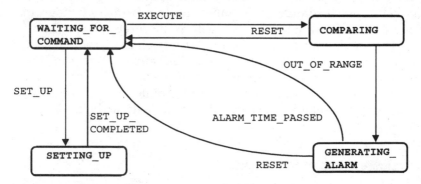

Figure 4.3 States, transitions, and event triggers.

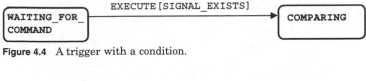

Figure 4.4 A trigger with a condition.

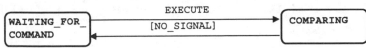

Figure 4.5 A condition as a trigger.

In the EWS example, we may want to prevent the transition between WAITING_FOR_COMMAND and COMPARING from being taken unless the sensor is connected to the system and there is a signal coming from the sensor. We could do this as in Fig. 4.4, by enriching the statechart of Fig. 4.3, with an appropriate condition.

In fact, a similar effect could be achieved differently by using a condition to trigger a transition, rather than as a guard on a triggering event. In Fig. 4.5, we take the transition to COMPARING when the EXECUTE command is issued, but once in COMPARING, we continuously monitor the condition NO_SIGNAL, returning to WAITING_FOR_COMMAND the instant we detect that it is true. In this way, if the sensor is not connected and there is no signal coming from the sensor when we enter COMPARING, we will immediately return to WAITING_FOR_COMMAND. However, if there is a signal, we will stay in COMPARING until the sensor is disconnected and the signal ceases.

A transition can be labeled not only with the trigger that causes it to be taken, but also, optionally, with an action, separated from the trigger by a slash as follows: *trigger/action*. If and when the transition is taken, the specified action is carried out instantaneously. Some actions simply generate an event, but they may also cause other effects. We shall see that actions can modify values of conditions and data-items; they can start and stop activities, and more. Several actions can be performed when a transition is taken. The actions are written after the slash in a sequence, separated by a semicolon (e.g., E/A;B;C).

A simple action incorporated into the EWS example is shown in Fig. 4.6. Here, we have decided that when the ALARM_TIME_PASSED event occurs in the GENERATING_ALARM state, two things happen simultaneously:

- The system returns to the WAITING_FOR_COMMAND state.
- The event PRINT_OUT_OF_RANGE, which is really an internal command to print a fault report on a printing device, is generated.

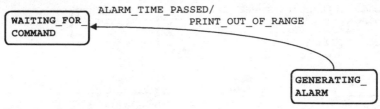

Figure 4.6 A simple action.

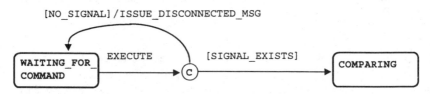

Figure 4.7 A condition connector.

Another way of using conditions to guard transitions is to employ the *condition connector*. An arrow enters the connector, labeled with the triggering event, and the connector may have several exit arrows, each labeled with a condition enclosed in square brackets and optionally also with an action. In general, any number of exit arrows from a condition connector is allowed.

Figure 4.7 shows how the EXECUTE event causes a transition from WAITING_FOR_COMMAND, with the two mutually exclusive conditions NO_SIGNAL and SIGNAL_EXISTS, that determine whether the system enters COMPARING or returns to WAITING_FOR_COMMAND. In the latter case, we have also specified that the event ISSUE_DISCONNECTED_MSG will be generated, causing an error message to appear.

Although the mechanisms of states and transitions labeled by triggers and actions allow rich and complex behavioral descriptions, they are not always enough. Later we will discuss the ability to specify reactions that do not involve transitions between states and to associate them with a specific state. These reactions, as well as the information about the activities that are active in a state, are attached to the state through the Data Dictionary. Like the other elements appearing in statecharts, such as triggers and actions, each state also has an associated entry in the Data Dictionary. Transitions, however, do not have Data Dictionary entries, mainly because they are not identifiable by name.

4.3 The Hierarchy of States

As it turns out, highly complex behavior cannot be easily described by simple, "flat" state-transition diagrams. The reason is rooted in the unmanageable multitude of states, which may result in an unstructured and chaotic state-transition diagram. To be useful, the state machine approach must be modular, hierarchical, and well structured. In this section we show how states can be beneficially *clustered* into a hierarchy.

Recall Fig. 4.2. Since event F takes the system to state U from either state S or state T, we may cluster the latter into a new state, call it V, and replace the two F transitions with one, as in Fig. 4.8.

The semantics of the new state V is as follows: to be in V is to be, exclusively, in either of its *substates,* S or T. This is the classical exclusive-or applied to states. V is called an *or-state,* and it is the *parent* of the two sibling states S and T. The F transition now emanates from on V, meaning that whenever F occurs in V, the system makes a transition to U. But because being in V is just being in S or T, the new F arrow precisely abbreviates the two old ones.

Applying this feature to our example, we may cluster the states COMPARING and GENERATING_ALARM into a new state (which does not need to have a name), simply because of the common exit transition triggered by the operator command RESET. (See Fig. 4.9.)

We can also achieve results similar to those shown in Figs. 4.8 and 4.9 not by clustering, which is a bottom-up operation, but by *refinement,* which is top-down (as in the functional decomposition that is presented in Chap. 2). For example, we could have started the EWS behavioral description with the two-state decomposition of Fig. 4.10, in which one top-level state, EWS_STATES, is decomposed into two

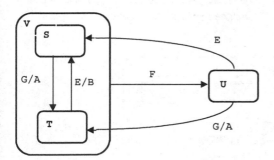

Figure 4.8 Clustering of states.

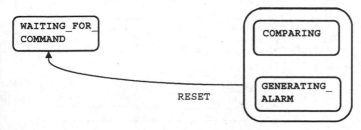

Figure 4.9 Clustering of EWS states.

substates, OFF and ON. These states are connected by two transitions, labeled POWER_ON and POWER_OFF.

We specify that the initial state of the system is OFF by using a *default transition,* specified by a small arrow emanating from a small solid circle. We can then zoom in to the ON state, and show the next-level state decomposition of the EWS. This results in the multilevel statechart of Fig. 4.11. The EWS states from Fig. 4.3 appear here as substates of the state ON. The default transition to WAITING_FOR_COMMAND indicates that this state is the default entrance of the ON state. This means that when there is a transition that leads to the borderline of the parent state, without indicating which of the substates is to be entered, like the one triggered by POWER_ON, the system enters the default substate.

The main advantage of using default transitions is in cases where there is more than one entrance to the parent state. Note that the top level of each parent state can have only one default entrance. A default transition usually leads to a substate in the first level of the state decomposition, but it can be made to directly enter a state on a lower level, as shown in Fig. 4.12.

Some terms and conventions that we use for the hierarchy of statecharts are similar to those used for activity-charts. A state that has no substates, such as WAITING_FOR_COMMAND, is referred to as a *basic state.* The state EWS_STATES is an *ancestor* of its *descendants,* which consist of all other states in Fig. 4.11. As in activity-charts, we say that a transition exits from its *source state* and enters its *target state.*

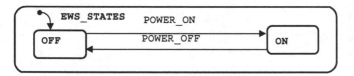

Figure 4.10 Top-level state decomposition of EWS.

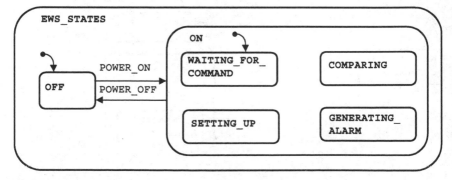

Figure 4.11 A multilevel statechart.

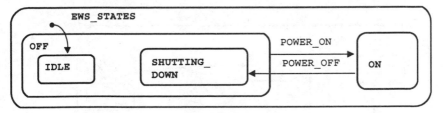

Figure 4.12   Default entrance to a lower-level state.

4.4   Orthogonality

4.4.1   And-states and event broadcasting

One of the main problems with descriptions of behavior is rooted in the acute growth in the number of states as the system is extended. Consider a statechart with 1000 states that describes certain control aspects of a flight-control system. Suppose that the behavior is now enriched by making its details depend to a large extent on whether the aircraft is in autopilot mode. With the features we have so far we might have to double the number of states, obtaining two versions of each of the old states—one with autopilot and one without—altogether 2000 states. As more additions are made, the number of states grows exponentially.

An additional problem arises when we want to describe independent or almost independent parts of the behavior (e.g., the behavior of several different subsystems) in a single statechart.

Statecharts handle these cases by allowing the *and-decomposition* of a state. This means that a state S is described as consisting of two or more *orthogonal components,* and to be in state S entails being in all of those components simultaneously. S is then called an *and-state.* The notation used is a dashed line that partitions the state into its components. The name of the and-state is attached to the state frame. The orthogonal components are named like regular states.

Figure 4.13*a* shows a state S consisting of the two components R and T, and being in S is being in both. However, because each component is an or-state, the first consisting of U and V and the second consisting of W, X, and Y, it follows that to be in S is to be in one of U or V as well as one of W, X, or Y. Such a tuple of states, each from a different orthogonal component, is called a *state configuration.* We say that S is the *parent* of its components R and T, or that R and T are the *sub-states* of S, as in the case of or-decomposition. The components R and T are no different from any other states; they may have their own sub-states, default entrances, internal transitions, and so on.

Entering S from the outside is tantamount to entering the configuration (U, X) by the default arrows. If E occurs in (U, X), the system transfers simultaneously to (V, Y), a transition that is really a form of synchronized concurrence—a single event triggering two simultaneous

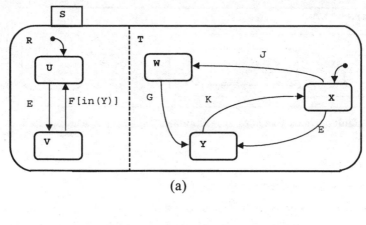

(a)

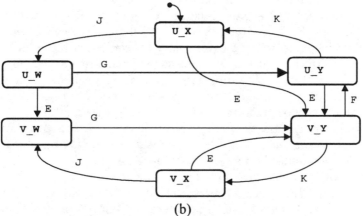

(b)

Figure 4.13 Orthogonality using and-decomposition. (*a*) An and-state. (*b*) A nonorthogonal equivalent.

happenings. If K now occurs, the new configuration is (V, X), yielding a form of independence—a transition is taken in the T component, independently of what might be happening in the R component. Notice the in(Y) condition appearing in R. It signifies that the F transition from V to U is taken only if the system is in (V, Y). Thus one component is allowed to sense which state the other is in.

Figure 4.13*b* is the conventional "and-free" equivalent of Fig. 4.13*a*, and while it is not much larger than Fig. 4.13*a*, it illustrates the blow-up in the number of states: if Fig. 4.13*a* had 100 states in each component, giving a total of 200 bottom-level (basic) states, Fig. 4.13*b* would have had to contain all 10,000 combinations explicitly!

Returning to our EWS example, consider Fig. 4.14. Here we have added an orthogonal component to the ON state named PROCESSING. Its role is to describe the processing aspects of the raw signal read from the external sensor.

The conditions SENSOR_CONNECTED and SENSOR_DISCONNECTED in the PROCESSING component indicate the status of the connection with the sensor. They are set by the operator and are thus external. The OPERATE and HALT events, on the other hand, being generated by the MONITORING component, are internal. They are generated by actions when the system enters and exits the COMPARING state, respectively, and serve to indicate to the processing unit whether the system has completed the comparing of the processed signal.

Notice how these events are sensed immediately by the orthogonal component. Moreover, events generated by actions in one component are sensed by all other orthogonal components. For example, if there were more than one sensor, each with a corresponding signal processing unit, we could have modeled each of them by its own component, and the OPERATE and HALT events would have then been broadcast automatically to each one of them.

4.4.2 Conditions and events related to states

It is interesting to note that some of the events and conditions that label transitions in the EWS example now depend on and refer to states in the orthogonal component. Thus we may replace the conditions NO_SIGNAL and SIGNAL_EXISTS in Fig. 4.14 with in(CONNECTED) and in(DISCONNECTED), respectively. In fact, we may refer not only to the status of being or not being in a state as a condition but to the moment of entrance or exit as an event. The syntax is entered(S) and exited(S), with en and ex abbreviating the verbs. We may thus replace the OPERATE and HALT events in the CONNECTED state by en(COMPARING) and ex(COMPARING), respectively, and

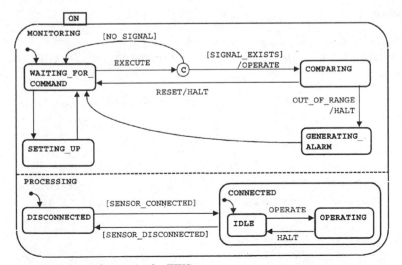

Figure 4.14 An and-state in the EWS.

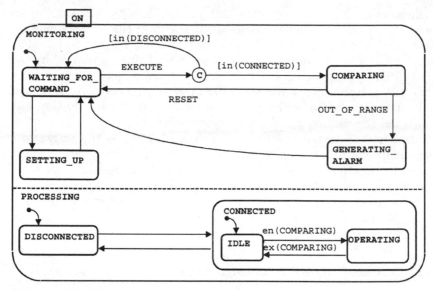

Figure 4.15 Conditions and events related to states.

the two events need no longer be explicitly generated by actions along transitions. The resulting statechart is shown in Fig. 4.15.

Note that the meaning of the and/or decomposition of states implies the following:

- If the system is in a state S, then not only is in(S) true but in(T) holds for each ancestor T of S.

- Entering a state S will trigger the event en(S), as well as en(T) for every ancestor T of S in which the system did not reside when S was entered.

- Exiting a state S will trigger the event ex(S), as well as ex(T) for each ancestor T of S in which the system does not reside after the transition.

Even in cases where states are exited and entered by looping transitions, such as the transition from or to WAITING_FOR_COMMAND shown in Fig. 4.7, the corresponding events ex(S) and en(S) occur. Section 5.4 contains further explanation about when these events occur.

The condition in(S) and the events en(S) and ex(S) may not be applied to an and-component such as PROCESSING. Instead, they should be applied to the parent and-state (in this case, the state ON).

4.4.3   Multi-level state decomposition

Orthogonal break-up into components is not restricted to a single level. For example, we might have further refined the OPERATING state of the

EWS, within CONNECTED, into two components: one deals with the clock rate of the signal sampling and the other with the computation mode. This is shown in Fig. 4.16.

Note that "high-level" transitions continue to apply, regardless of whether a state has orthogonal components. Thus the HALT event, for example, takes the system out of whatever state configuration within OPERATING it is in and causes entry into IDLE.

An important point is that there are no scoping restrictions within a single statechart, so any state can be referred to anywhere in the state-chart, even if the state referred to appears in some level lower down.

As with activities, two states may have the same name if they have different parent states, in which case their names are distinguished by using *path names,* that is, by attaching their ancestors' names separated by periods. Thus had we chosen to rename CONNECTED and DISCONNECTED simply by ON and OFF, we would have to write PROCESSING.ON and PROCESSING.OFF whenever they had to be distinguished from the ON and OFF that reside within the top-level state. This convention is not limited to a single level; a sequence of several state names can be given, separated by periods, such as S1.S2.S3. Notice that no particular relationship is implied between states that have the same name.

4.5   Connectors and Compound Transitions

As in activity-charts, we allow several kinds of connectors in state-charts. They are used to help economize in arrows to clarify the specification.

4.5.1   Condition and switch connectors

As mentioned earlier, statecharts may employ *condition connectors,* also called *C-connectors.* Figure 4.7 showed an example. In general, the conditions along the branches emanating from the C-connector

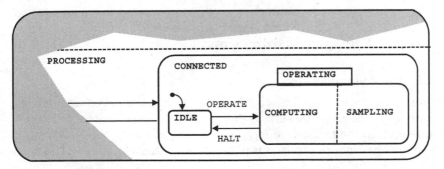

Figure 4.16 And-decomposition on any level.

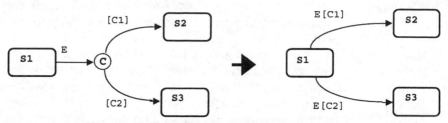

Figure 4.17 A condition connector and compound transitions.

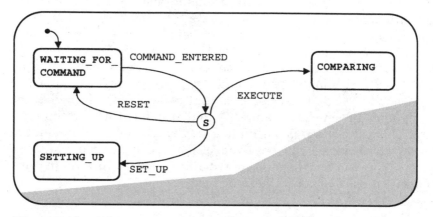

Figure 4.18 A switch connector.

must be exclusive, but there can be more than two such branches. When the conditions are not exclusive, a situation of nondeterminism ensues, which is discussed in more detail in Sec. 6.3.

Figure 4.17 shows a simple case of using the C-connector and the equivalent *logical transitions*. Each logical transition is represented by a *compound transition* consisting of two simple transitions. The transition labeled E is part of both.

Another connector, similar to the C-connector, is the *switch connector,* also called the *S-connector,* which is usually used with events rather than conditions. In our EWS example, we may define a named event, COM-MAND_ENTERED, as the disjunction of three command events: EXECUTE or SET_UP or RESET. (Named events are discussed in Chap. 5.) We may then deal with the command-driven transitions of Fig. 4.3 as in Fig. 4.18.

4.5.2 Junction connectors

Transition arrows can be joined using *junction connectors,* and the labels along them can be split as desired. This makes it possible to economize both in the number of lengthy arrows present in the chart and in the number of identical portions of labels. For example, Fig. 4.19*a* shows how to use a junction connector if the same event (RESET, in this case) causes exit from two states, but we do not want to cluster the two states into one.

Figure 4.19*b* shows a more subtle case, in which two events lead out of a state into two separate states, but there is a common action that is to be carried out along both. As this last example shows, the order in which events and actions appear along the parts of the compound transitions formed by using junction connectors is unimportant. However, all the triggers appearing along the parts of a compound transition must occur at exactly the same time for the transition to be taken. If and when that happens, all the actions appearing along the transition are carried out. As an example, the two parts of Fig. 4.20 are actually equivalent.

Multiple entrances and exits may be attached to a junction, and the semantics prescribes creation of logical compound transitions from all possible combinations of paths. The same is true of C-connectors and S-connectors.

The different connectors are meant to visually emphasize the distinction between different kinds of behavior: a C-connector indicates branching by conditions, an S-connector branches by events, and junction connectors are used for the remaining cases.

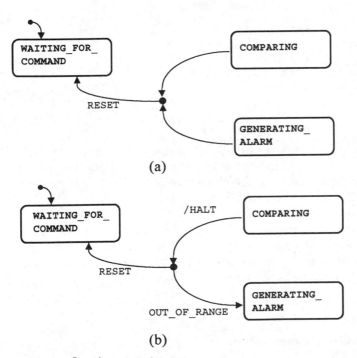

(a)

(b)

Figure 4.19   Junction connectors.

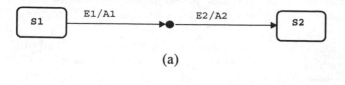

(a)

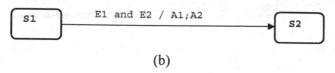

(b)

Figure 4.20 Two equivalent transition constructs.

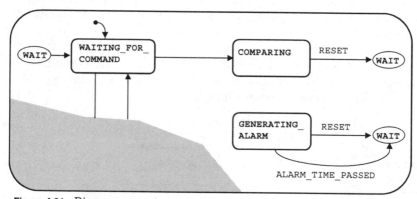

Figure 4.21 Diagram connectors.

4.5.3 Diagram connectors

As in activity-charts, statecharts also allow diagram connectors. These are simply a means for eliminating lengthy arrows from the chart in favor of marking two points in the chart and indicating that the arrow flows from one point to the other. See Fig. 4.21.

Any legal name may be used to label the diagram connectors (see App. A.1), as can any integer. Each occurrence must have only entering arrows or only exiting ones. Triggers and actions are concatenated along all possible combinations of paths that constitute compound transitions, as with other connectors.

4.6 More about Transitions

4.6.1 Transitions to and from and-states

Recall that being in an and-state is being in a configuration of states—one from each component. As a consequence, the Statecharts language allows splitting and merging arrows to denote entries to and exits from state configurations.

Figure 4.22 shows an alternative way of describing the transition from OFF to ON in our EWS example. Instead of having a default entrance in each component (as in Fig. 4.14), we have a *fork construct* that depicts the entrance to the default configuration directly. We may view a fork as another kind of compound transition, with the splitting point of the two branches as a special *joint connector.*

Such a transition is taken if and when all of its triggers occur, and when taken, all of its actions are performed. Thus Fig. 4.23, for example (while possibly misleading), shows a case in which the transition is not taken unless all of E, E1, and E2 occur simultaneously. When it is taken, both actions A1 and A2 are performed.

A dual kind of arrow can be used to exit a state configuration. Figure 4.24 shows a case in which the system will enter S5 if it was in the configuration (S2, S4) and E occurred. This is a *merge construct.*

If one portion of the transition is missing, the meaning is quite different. Figure 4.25 illustrates this case, in which the and-state is exited, and S5 is entered when E occurs and the system is in S2. The

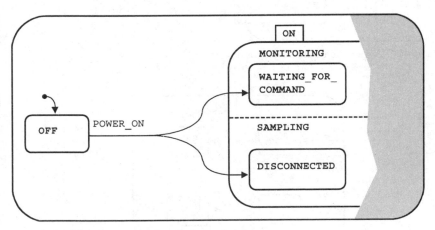

Figure 4.22   A joint connector in a fork construct.

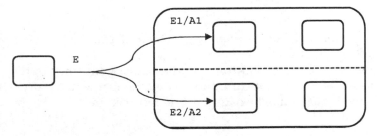

Figure 4.23   Triggers and actions on a fork construct.

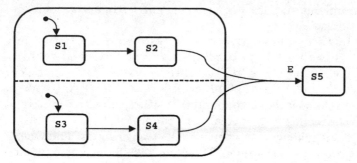

Figure 4.24 A joint connector in a merge construct.

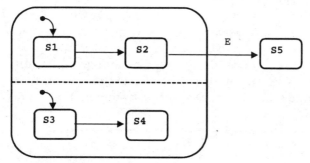

Figure 4.25 A transition from an and-state.

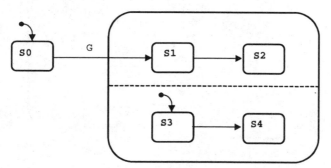

Figure 4.26 A transition into an and-state.

transition is performed independently of which of the substates in the other component the system is in (S3 or S4).

Figure 4.26 shows a transition from S0 that causes entrance to the configuration (S1, S3). The entrance to S1 is by the arrow itself, overriding any default that might exist, and the entrance to S3 is by the default transition.

4.6.2   History entrances

An interesting way to enter a group of states is by the system's history in that group. The simplest kind of this "enter-by-history" feature is to enter the state most recently visited within the group. This is depicted by the special *history connector,* also called an *H-connector.*

Returning once again to our EWS example, consider Fig. 4.27. Here we have decided that once the sensor is connected when we are in state DISCONNECTED, we make a transition to state CONNECTED and enter the inner state that was visited most recently, which will be either IDLE or OPERATING. The arrow leads to an H-connector; thus the mode the EWS reenters is the mode it left when the sensor was disconnected. Notice that the H-connector also has a regular outgoing transition leading to IDLE. This signifies that IDLE is the state to be entered if there is no history (e.g., when the CONNECTED state is entered for the first time).

The history connector specified in Fig. 4.27 indicates an entrance by history on the first level only. If state OPERATING, for example, had substates SLOW and FAST, the history entrance would not extend down to these. In other words, it would not "remember" which of these two substates the system last resided in, and the entrance would be to the one specified as default. To extend a history entrance down to all levels, the H-connector can appear with an asterisk attached, indicating an entrance to the most recently visited state (or configuration) on the lowest level. This is a *deep history connector,* and it is illustrated in Fig. 4.28. If the system was last in OPERATING.FAST, that would be the state entered, despite the fact that SLOW is the internal default.

Once we have history entrances, we must provide the ability to "forget" the history at will. In our example, we may wish to specify that when the HALT event is generated the slate will be cleaned, and the next entrance to OPERATING will be to the default state SLOW, regardless of past behavior. We have special actions for this purpose, which can be used along the appropriate transitions:

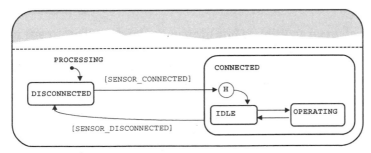

Figure 4.27   A history connector.

5.1.1 Event expressions

Most of the transition triggers shown in Chap. 4 consisted of just an event name. However, a trigger can be any event expression, as described here. Figure 4.15 showed events that occur upon entering or exiting a state, en(S) and ex(S). Other events indicate changes in the status of other elements, such as changes in the values of conditions and data-items, and in the status of activities. These will be discussed when the manipulation of the relevant elements is presented.

Expressions for *compound events* can be constructed by using the Boolean operations and, or, and not. In the EWS example, the two transitions from GENERATING_ALARM to WAITING_FOR_COMMAND in Fig. 4.3 may be combined, using an event disjunction, as in Fig. 5.1. The transition labeled with the event disjunction is taken when at least one of the events occurs.

The negation of an event using the *not* operation must be approached with caution. This negation means that the specified event did *not* occur, and it makes sense only when the negated event is checked at a specific point in time, that is, when combined with other events. This is achieved by using an *and* operation or a compound transition. Thus, for example, if the event E has been defined as E1 or E2 or E3 or E4 or E5 (using the Data Dictionary, as explained in the next section), then we may use either Fig. 5.2a or Fig. 5.2b instead of Fig. 5.2c. Recall that the junction connectors used in this figure denote the conjunction of triggers.

Note also that the combination of an event and a condition, E[C] (even if the event is absent, as in the trigger [C]), is considered an event, so that E1[C1] and [C2] or E2, for example, is an event expression, too.

Event expressions are evaluated according to the conventional precedence rules of logical operations, and parentheses can be used in the usual way to override the default orderings. See App. A for detailed information about precedence of operations.

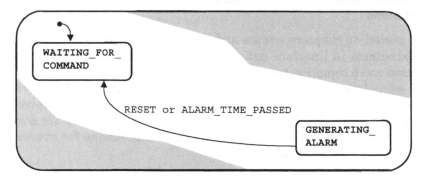

Figure 5.1 Disjunction of events.

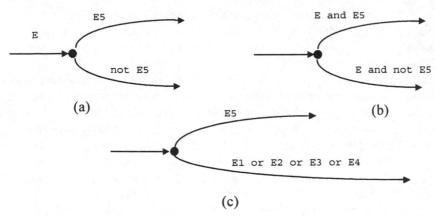

Figure 5.2 Negating an event.

All the aforementioned event expressions evaluate to yield a single event (as opposed to an event array). A component of an event array can be used whenever an event expression is allowed, and it is identified by its index, for example, `DIGIT_PRESSED(1)`.

Very often we want to detect the fact that some unspecified component of an event array has occurred. We use the operator `any` for this. For example, the event expression `any(DIGIT_PRESSED)` refers to the event array defined in Fig. 3.1, and captures the pressing of any one (or more) of the ten digit keys on the operator keyboard of the EWS. Similarly, although rarely used, the `all` operator captures the simultaneous occurrence of all events in the array.

5.1.2 Condition expressions

Some of the transition labels presented in Chap. 4 include condition expressions. In the simplest case, the condition expression is just the condition name, such as `SIGNAL_EXISTS` in Fig. 4.4, but we also saw the condition expression `in(CONNECTED)` used in Fig. 4.15. Other condition expressions are also related to the status of other kinds of elements, and they will be presented as we go along.

We often want a condition to compare data-items in one of several ways. To do so, we allow the following comparison conditions, where # depicts inequality:

```
exp1 = exp2,     exp1 # exp2,
exp1 > exp2,     exp1 < exp2,
exp1 <= exp2,    exp1 >= exp2
```

Assume that we have chosen to represent the operator command of the EWS by a string data-item `COMMAND` that has three possible values, namely, `` `execute` ``, `` `set-up` `` or `` `reset` ``. The exit from the

WAITING_FOR_COMMAND state would be triggered by the event COM-MAND_ENTERED, denoting the assignment of a value to this data-item, and would be channeled to the appropriate state, depending on that value. See Fig. 5.3.

The expressions on both sides of the comparisons must be of the same type, both numeric or both strings. They can also be arrays or records and are then compared component-wise. Arrays must be of the same length and component type, and records can be compared only if they are of the same user-defined type. For strings we allow only = and #.

As in the case of events, the Boolean operations and, or, and not can be used to construct *compound conditions.* Figure 5.4 shows two alternative ways to restrict the transition from WAITING_FOR_COMMAND to COMPARING by using the conditions SET_UP_DONE and in(CONNECTED).

Because conditions can be organized in arrays or constitute fields in a record, the condition expression can have the corresponding syntax. For example, if the EWS monitors an array of sensors and SENSORS_CONNECTED is the array of conditions representing their connection status, then SENSORS_CONNECTED(I) is a legal condition expression specifying the status of the Ith component. To capture the condition of at least one of the sensors being connected or all of them, we may use the any and all operators, respectively, as in any(SENSORS_CONNECTED). These operators can also be used to refer to a slice of the array, as in all(SENSORS_CONNECTED(1..3)), which is true when the three first sensors are connected.

5.1.3 Data-item expressions

We mentioned conditions that compare data-item expressions. Data-item expressions can also be used in other places in the textual language, such

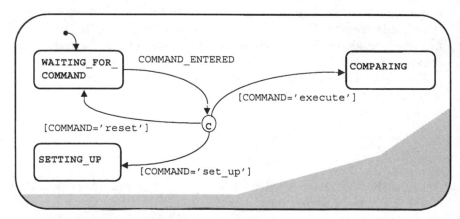

Figure 5.3 Comparison conditions.

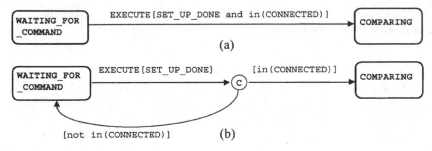

Figure 5.4   Condition expressions.

as in assignment actions, and can be of different types: numeric (integer, real, bit, and bit-array), strings, and structured.

Numeric expressions consist of constants and numeric data-items (or numeric components of structured data-items), combined by conventional arithmetic and bit-wise operations with the usual precedence rules. An example is $Y+3*R.X-A(I+J)$. There is also a set of predefined functions that can be used within numeric expressions, such as arithmetic and trigonometric functions (e.g., abs(X), sin(A)), bit-array operations (e.g., the logical shift-left operation lshl(B)), and random number generators (e.g., rand_normal(R,S)). See App. A.

In addition, in numeric expressions we allow the use of functions that are not predefined. These are called *user functions*, and may employ data-item and condition parameters that come from the model. These functions usually denote parts of the system whose details are not currently essential. They may remain unspecified, and eventually could be taken from an existing implementation.

Numeric expressions can involve the various numeric types, and type conversion is carried out as needed. Integer and bit-array constants can use bases other than the decimal base, such as binary (e.g., 0B00101011), octal (e.g., 0O0053), and hexadecimal (e.g., 0X2B). Real constants can be represented in exponential format (e.g., 2.5e-3).

As mentioned earlier, string constants are enclosed in quotes, (e.g., `abc`). There are no operations on strings, but the language offers several functions for string manipulation, such as concatenation, substring search in another string, and conversion between integer and string. See App. A.

Structured data-items (i.e., arrays, records, and unions) do not support operations, either. There is a special representation for array constants that uses commas between the components. An asterisk for repetitions is also allowed. For example, {20*0} is an array constant consisting of 20 zeros, while {1,2,3,10*1,0,0} is an array constant consisting of 15 integer components. However, the language provides no record or union constants.

Appendix A describes the full set of operations and functions that can be applied to data-items and their relative precedence.

5.1.4   Named expressions

We mentioned earlier that an element expression can be abbreviated by a simple element name. This is carried out by associating a *definition* with an element in the Data Dictionary, and here are the most common reasons for doing so:

- To shorten a lengthy expression that appears many times in transitions or in other places where the textual language is used. A short definition in the Data Dictionary prevents errors of inconsistency, enhances clarity, and economizes in writing. In the EWS example, we can define the condition READY to be SET_UP_DONE and in(CONNECTED). This will shorten the trigger on the transition in Fig. 5.4*a,* yielding EXECUTE[READY].

- To abstract away the expression, hiding details that we might not have decided upon yet or might want to change later on. In the EWS example, we can define a data-item ALARM_DURATION whose value will be specified later. In this example, the reason could be our desire to be able to change the duration in a flexible way. Also, the exact time is not really important in an early stage of the specification.

Such an abbreviating definition can be associated with any event, condition, or data-item. An element with no definition is called a *primitive element,* or a *variable,* and can be generated (in case of an event) or modified (in case of a condition or a data-item) in the model in the usual way. An element that has an expression definition is called a *compound element* (see Fig. 5.5*a*). The element is referred to as a compound element even when the expression is just the name of some other element. For example, the event E is defined to occur when event G occurs. An element, a data-item, or condition, is referred to as a *constant* when its definition is a literal constant expression (see Fig. 5.5*b*).

Because compound elements or constants depend for their values on their associated expressions, they cannot be affected directly by actions. For example, such an element cannot appear on the left-hand side of an assignment action, cannot label a flow-line, and cannot be a component of an information-flow.

These limitations do not apply to the special case of attaching an *alias* to a bit-array slice, which can be useful in applications such as digital chip design and communication protocol specification. In such applications an individual bit or a slice of a bit-array might carry special meaning, and it helps to be able to refer to the bit-array portion by a special name. For example, a message can be composed of a series of bits divided into groups that denote the message type, command code, data fields, etc. Assume that MSG is a message that is implemented by a bit-array of 64 bits, indexed from 0 to 63. The first three bits, MSG(0..2), denote the message type. An integer data-item MSG_TYPE will be defined to be an alias of MSG(0..2) (see Fig. 5.5c). Now the message sender can assign a value to MSG_TYPE, which is just like assigning a value to MSG(0..2), and the message reader can check the value of MSG_TYPE in the decoding process. A lower level of the communication protocol that handles these messages can be made to access the individual bits, with no extra conversion to another data structure.

It is possible to define a data-item of type integer, bit, or bit-array to be an alias of an expression for a bit-array slice with a constant range of indices. As mentioned, an alias is treated like a variable and can be used wherever a variable is allowed, unlike compound and constant data-items.

Any occurrence of the element that has an expression definition can be viewed as if the expression were written out in full. Moreover, the expression is reevaluated whenever there is need to evaluate the element.

It is also possible to define named actions, as discussed in the next section.

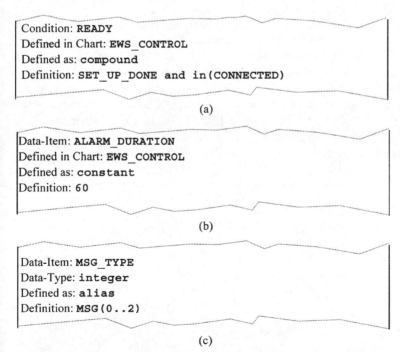

(a)

(b)

(c)

Figure 5.5 Elements with definitions in the Data Dictionary: (a) compound, (b) constant, and (c) alias elements.

5.2   Actions

In addition to the transitions between states, other things may happen during execution of the model. They are usually specified by the *actions.* We saw some examples of actions written along transitions. In addition, actions can appear in *static reactions,* as described later in this chapter, and in *mini-specs* of activities, as described in Chap. 7.

The textual language allows various types of actions, which are described in the following sections. They can be classified as follows:

- Basic actions that manipulate elements, causing changes that can be checked and triggering other happenings in the system.

- Conditional and iterative actions, similar in structure to those in conventional programming languages.

5.2.1   Element manipulation

The most basic actions manipulate three types of elements: events, conditions, and data-items.

Event manipulation is really just sending the event. This is performed by the action that is simply the name of the event. We saw examples of actions that send events in Fig. 4.14: the events OPERATE and HALT are sent when the transitions to and from the COMPARING state are taken, respectively.

Condition manipulation is a little more flexible. Special actions can cause a condition to become true or false. In our EWS example, we may want to distinguish between success and failure of the setting-up procedure to ensure that we start comparing values in the COMPARING state only if the set-up succeeded. This may be achieved as follows. In Fig. 5.4, we added theguarding condition SET_UP_DONE to the transition from WAITING_FOR_COMMAND to COMPARING. Now, in Fig. 5.6, we add the two self-explanatory events SET_UP_SUCCEEDED and SET_UP_FAILED, which label two separate exits from the SETTING_UP state. In the case

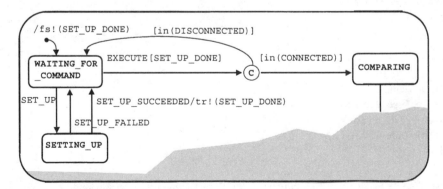

Figure 5.6 Actions on conditions.

of success—and in that case only—we carry out the action `make_true` (`SET_UP_DONE`) (abbreviated `tr!(SET_UP_DONE)`).

In general, the action `tr!(C)` has the effect of setting the truth value of condition C to true, and the corresponding action `make_false(C)` (abbreviated `fs!(C)`) sets it to false. The default entrance to `WAITING_FOR_COMMAND`, for example, is labeled with a `make_false` action that assigns a false value to `SET_UP_DONE`. So the system will react to the `EXECUTE` command only if the setting-up procedure ended successfully at least once.

Instead of the actions `tr!(C)` and `fs!(C)` we may use the assignment actions `C:=true` and `C:=false`, respectively. In general, the right-hand side of such a condition assignment can be any condition expression.

In addition to these actions, a condition C has two associated events, `true(C)` and `false(C)`, which occur precisely when C changes from false to true and from true to false, respectively. We abbreviate them as `tr(C)` and `fs(C)`. The condition C can be a condition expression that depends on other conditions or data-items. Interestingly, this makes it possible to replace events by conditions. In Fig. 4.10, for example, instead of the two events `POWER_ON` and `POWER_OFF`, we could have a single condition, `POWER_IS_ON`, and use the two events `true(POWER_IS_ON)` and `false(POWER_IS_ON)`.

A subtle point concerns the precise relationship between the actions `tr!(C)` and `fs!(C)` and the events `tr(C)` and `fs(C)`. For example, does `tr(C)` always occur when `tr!(C)` is executed? The answer is no. The events occur only when the truth value of C changes value, but the actions can be executed without changing the truth value if it was the desired one to start with. Thus, for example, if the setting-up procedure completed successfully twice in succession, then the first execution of the action `tr!(SET_UP_DONE)` will trigger the event `tr(SET_UP_DONE)`, but the second execution will not.

Assignment actions can also be used to manipulate data-items, and as in the case of conditions, there are events and conditions associated with them. In the EWS example, we may be interested in producing an alarm only after three occurrences of `OUT_OF_RANGE`. This may be achieved as in Fig. 5.7.

All types of data-items can be involved in assignments. The right-hand-side expression of the assignment must be type consistent with the assigned data-item on the left-hand side. Both sides must be either numeric or string. They can also be arrays, in which case their lengths must be the same and the component types must be consistent. Assignments of an entire structured data-item (record or union) are also allowed, but both sides must be of exactly the same user-defined type.

Whenever an assignment to X takes place, the event `written(X)` (abbreviated `wr(X)`) occurs. Thus, we may replace the trigger `COMMAND_ENTERED` in Fig. 5.3 with the event `wr(COMMAND)`. The exit

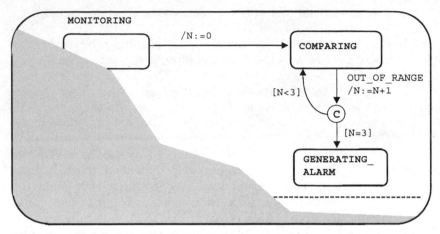

Figure 5.7 Actions and conditions on data-items.

from the WAITING_FOR_COMMAND state would be triggered by an (external) assignment to COMMAND, and would be channeled to the appropriate state, depending on its value. See Fig. 5.8.

A similar event is changed(X) (abbreviated ch(X)), which occurs when and if there was a change in the value of the data-item expression X. Thus, in our example, we cannot replace the event wr(COMMAND) by ch(COMMAND) (as a trigger of the transition from WAITING_FOR_COMMAND), because that would make it impossible to carry out two successive entries to SETTING_UP.

We may also use the actions write_data(X) and read_data(X) (abbreviated wr!(X) and rd!(X), respectively). These actions apply to all types of data-items, including ones that are structured, and even to conditions. These actions cause the occurrence of the events written(X) and read(X), respectively. They will be discussed further in Chap. 8.

Note that we do not allow actions to be carried out on named compound elements. It makes no sense to perform the action tr!(C) when C is defined as C1 or C2, or similarly to assign a value directly to X1+X2. (Of course, these changes can be achieved by operating on the components, i.e., by changing the values of C1, C2, X1, or X2.)

5.2.2 Compound actions and context variables

We already mentioned that it is possible to perform more than one action when a transition is taken. This compound sequential action is written by separating the component actions by a semicolon (e.g., A1;A2;A3).

Another kind of compound action is the *conditional action,* in which the actual action carried out depends on a condition or an event. The two cases differ in their format:

```
if C then A else B end if
when E then A else B end when
```

where A and B are actions, C is a condition expression and E is an event expression. The meaning of these is self-explanatory. In both cases the else B part is optional.

For example, in the EWS we may define an event SET_UP_COM-PLETED to be the disjunction SET_UP_SUCCEEDED or SET_UP_FAILED. Figure 5.9 may then be used to specify the transitions from SETTING_UP to WAITING_FOR_COMMAND concisely, and it should be compared with Fig. 5.6.

Actions can be lengthy sequences of compound actions, and may involve complex expressions. It is thus helpful to attach a name to an

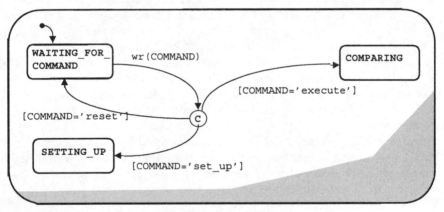

Figure 5.8   An event related to a data-item.

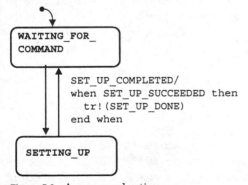

Figure 5.9   A compound action.

action, using the Data Dictionary. For example, the conditional action in Fig. 5.9 can be named SET_SUCCESS, shortening the transition label to SET_UP_COMPLETED/SET_SUCCESS.

When a sequence of actions involves assignments, the timing in which the left-hand-side variable gets its new value is significant. As explained in Chap. 6, the model is executed in steps, and the actual assignment is performed only at the end of the step using the values from the end of the preceding step. Therefore, an action like X:=1;Y:=X will result in Y becoming equal to the value that X had *before* the action execution, which may not necessarily be 1. Moreover, if we check the value of a variable X in a conditional action that follows an assignment to X, the value used will be the one from the preceding step. For example, in the action sequence X:=Y; if X=Y then A1 else A2 end if, the action A1 is *not* necessarily carried out because X and Y might have had different values before the action.

This method of computation is sometimes inconvenient, especially when true sequentiality is required. For this purpose we provide *context variables*, identified by a prefixed $. In contrast to regular data-items and conditions, context variables get their values immediately, so that $X:=1; Y:=$X results in Y being equal to 1, and $X:=Y; if $X=Y then A1 else A2 end if causes A1 to be performed in any case.

Context variables have limited scope. They are recognized only within the action expression in which they appear, and their value is not saved between different invocations of the same action. Thus context variables used in the definition of a named action A are not recognized in an action instantiating A, and vice versa. Also, actions that appear in labels of different transition segments connected by a connector do not share the context variables, even when they are performed in the same step. Context variables have no entry in the Data Dictionary; thus they inherit their type from the expression first assigned to them.

5.2.3 Iterative actions

We have seen how to define arrays of events, conditions, and data-items. To help manipulate these arrays we provide iterative actions. In particular, the *for loop* action makes it possible to access the individual array components in successive order. The for loop action has the following syntax:

```
for $I in N1 to N2 loop
    A
end loop
```

Here, $I is a context variable, N1 and N2 are integer expressions, and A is an action. For example, assume that there is an array of sensors monitored by the EWS. For each sensor I, there is a corresponding SAMPLE(I) whose value is checked for being in the desired range, producing an array of self-explanatory IN_RANGE conditions. This can be done as follows:

```
for $I in 1 to NUMBER_OF_SENSORS loop
    IN_RANGE($I):=(SAMPLE($I) => LEGAL_RANGE.LOW_LIMIT)
                and (SAMPLE($I) =>LEGAL_RANGE.HIGH_LIMIT)
end loop
```

The iterations can be carried out with the context variable repeatedly decremented, by using the keyword downto instead of to in the range designation.

Assume now that instead of producing the IN_RANGE values for all the sensors, it suffices to identify one sensor for which the value is out of legal range. When this happens, the OUT_OF_RANGE event should be produced. This can be done by the following for loop action:

```
for $I in 1 to NUMBER_OF_SENSORS loop
    if ((SAMPLE($I) < LEGAL_RANGE.LOW_LIMIT) or
        (SAMPLE($I) > LEGAL_RANGE.HIGH_LIMIT)) then
        OUT_OF_RANGE;
        break
    end if
end loop
```

The action break, which is performed when an out of range situation is detected, will skip the rest of the loop's iterations, and the action that follows the loop construct (if there is such an action) will be the next one to execute.

Another iterative action, the *while loop* construct, iterates until some condition becomes false. The preceding operation for the sensors can be implemented with this construct as follows:

```
$I:=1;
$ALL_IN_RANGE:=true;
while
        (($I =< NUMBER_OF_SENSORS) and $ALL_IN_RANGE) loop
    if ((SAMPLE($I) < LEGAL_RANGE.LOW_LIMIT) or
            (SAMPLE($I) > LEGAL_RANGE.HIGH_LIMIT)) then
        OUT_OF_RANGE;
        $ALL_IN_RANGE:=false
    end if;
    $I := $I+1
end loop
```

The break action can also be used in the while loop to jump out of the loop without completing the iteration.

Notice that the iteration counter in the for loop action and the iteration condition in the while loop involve context variables. The reason is that the values of these expressions must change during the execution of the action, that is, within the same step.

Iterative actions can be used wherever any other action can be written, particularly inside another iterative action. No limit is set on the level of nesting of iterations.

5.3   Time-Related Expressions

Many kinds of reactive systems have timing restrictions, and their behavioral specification must involve reference to time delays and timed-out events. Our textual language provides several constructs to deal with timing.

5.3.1   Timeout events

One way to introduce explicit timing information into a statechart is by using the *timeout event*. The general form is `timeout(E,T)` (abbreviated as `tm(E,T)`), where `E` is an event and `T` is an integer expression. This expression defines a new event, which will occur `T` time units after the latest occurrence of the event `E`. In the EWS example, we may replace the event `ALARM_TIME_PASSED` of Fig. 4.3 by the more informative and detailed event: `tm(en(GENERATING_ALARM),AL ARM_DURATION)`. The new event will occur `ALARM_DURATION` time units after the state `GENERATING_ALARM` is entered. The waiting time, `ALARM_DURATION`, is measured in some abstract time unit. The way these units refer to concrete time units, such as seconds or minutes, is not part of the language and may be specified informally in the Data Dictionary. In addition, the relationship can be fixed in related tools, such as simulators, where concrete units are meaningful. In any case, the same abstract time units are used in all timing expressions throughout the entire statechart.

A subtle point related to the `timeout(E,T)` event is that the clock that "counts" the time from the occurrence of `E` is reset to zero each time `E` occurs. Thus if less than `ALARM_DURATION` time units elapsed since the system entered the `GENERATING_ALARM` state, and in the meantime that state was left and reentered, thus retriggering the event `en(GENERATING_ALARM)`, the counting of `ALARM_DURATION` will restart and the alarm will last until this new duration ends.

5.3.2   Scheduled actions

A construct that is in a way dual to the timeout event is the *scheduled action*. The general format is `schedule(G,T)` (abbreviated as `sc!(G,T)`), where `G` is an action and `T` is an integer expression. It schedules `G` to be performed `T` time units from the present instant. Referring to Fig. 4.7 of the EWS example, we can define the action that should be taken if `NO_SIGNAL` is true to be `sc!(if NO_SIGNAL then ISSUE_DISCONNECTED_MSG,3)`. This will cause the system to wait for 3 time units and then check whether there is still no signal before issuing the message.

It is interesting to compare two ways of specifying that `G` is to occur `T` time units from a present occurrence of the event `E`. If we do this by using E/sc!(G,T), then indeed nothing can prevent G from being carried out on time. In contrast, if we use tm(E,T)/G, then, as mentioned earlier, a second occurrence of E before T units elapse resets the clock to zero, and G might take longer to occur or might never get around to doing so.

5.4 Static Reactions
5.4.1 Reactions on entering and exiting a state

We are often interested in associating actions with the event of entering or exiting a particular state. This may be done by adding the required actions to all entering or exiting transitions. A better way, especially when there are many such transitions, is to associate corresponding reactions with the state in the Data Dictionary. These reactions are triggered by entering and exiting events (abbreviated by ns and xs).

To use the EWS as an example, refer to Fig. 4.14. The event OPERATE is generated on all transitions entering the COMPARING state, and the event HALT is generated on the exiting transitions thereof. We may instead omit these actions from the chart and associate two reactions with the COMPARING state in the Data Dictionary (separated by a double semicolon), as shown in Fig. 5.10.

Exactly when the events of entering and exiting a state occur in standard cases was explained in Sec. 4.4.1. However, there is a somewhat more subtle case—that of looping transitions. In Fig. 5.11, assume we are in state S2. In Fig. 5.11a the only entering and exiting events that occur when the transition is taken are those related to S2, but, in contrast, in Figs. 5.11b and 5.11c the ones related to S occur, too.

5.4.2 General static reactions

The reactions attached to a state in the Data Dictionary are called *static reactions*. The general static reaction construct makes it possible to define the reaction of the system to an event within a particular state, even without associating it with a transition between states.

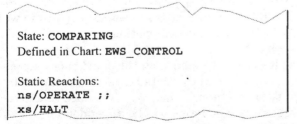

State: **COMPARING**
Defined in Chart: **EWS_CONTROL**

Static Reactions:
ns/OPERATE ;;
xs/HALT

Figure 5.10 Reactions on entering and exiting a state.

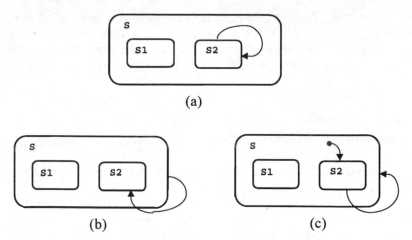

(a)

(b)   (c)

Figure 5.11 Looping transitions.

Associating the reaction `trigger/action` with state S in the Data Dictionary means that as long as the system is in state S, the action is performed whenever the trigger occurs. As in the case of a label of a transition, the trigger can be any event expression (not only `entering` and `exiting`, which are special cases), and the action can be any action expression.

In the EWS example, assume that there is no built-in clock that allows us to use the event `tm(en(GENERATING_ALARM),ALARM_DURATION)` to exit from the GENERATING_ALARM state. We may instead employ a "self-made" clock that, from the moment GENERATING_ALARM is entered, generates an event TICK every time unit. We can then introduce the data-item NO_OF_TICKS, and associate two static reactions with the GENERATING_ALARM state, as shown in Fig. 5.12.

We may then exit from GENERATING_ALARM when we have "seen," say, three ticks. This could be achieved by a transition exiting from GENERATING_ALARM, and labeled with the condition [NO_OF_TICKS=3].

It is often tempting to replace a static reaction with a self-looping transition labeled with the reaction, so as to depict more of the specification graphically. This should be done with care. For example, we cannot naively replace the second static reaction for the GENERATING_ALARM state with the transition in Fig. 5.13 because each time we reenter GENERATING_ALARM, the first static reaction will set the data-item NO_OF_TICKS to zero.

Finally, let us note that it is useful to mark on the chart those states that have associated static reactions in the Data Dictionary. We use the > character for this. Thus, for instance, when we add static reactions to the GENERATING_ALARM state, the name will be appended with a >, to mark the existence of additional information. See Fig. 5.14.

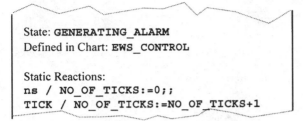

State: **GENERATING_ALARM**
Defined in Chart: **EWS_CONTROL**

Static Reactions:
```
ns / NO_OF_TICKS:=0;;
TICK / NO_OF_TICKS:=NO_OF_TICKS+1
```

Figure 5.12   General static reactions in a state.

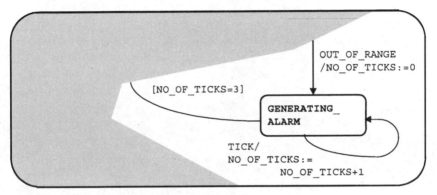

Figure 5.13   Looping transition instead of static reaction.

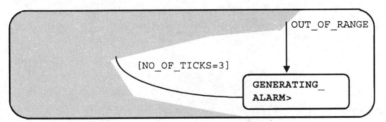

Figure 5.14   Marking a state having static reactions.

6

The Semantics of Statecharts

In the two preceding chapters we described the language of Statecharts and the associated textual expression language. The meaning of the various notational constructs in these languages was discussed on an intuitive level to help the reader grasp how they are used to specify behavior. This chapter defines the semantics of Statecharts more rigorously and addresses some of the delicate issues that arise in working out such a definition. A fuller discussion of the semantics can be found in Harel and Naamad (1996).

Later chapters of the book introduce additional features of our languages, and their behavioral meaning is defined in those places in a way that is consistent with the general principles of the semantics presented here.

6.1 Execution of the Model

A semantic definition of a language for specifying behavior must be sufficiently detailed to give rise to a rigorous prescription of how the model is executed, that is, how it reacts to the inputs arriving from the environment to produce the outputs. Several times we mentioned that a model is executed in steps, and in this chapter we explain what exactly that means. We first present an intuitive view and then get into a more detailed description.

6.1.1 External changes and system reactions

The input to a reactive system consists of a sequence of stimuli—events and changes in the values of data elements—that are generated by the system's environment. We call them *external changes*. The system senses these changes and may respond by moving from state to state along a transition, by performing some actions, or both.

In general, a model can be viewed as a collection of reactions, which are `trigger/action` pairs. When external changes occur, they may cause some of these triggers to be *enabled,* which causes the corresponding actions to be performed. We have seen two kinds of reaction so far:

- A reaction related to a transition. Its trigger labels the transition, and there are three kinds of implied actions: the transfer from state to state, the actions connected with the exit from and entrance to the appropriate states, and the actions that appear on the transition itself. (Recall that when we talk about transitions, we mean the logical compound transitions; see Sec. 4.5.)

- A static reaction associated with being in a state.

At any given moment, only some of the reactions are *relevant,* depending on the current states of the system. Later we shall also see reactions that are associated with activities by mini-specs. These become relevant when their holding activities become active.

In Fig. 6.1, for example, two transition reactions are relevant in state S1, triggered by E[C1] and by E[not C1], respectively. The actions that are performed if E occurs when the system is in state S1 and condition C1 is true, are: `make_false(P1)`, generate G, and `make_true(P2)`. (Also, of course, S1 is exited and S2 is entered.) Note that the exiting and entering reactions are linked with all respective exiting/entering transitions, as if they were part of their labels. Also, note that because the reaction E/K is associated with S2 and the event E "lives" only for an instance, the event K is not generated. Similarly, F/L is active only in S2, and if the event F occurs when the system is in S1, it will be lost and will have no effect.

We say that the system executes a *step* when it performs all relevant reactions whose triggers are enabled. As a result of a reaction, the sys-

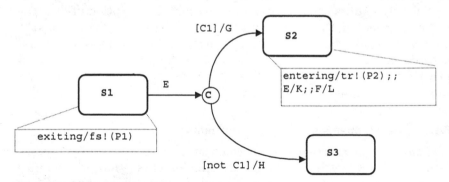

Figure 6.1 A transition reaction.

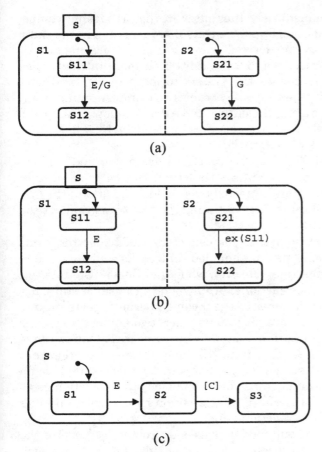

Figure 6.2   Chain reactions.

tem may change its states, generate events, and modify values of internal data elements. In addition, these can cause *derived events* to occur (e.g., changed(D) , if the data-item D changes value) and conditions to change their value (e.g., in(S) , if state S is entered). Any of these resulting changes may, in turn, cause other triggers to be enabled and, subsequently, other reactions to be executed in the next step. This has the effect of a *chain reaction,* and some of the generated events and value changes can become outputs of the system. A series of steps representing the system's responses to the sequence of external stimuli and their subsequent internal changes is called an *execution scenario,* or a *run.*

Figure 6.2 illustrates three cases of chain reactions, each consisting of two steps. All start with the system in S1 when the external event E occurs. The first one, Fig. 6.2a, shows an event G generated by the reaction E/G in one state component S1 and triggering another reaction (a state transition) immediately thereafter in the orthogonal component S2 . In the second case, Fig. 6.2b, the subsequent step in the chain takes place, triggered by the derived event ex(S11) indicating an exit from S11 . The third case, Fig. 6.2c, is a little bit more intricate. The reaction triggered by E causes the system to move to S2, and as a result the transition labeled by [C] becomes relevant. Assuming that the condition C is true during the entire scenario, the following step will take the system to state S3 . See also Figs. 4.14 and 4.15, which show chain reactions in the EWS example.

In all three parts of Fig. 6.2, the reactions are performed sequentially because each somehow entails the other. However, more than one reaction can occur simultaneously, as in Fig. 6.3. Being in S11 and in S21 when E occurs results in taking the two transitions at the same time.

Because multiple external changes can occur exactly at the same time, multiple reactions may be enabled and performed in parallel components at the same time, too, even when they depend on different triggers. Moreover, static reactions, even when in the same state, are not exclusive; that is, a number of them can be performed simultaneously. Nevertheless, there are situations when two enabled reactions *are* exclusive and cannot both be taken in the same step. One example involves two transitions exiting from the same state, a situation that is dealt with in the last section of this chapter. Another example is an enabled transition exiting a state and an enabled static reaction associated with the same state. Here, the transition has priority, and it is taken, whereas the static reaction is not.

The parallel nature of our models raises a problem regarding the order in which the actions are performed. Consider Fig. 6.4, in which the preceding example is enhanced with actions along the transitions. When E occurs, both actions are to be performed in the same step. The value of Y after carrying out the assignment Y:=X in this step depends upon whether or not the assignment of 1 to X was performed before. Our semantics resolves this dilemma by postponing

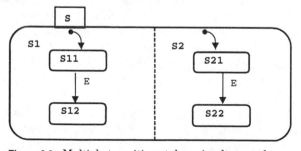

Figure 6.3 Multiple transitions taken simultaneously.

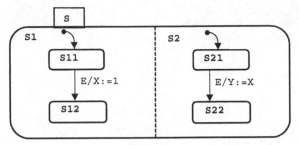

Figure 6.4   Multiple actions performed simultaneously.

the actual value updates until the end of the step, when they are carried out "at once," as we explain shortly. In this way, the evaluation of expressions that are used in actions is based on the "old" values of the variables.

It is important to realize that, by our semantics, different actions in a step are not carried out in any particular order, even when they are specified in a way that appears to prescribe such an order. For example, this includes the three kinds of actions appearing in Fig. 6.1—those associated with exiting a state, those appearing along transitions, and those associated with entering a state. The exceptional behavior of context variables, which are the ones that change their value immediately during the step (see Sec. 5.2.2), does not destroy the true concurrency among different actions performed in the same step. The scope of a context variable is the compound action it is in, and as such, it influences only the sequential evaluations carried out inside that action.

In summary, all calculations taking place in a step—both those that evaluate the triggers and determine the reactions that will be taken and those that affect the results of the actions—are based on what we call the *status* of the system prior to the step execution. The status includes the states the system is in, the values of variables at the beginning of the step, the events that were generated in the preceding step and since then, and some information about the past that we will discuss later.

Thus an execution scenario consists of a sequence of statuses, starting with the initial (default) one, separated by steps that transfer the system from one status to another, in response to external stimuli, to the actions generated in the preceding step, or both. See Fig. 6.5.

6.1.2   The details of status and step

In this section, we describe the contents of the system status and the algorithm for executing a step. Note that this description does not

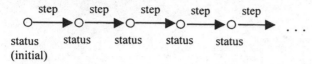

Figure 6.5 An execution scenario.

cover the behavioral aspects related to activities, although where the additional information is straightforward and does not complicate the description, we include it. This additional information will be given in Chaps. 7 and 8.

The *status* includes:

- A list of states in which the system currently resides.
- A list of activities that are currently active.
- Current values of conditions and data-items.
- A list of regular and derived events that were generated internally in the preceding step.
- A list of timeout events and their time for occurrence.
- A list of scheduled actions and their time for execution.
- Relevant information on the history of states.

The *input* to the algorithm for executing a step consists of:

- The current system status.
- A set of external changes (events and changes in the values of conditions and data-items) that occurred since the last step.
- The current time (see the discussion of time in Sec. 6.2).

The *step* execution algorithm works in three main phases:

1. First phase:
   - Calculate the events derived from the external changes and add them to the list of events (e.g., if a false condition C is set to be true, the event tr(C) is added to the list).
   - Perform the scheduled actions whose scheduled time has been exceeded, and calculate their derived events.
   - Update the occurrence time of timeout events if their triggering events have occurred.
   - Generate the timeout events whose occurrence time has been exceeded.

The first phase may modify the input status, and the new status is the one used in the following phases.

2. Second phase:
   - Evaluate the triggers of all relevant transition reactions to compute the enabled transitions that will be taken in this step (see following for how conflicts are dealt with).
   - Prepare a list of all states that will be exited and entered. This may involve the use of default entrances and history information. Note that the lists may contain nonbasic states.
   - Evaluate the triggers of all relevant static reactions to compute the ones that are enabled. Static reactions in states that are exited in this step are not included here.

The second phase ends with a list of actions to be performed in the current step. Actions specifying the exit from and entrance to states are included.

3. Third phase:
   - Update the information on the history of states.
   - Carry out all computations prescribed by the actions in the list produced in the second phase but without event generation or the value updates called for by the assignments to data-items and conditions (except for context variables, which are assigned their new values as the relevant actions are carried out).
   - Add scheduled actions from the list produced in the second phase to the list of scheduled actions.
   - Carry out all updates called for by the actions on the list produced in the second phase. This includes actually making the value assignments to data-items and conditions, and updating the list of events (i.e., removing all current events and adding the newly generated ones).
   - Update the list of current states.

The second phase can end with no enabled reactions. If this occurs, we say that the system has reached a *stationary status,* and the third phase is not performed at all. In such cases, execution will remain suspended until new external changes occur or time is advanced.

6.2 Handling Time

In reactive systems, as opposed to transformational systems, the notion of sequentiality and its relationship with time is of central importance. We now discuss this issue.

6.2.1 Sequentiality and time issues

We saw earlier that an execution scenario consists of steps triggered by external changes and the advancement of time. We also saw that reactions triggered by such happenings may continue to generate a chain of steps caused by internal changes. This raises the following questions:

- Can external changes interleave with internal chain reactions or are the former sensed by the system only after all the internal happenings end?
- When do external changes stop being accumulated to make place for the execution of a step?

These questions deal only with the order in which things occur during execution and do not get into detailed issues involving the quantitative nature of elapsed time. They are relevant to all kinds of models. On the other hand, quantitative issues cannot be ignored when the model contains timeout events and scheduled actions, because time quantification appears within them explicitly and the current time must be used to determine whether these elements affect a particular step. When such elements are present in a model, we may also ask who causes time to progress during execution and how does this occur?

The time calculated in dealing with the explicit time expressions appearing in timeout events and scheduled actions is measured in terms of some abstract time unit common to an entire statechart. Different statecharts can have different time units, in which case the relation between them must be specified prior to model execution. When the model runs in a real environment or participates in a simulation in which concrete time units, such as seconds and minutes, are meaningful, the relationship between the model's time units and the real clock must be provided.

6.2.2 Time schemes

We now propose two time schemes and show how each of them addresses these questions. In both schemes we assume that time does not advance during the step execution itself, which can be viewed as taking zero time. The actual meaning of this assumption is that no external changes occur throughout the step, and the time information needed for any timeout events and scheduled actions in a step is computed using a common clock value.

The *synchronous time scheme* assumes that the system executes a single step every time unit. This time scheme is particularly fitting for modeling electronic digital systems, in which the execution is synchronized with clock signals and external changes can occur between any two steps. The execution proceeds in cycles, in each of which time is incremented by one time unit, all external changes that occurred since the last step are collected, and a step is executed. When different clocks are assumed for the various components of the model, time is advanced to the nearest next clock value and only the relevant components perform a step.

The *asynchronous time scheme* is more flexible regarding the advancement of time, and it allows several steps to take place within a single point in time. In general, external changes can occur at any moment between steps, and several such changes can occur simultaneously. Actually, any implementation of this scheme can choose how it deals with these possibilities. An execution pattern that fits many real systems responds to external changes when they occur by executing the sequence of all steps these changes entail, as in a chain reaction, until it reaches a stationary, stable status. Only then is the system ready to react to further external changes. Such a series of steps, initiated by external changes and proceeding until reaching a stable status, is called a *super-step,* and when adopting this execution pattern, time does not advance inside a super-step.

6.3   Nondeterministic Situations

This section discusses the nondeterministic situations that a model might run into during execution.

6.3.1   Multiple enabled transitions

Consider the simple statechart of Fig. 6.6. When the system is in S1, there are two relevant outgoing transitions. If E occurs and both C1 and C2 are true, the system does not know which transition to take, and *nondeterminism* occurs.

Such a situation occurs when several transitions that cannot be taken simultaneously are enabled, and no added criterion has been given for selecting only one. Tools executing the model can make an arbitrary decision in these situations or can ask the user to decide.

Now consider Fig. 6.7, which shows a portion of the main statechart of the EWS example. Assume that we are in the COMPARING state, which is one of the substates of ON. If the event POWER_OFF occurs at the same time as OUT_OF_RANGE, two conflicting transitions will be enabled. However, in this case, a nondeterministic situation will *not* occur, because the higher-level transition (i.e., the one from ON to OFF) has *priority* over the internal transition. The

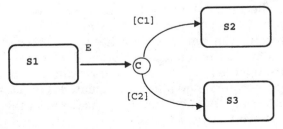

Figure 6.6 Potential nondeterminism.

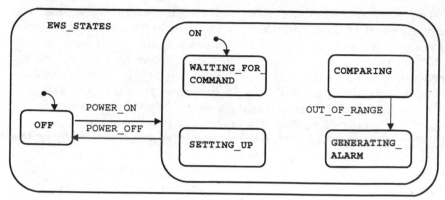

Figure 6.7 Priorities on transitions.

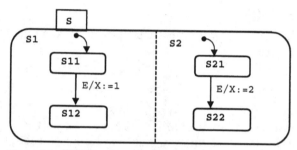

Figure 6.8 Write-write racing situation.

criterion for priority of transitions prefers the transition whose source and target have a higher common ancestor state, if possible. If the common ancestors of both transitions are identical, then non-determinism indeed occurs.

6.3.2 Racing

We say that a *racing situation* occurs if during execution an element is modified more than once or is both modified and used at a single point in time. Situations like this usually indicate some problem in the preparation of the model.

Figure 6.4 showed a case where data-item X is both assigned a value and used in the same step. It is an example of what we call a *read-write racing situation*. Figure 6.8, in contrast, presents a *write-write racing situation*. According to the definition of a step presented earlier, it is clear that multiple assignments to a data-item or a condition in a single step are meaningless, because the values are updated only at the end of the step. In a write-write racing situation, the element will be assigned one of the values arbitrarily.

More information on racing situations can be found in Harel and Naamad (1996).

7

Connections between the Functional and Behavioral Views

In Chap. 2 we discussed the functional view and the language of Activity-charts, which is used to specify it. As explained there, each activity in the chart may contain a control activity whose role is to supervise the behavior of its sibling activities. The internal descriptions of control activities are given by Statecharts, the language for the behavioral view discussed in Chap. 4.

In this chapter, we provide the link between the two languages, by describing the mechanisms that a statechart may use to control those parts of the activity-chart for which it is responsible. We discuss the actions used by the statechart to control activities and the events and conditions used by it to sense their status.

In addition, we show how the behavior of a basic activity (i.e., one that is not further decomposed into other activities) can be specified by a mini-spec, using the textual language described in Chap. 5.

Behavioral aspects of the communication between the activities are described in Chap. 8.

7.1 Dynamics in the Functional Decomposition

The activities participating in the functional decomposition are not necessarily always active. They may be constantly active when the functional components represent blocks of electronic design, as happens in chip-level modeling. However, in most kinds of systems many of the activities have limited periods in which they are active.

Here are some examples. Procedures and functions in software programs start when they are "called" by another part of the code, and upon completion they stop and return to the calling statement. In multitasking or multiprocessing systems, tasks (or processes) are invoked, do their job, and then are "killed" or "kill" themselves. Tasks with lower priorities are interrupted and delayed when a mission of higher priority arrives, and they are resumed when the more urgent mission completes. Interactive user interface is specified by "callback functions" of limited execution time, performed as a reaction to keyboard and mouse events. In object-based decomposition, objects are dynamically created and deleted, and operations related to an object are activated only when needed.

Let us examine the dynamic and timing issues related to the activities in our EWS example. Most of the details are obtained from the textual description of the example in Chap. 1, and others reflect decisions made later on in the text.

SET_UP	Activated by an explicit request of the operator when the system is waiting for a command. It terminates on its own.
COMPARE	Starts when the operator invokes an EXECUTE command, and stops when the event OUT_OF_RANGE occurs or when the operator stops it with the RESET command.
PROCESS_SIGNAL	Active only when the system is in the usual execution mode and the COMPARE activity is active and is consuming its output for comparison.
DISPLAY_FAULT	Starts when the processed signal has become out of range and is stopped either by the operator or after a predefined time period.
PRINT_FAULT	Activated if the predefined time period has passed and has caused DISPLAY_FAULT to stop. It terminates on its own.

Obviously, merely listing the activities and their connections, as is done in the functional view, is not sufficient. We have to specify the dynamics of controlling these activities, including the starting and stopping of the subactivities of a nonbasic activity. In the following sections we shall see how these aspects are covered in our models using the control activities and their describing statecharts. But nonbasic activities are not all we have. To complete the specification, we have to add something to describe the behavior of the basic activities, those that have no subactivities, not even a control activity. In Sec. 2.4.2 we examined the different types of basic activities—reactive event-driven, procedure-like, and data-driven—and mentioned that their behavioral description is provided in the Data Dictionary. In the last section of this chapter we show in detail how this is done.

Behavior related to the communication between activities, which deals not only with reading the inputs and sending the outputs but with synchronization aspects, is discussed in Chap. 8.

We should emphasize that the order in which the functional and behavioral views and their connections are developed depends on the nature of the system and on the specification methodology. One can start by carrying out a functional decomposition in activity-charts, and then add the timing and other dynamic information in statecharts to capture behavior. In contrast, it is possible to start by using statecharts to describe the system's modes of operation, a collection of use-cases (scenarios), or both and then construct an activity-chart from the activities performed in these modes or scenarios.

7.2 Dynamics of Activities

To capture the dynamic behavior of nonbasic activities, that is, to manage and control their subactivities, our models employ control activities that are associated with statecharts. In this section and the next, we discuss how this controlling is carried out.

7.2.1 Statecharts in the functional view

In general, when a nonbasic activity that contains a control activity starts its execution, the statechart associated with that control activity becomes active, that is, the system enters the top-level state of this statechart, and it starts reacting to external and internal happenings, as described earlier.

Associating a statechart with the control activity is accomplished by using the @ symbol. Figure 7.1 shows a control activity named CNTRL_ACT, which is associated with the statechart CNTRL_SC. (The special dashed lines in this and similar figures are not part of our graphical languages; they are used to denote associations between boxes and charts.)

Very often the name of the control activity itself is omitted. (See Fig. 7.2 below), in which case it is referred to by the name of its associated statechart.

An activity with a reactive behavior pattern can be described by a statechart even though it is not further decomposed so that it has no

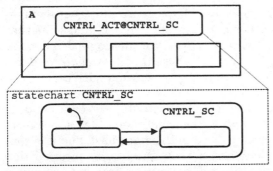

Figure 7.1 Associating a statechart with a control activity.

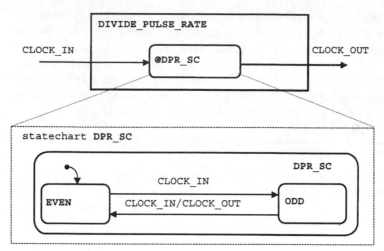

Figure 7.2 A statechart describing a simple activity.

subactivities to control; that is, its only subactivity is the control activity. See Fig. 7.2. The activity in this example doubles the rate of a clock pulse.

In some cases, the control behavior of an activity can be captured by static reactions alone, without the need for states and transitions. In such cases, the controlling statechart will consist of a single top-level state with the static reactions given in its Data Dictionary entry. If this behavior does not involve the control of sibling activities, a mini-spec can be used instead; see Sec. 7.4.

Finally, we should mention that while the controlling statechart may consume and produce external (control and data) information, its interface does not appear in the statechart itself. Rather, it shows up in the activity-chart as the interface of the control activity with which it is associated. This issue is also discussed in Chap. 8.

7.2.2   Termination type of an activity

In the discussion of dynamics in earlier chapters we saw several examples of activities that stop by themselves, from "within," and some that are stopped only from the "outside." We thus distinguish between activities that have *self-termination* and those that have *controlled termination*. (Of course, some can have both; we consider such cases to be self-terminating.)

If a self-terminating activity has a control activity, the corresponding statechart must contain a *termination connector,* also called a *T-connector.* This connector can appear anywhere in the statechart, and it is considered a final state; in particular, it has no exits. Upon entering this connector, the statechart "stops," its parent activity—call it A—becomes deactivated, and the event stopped(A) (abbreviated by sp(A)) occurs.

In the EWS example, the activities SET_UP and PRINT_FAULT are self-terminating. Figure 7.3 shows the controlling statechart of SET_UP, and it contains a termination connector. In contrast, COMPARE and PROCESS_SIGNAL are periodic activities with controlled termination. Also, DISPLAY_FAULT, which produces an alarm sound and displays a message on the screen, continues to do so until it is stopped (as we shall see later) by the controlling statechart of EWS_ACTIVITIES.

While reactive activities, whether data-driven or event-driven, can have either controlled termination or self-termination, procedure-like activities are always self-terminating. When invoked, a procedure-like activity performs a sequence of actions and stops. It is always a basic activity and lasts for one step of execution only.

The distinction between the two termination types can be made for both basic and nonbasic activities, and it is recorded in the Data Dictionary entry of the activity. An important point is that when a nonbasic activity stops, either because its statechart moves to a termination connector or it is stopped from the outside (e.g., by an explicit stop action, as we shall see), all its subactivities stop immediately, too.

7.2.3   Perpetual activities

We mentioned activities whose components are "always active." Because this kind of behavior pattern is very common in the specification of hardware systems, we refer to it as *hardware activation style*. This is a case in which an activity does not need to have a control activity. For nonbasic activities that do not have a control activity, we provide special default behavior: all the subactivities start when the parent activity starts, and they all stop when it stops. (The latter is always true, even in the presence of a control activity.)

In the EWS example, we may decompose DISPLAY_FAULT into two subactivities with no control activity, as shown in Fig. 7.4. When

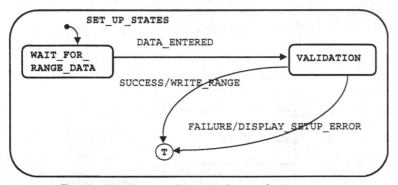

Figure 7.3   Termination connector in SET_UP's statechart.

DISPLAY_FAULT is activated, both DISPLAY_FAULT_MESSAGE and PRODUCE_ALARM_SOUND start simultaneously. They stop when DISPLAY_FAULT is stopped.

7.3   Controlling the Activities

We now show how the controlling statecharts affect and sense the status of their sibling activities.

7.3.1   Starting and stopping activities

One of the main mechanisms that statecharts use to control activities is the ability to activate (start) and deactivate (stop) them explicitly. This is usually carried out via the actions start(A) and stop(A), which are abbreviated as st!(A) and sp!(A), respectively.

To exemplify these actions, let us return to the dynamic and timing issues related to our EWS example, as described in Sec. 7.1. Here is how these decisions can be specified in the controlling statechart. Consider the statechart of Fig. 4.6 and compare it with Fig. 7.5. The event PRINT_OUT_OF_RANGE, which is generated on the transition from GENERATING_ALARM to WAITING_FOR_COMMAND, is replaced by the action st!(PRINT_FAULT).

This takes care of the activation of PRINT_FAULT. For all other activities, we can link their activation with the entrance to a state. For example, SET_UP is started by carrying out the action st!(SET_UP) upon entering the state SETTING_UP. A good way to achieve this effect is to attach a static reaction: ns/st!(SET_UP) to the SETTING_UP state. (Recall that ns abbreviates the entering event.) Similarly, the activities COMPARE, PROCESS_SIGNAL, and DISPLAY_FAULT are started upon entering the states COMPARING, OPERATING, and GENERATING_ALARM, respectively. The existence of the static reactions attached to these states is marked by a > symbol affixed to the state name, as shown in Fig. 7.6. Notice that entering these states is triggered by the events that were stated above to start the corresponding activities. For example, the SET_UP command causes entrance to the SETTING_UP state and therefore causes activation of the SET_UP activity.

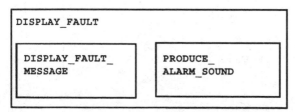

Figure 7.4 A nonbasic activity with no control activity.

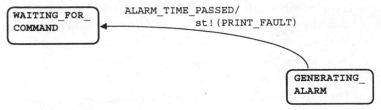

Figure 7.5 An action that starts an activity.

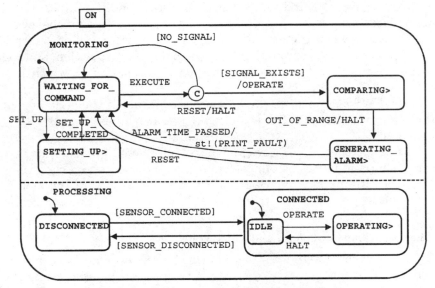

Figure 7.6 States marked as having entering and exiting reactions.

The COMPARE activity is stopped when the COMPARING state is exited by the reaction xs/sp!(COMPARE) that appears in the Data Dictionary entry of this state. (Recall that xs abbreviates the exiting event.) Note that the events OUT_OF_RANGE and RESET cause the system to exit the COMPARING state, and therefore they stop the COMPARE activity.

It is noteworthy that the action st!(A) has no effect if A is already active, and sp!(A) has no effect if it is not. Thus, for example, no message will be printed if st!(PRINT_FAULT) was executed a second time before the last activation of PRINT_FAULT terminated.

Starting an activity that has a controlling statechart with the start action will cause the statechart to begin "running" in parallel to all other statecharts that might be active in the model at that time. Similarly, stopping an activity by the stop action causes the controlling statechart of the stopped activity to abort and to remain dormant until its next activation, when it will restart in its top-level state. Moreover, if the stopped activity is nonbasic, all its subactivities stop, too.

Recall that the control activity can control only its sibling activities. Therefore, all actions that appear in its statechart may refer to the sibling activities only.

7.3.2   Sensing the status of activities

The statechart that describes a control activity is not limited to causing activities to start and stop. It can also sense whether such happenings have indeed taken place. Specifically, the control activity can sense the events started(A) and stopped(A), and the condition active(A), abbreviated as st(A), sp(A), and ac(A), respectively. The event st(A) occurs when the activity A starts, sp(A) occurs when A terminates either by self-termination or by an external stop action, and the condition ac(A) is true for the duration of the period in which A is active.

In the EWS example, we can be more specific about the actual event that triggers the exit from SETTING_UP. It will be sp(SET_UP), rather than SET_UP_COMPLETED. (See Fig. 7.7.)

Just as the control activity can control only its sibling activities, so can it sense only these siblings. Therefore, the events and conditions in the describing statechart are allowed to refer only to the sibling activities.

7.3.3   Activities throughout and within states

Often, we wish an activity A to start when a certain state S is entered and to stop when S is exited. This can be specified by associating the action st!(A) with the entering event ns as a static reaction in the Data Dictionary entry for S and the action sp!(A) with the exiting event xs therein. To cater for such cases in a more compact way, we may specify in the Data Dictionary entry for S that A is *active throughout* S. For example, the COMPARE activity can be specified as being active throughout the COMPARING state and PROCESS_SIGNAL as being active throughout the OPERATING state. See Fig. 7.8.

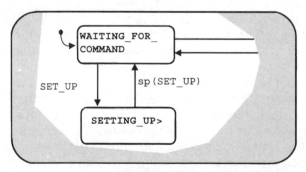

Figure 7.7 An event signifying termination of an activity.

State: **COMPARING**
Defined in Chart: **EWS_CONTROL**

Activities in State:
        COMPARE (throughout)

State: **OPERATING**
Defined in Chart: **EWS_CONTROL**

Activities in State:
        PROCESS_SIGNAL (throughout)

Figure 7.8 Activities active throughout states in the Data Dictionary.

The throughout correspondence between a state and an activity is natural for activities with controlled-termination because exiting the state will stop the activity. However, a self-terminating activity A may also be specified as being active throughout a state S. In such a case, there is usually an exit transition from S triggered by the event sp(A); this implies that if and when A stops of its own accord S will be exited via this exit. If A stops and there is no such exit transition, the specification is misleading, but it is not a language error. If S is exited before A terminates on its own, A will stop as a result, just as if A had been of the controlled-termination type.

The following example illustrates this case. Assume that the self-terminating activity SET_UP is specified as active throughout the SETTING_UP state. Figure 7.9 shows an exit transition from this state, labeled sp!(SET_UP). We have also added another exit transition, triggered by the RESET command, that enables the operator to abort the SET_UP activity during its execution.

Another similar association is *active within,* which represents a looser connection between an activity and a state. Again, we use the Data Dictionary to assert that activity A is active within state S. This is mainly done as a temporary specification to indicate that the activity is activated sometime during the time the system is in S but that we cannot be more concrete at present. One of the technical ramifications of this association is that when S is exited A stops (unless, of course, it had stopped earlier for some other reason). However, in contrast to the throughout connection, A does not necessarily start when S is entered.

For example, in Fig. 7.6, the activity PROCESS_SIGNAL can be defined as active within the CONNECTED state before that state is further decomposed into IDLE and OPERATING. The reason is that

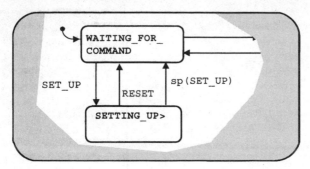

Figure 7.9 Self-terminated activity active throughout a state.

even before the decomposition we do know that it is meaningless to perform this activity when the sensor is disconnected. Later on, we can be more concrete and define the activity PROCESS_SIGNAL as being active throughout OPERATING.

7.3.4   Suspending and resuming activities

In addition to being able to start and stop activities, control activities can cause an activity to "freeze," or *suspend,* its activation, and to later *resume* from where it stopped. The relevant actions are suspend(A) and resume(A) (abbreviated as sd!(A) and rs!(A), respectively). Associated with these actions is the condition hanging(A) (abbreviated as hg(A)), which is true as long as A is suspended without being resumed or stopped. It should be emphasized that an activity is considered active even when suspended. Thus whenever hg(A) is true, so is ac(A).

Suspension may be used, for example, when we want to interrupt the progress of an activity in favor of another activity with a higher priority. Figure 7.10 shows a simple activity and its controlling statechart. The event E causes A to be suspended, while the preferred activity B is carried out to completion, at which time A is resumed.

If A is suspended, its descendant subactivities, including all descendant control activities, become suspended, too. This means that the corresponding statecharts stop in their tracks: they remain in the state configurations they were in at the instant of suspension. Upon resuming, all such control activities continue in a normal fashion from those configurations. While suspended, the statechart does not react to events. In fact, all events that occur during the suspension period are "lost" and have no effect on the suspended statechart.

Resuming a suspended activity sounds very much like entering a state via a history entrance (see Sec. 4.6.2). However, these notions should not be naively interchanged. To illustrate the difference, compare the statechart of Fig. 7.10 with Fig. 7.11. In the absence of any additional static reactions, the exit from the AC_A state in Fig. 7.11 does not cause activity A to either stop or suspend. Now assume that we remove the starting action from the default entrance in that figure and the activity A is defined to be active throughout state AC_A. In this case, the event E will cause A to stop, and returning to AC_A will cause it to start at the beginning, which is not the case in Fig. 7.10. Thus one must remember that reentering a state via a history entrance is considered an entrance nonetheless, and actions that are to be performed on entry (such as starting activities that are defined throughout) are indeed carried out.

7.4 Specifying Behavior of Basic Activities

When carrying out functional decomposition, the lower-level building blocks of the description are the basic activities, those that

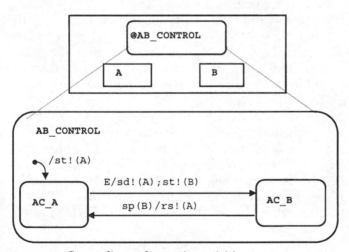

Figure 7.10 Suspending and resuming activities.

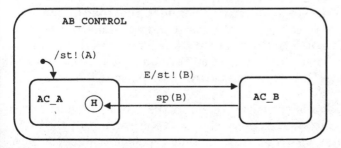

Figure 7.11 History entrance vs. resume activity.

require no further breakup. We may use the textual language of Chap. 5 to associate formal executable descriptions with basic activities without using the Statecharts language. These descriptions, called *mini-specs* and *combinational assignments*, are written in the Data Dictionary. (They were mentioned also in Sec. 2.4.2.) Basic activities that have additional textual descriptions in the Data Dictionary are marked by a > appended to their names, like states with static reactions.

7.4.1 Reactive mini-specs

In some cases the behavior of a basic activity can be described by a collection of reactions consisting of triggers and their implied actions. In these cases, a *reactive mini-spec* can be used.

The syntax of a reactive mini-spec is similar to that of a static reaction in a state; that is, it is a list of reactions of the form trigger/action, separated by a double semicolon (; ;). The meaning is obvious: as long as the activity is active, an action is performed whenever the corresponding trigger occurs.

It is also possible to associate actions to be carried out when the activity starts by using the event started (abbreviated by st) as the trigger in the mini-spec. This event occurs one step after the action st!(A) is performed, like the event started(A). Notice that the name of the activity does not appear in this event because the reaction is associated with the activity itself.

Figure 7.12 describes the PROCESS_SIGNAL activity of the EWS as a reactive mini-spec. This activity reads the sensor's output, SIGNAL, every SAMPLE_INTERVAL and transfers the read value to a processing user function COMPUTE(), which is unspecified in the model. The function's output, SAMPLE, is later checked for being inside the required range. The sampling cycle is implemented by an internal event TICK, which is first scheduled when the activity is started, and is then scheduled for the subsequent cycle.

A reactive mini-spec can be attached to both self-terminating or controlled-terminating activities. To stop a self-terminating activity, the stop action (abbreviated sp!), which also has no activity name, is used. The stopped activity becomes inactive in the next step. In the current step, it continues to apply other reactions if there are other enabled triggers, and it even completes the sequence of actions that follows the stop action (although it is probably bad practice to write action expressions with actions that follow a stop action).

To illustrate usage of the stop action in the EWS example, let us assume (over and above the original requirements) that the PROCESS_SIGNAL stops when it finds that the sensor signal is zero. This can be specified as in Fig. 7.13.

```
Activity: PROCESS_SIGNAL
Defined in Chart: EWS_ACTIVITIES
Termination Type: Reactive Controlled
Mini-spec: st/TICK;;
TICK/ $SIGNAL_VALUE:=SIGNAL;
        SAMPLE:=COMPUTE($SIGNAL_VALUE);
        sc!(TICK,SAMPLE_INTERVAL)
```

Figure 7.12 A reactive mini-spec in the Data Dictionary.

```
Activity: PROCESS_SIGNAL
Defined in Chart: EWS_ACTIVITIES
Termination Type: Reactive Controlled
Mini-spec: st/TICK;;
TICK/ $SIGNAL_VALUE:=SIGNAL;
        if ($SIGNAL_VALUE # 0) then
            SAMPLE:=COMPUTE($SIGNAL_VALUE);
            sc!(TICK,SAMPLE_INTERVAL)
        else
            sp!
        end if
```

Figure 7.13 The stop action in a mini-spec.

It is important to remember that states and activities cannot be referred to in the mini-spec. All the activities and states of the model are beyond the scope of an individual mini-spec.

7.4.2 Procedure-like mini-specs

Very often, an activity can be described as a sequence of actions, possibly with conditional branching and iterations. Such activities are called *procedure-like* and are actually similar to actions: they are described by a mini-spec that has an action syntax and are active for a single step only. Obviously, such activities are always self-terminating.

For example, let us return to the SET_UP activity, whose activity chart and controlling statechart are shown again in Fig. 7.14. The VALIDATE_RANGE subactivity is active throughout the VALIDATION state. It can be described by a very simple procedure-like mini-spec, as shown in Fig. 7.15. Notice the > marks in the statechart and activity-chart, which indicate that the VALIDATION state and the VALIDATE_RANGE activity have an additional behavioral description in the Data Dictionary.

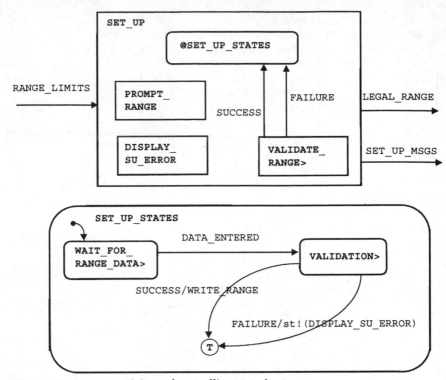

Figure 7.14   SET_UP activity and controlling statechart.

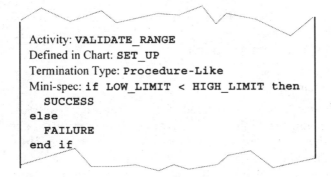

Figure 7.15   A procedure-like mini-spec in the Data Dictionary.

As in the case of reactive mini-specs, procedure-like mini-specs are not allowed to refer to states and activities.

7.4.3   Combinational assignments

Another typical behavior for an activity is that of a *data-driven* pattern. The activity is continuously ready to perform some calculations whenever the input changes its values. In principle, this pattern can be described by a reactive mini-spec in which the required calculations are performed when the activity starts and also whenever an event changed(X) occurs for any relevant data-item or condition X. We provide an alternative, more convenient way to describe data-driven activities: *combinational assignments.* These are associated with the activity via the Data Dictionary, just as mini-specs are.

The general syntax of a combinational assignment is:

```
X := Y1 when C1 else
     Y2 when C2 else
     . . .
     Yn
```

when X is a variable condition or data-item, Y1 to Yn are expressions, and C1 to Cn are condition expressions.

For example, let us define a subactivity COMPUTE_IN_RANGE of the COMPARE activity, with the following combinational assignment:

```
IN_RANGE:= false when (SAMPLE < LEGAL_RANGE.LOW_LIMIT)
           else false when (SAMPLE > LEGAL_RANGE.HIGH_LIMIT)
           else true
```

This combinational assignment was designed to illustrate the syntax of the construct, but there is actually a simpler way to obtain the same effect, using only a simple expression with no when clause, as shown in Fig. 7.16.

Whenever SAMPLE changes its value, the combinational assignment recomputes the value of IN_RANGE. (The OUT_OF_RANGE event will be generated by another action when IN_RANGE becomes false.)

The left-hand side of the assignment is called a *combinational element.* It can be of a numeric type, a string, or a condition. It can be an array component (with a constant index) or a record field. It can also be a bit-array slice but, again, only with constant range indices.

The combinational assignments are performed at the end of an execution step. If, during the step, a value of an element appearing on the right-hand side of some combinational assignment is changed, the assignment is carried out using the new values. If

```
Activity: COMPUTE_IN_RANGE
Defined in Chart: COMPARE
Termination Type: Reactive Controlled
Combinational Assignments:
IN_RANGE:= (SAMPLE > LEGAL_RANGE.LOW_LIMIT) and
           (SAMPLE < LEGAL_RANGE.HIGH_LIMIT)
```

Figure 7.16 Combinational assignments in the Data Dictionary.

doing so changes the value of an element in some assigned expression, an additional computation phase is called for. Of course, this chain of computations can be infinite, resulting in an unstable design.

8

Communication between Activities

Specifying the communication between activities consists of the what and the when, just as in other parts of the specification. The what is described by the flow-lines in the activity-charts (see Chap. 2) and relevant parts of the Data Dictionary (see Chap. 3). The "when" is to be specified by the behavioral parts of the model, that is, the statecharts and mini-specs. This dynamic aspect of communication is the subject of the present chapter. We discuss the parts of our languages that control the communication between activities and discuss how they are related to the flow-lines in the functional view. We also describe the queue mechanism in some detail.

8.1 Communication and Synchronization Issues

Functional components in systems communicate among themselves to pass along information and help synchronize their processing. A number of attributes characterize the various communication mechanisms, and different mechanisms are convenient for different application domains. The communication can be *instantaneous,* meaning that it is lost if not consumed immediately, or *persistent,* meaning that it stays around until it gets consumed (which can be achieved by queuing, for example). The communication can be *synchronous* (e.g., the sender waits for an acknowledgment or reply from the listener) or *asynchronous* (i.e., there is no waiting on the part of the sender). The communication can be *directly addressed* (i.e., the target is specified) or sent by *broadcasting*. And there are other issues. A flexible modeling and implementation environment will make it possible to use many variants of these communication patterns.

In our models, every element has a *scope* in which it is recognized. The scoping depends on the element's definition chart, and is described in Chap. 13. The central point here is that every change in the value of an element is broadcast to all activities and statecharts in the element's scope, and is thus "seen" by them all. These changes include the occurrence of an event, the assignment of a value to a data-item or condition, a change in the status of an activity, and entering or exiting a state.

In addition to events, which are instantaneous and last for one step only, all other elements keep their values until some explicit action causes a change. Therefore, for all communicated elements other than events, the receiver need not necessarily be active when the sender assigns them a value. Moreover, in all cases other than queues, the same information can be consumed an unlimited number of times.

The following sections discuss the elements related to the flow of information in our languages and illustrate how they can be used to model various communication patterns.

8.2   Controlling the Flow of Information

The statecharts and mini-specs are responsible, among other things, for controlling the flow of information between activities, and they are complemented by certain elements in the textual language. The description of the information flow given in the activity-charts completes the picture, and it should be consistent with the control specification.

8.2.1   Elements related to flow of information

Consider Fig. 8.1, in which X is specified to flow between activities A and B. When does X flow, and what triggers the flow?

Assume first that X is an event, and that the behavior of A is described by the statechart that constitutes A's control activity. This statechart may contain an action that generates X along a transition or in a static reaction, and at that instant the controlling statechart of B (or of any of B's descendants) can sense X and modify its behavior accordingly. See Fig. 8.2. Similarly, A and B can be described by mini-specs, which, respectively, contain an action that generates X and some reaction triggered by it. Many other alternatives are also possible.

If X is a condition or a data-item, it is considered to be continuous in time. This means that the value of X may change at any point in time

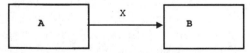

Figure 8.1   An information element flowing between activities.

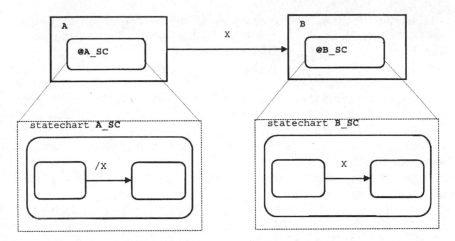

Figure 8.2 Producing and consuming an event.

as long as A is active, and B can sense and use this value at all times (even when A is no longer active). The actions and events that were described in the preceding chapters enable us to affect the values of the conditions and data-items and to sense when changes in such values occur. More specifically, if X is a condition, the source activity A (i.e., its controlling statechart or mini-spec and those of its descendants) can change X's value by the actions `tr!(X)` and `fs!(X)`. The change itself (via the events `ch(X)`, `tr(X)`, or `fs(X)`), and the current truth value of X, can be sensed anywhere in B. If X is a data-item or condition, it can be assigned values in A by actions such as `X:=E` for an expression E. In B, we can sense the event `written(X)` (abbreviated `wr(X)`), which may be viewed as occurring at the instant the assignment takes place. The value of X can also be used in any controlling statechart, mini-spec, or combinational assignment inside B.

If we are not interested in assigning a specific value to X, just in stating that some value has been assigned, A may execute the action `write_data(X)` (abbreviated `wr!(X)`), and B may sense the event `wr(X)`. Thus, informally, the action `wr!(X)` means assign a value to X but without specifying any specific value, and the event `wr(X)` means that X has been assigned a value. In a dual fashion, the target activity B of the data-item or condition X may perform the action `read_data(X)` (abbreviated `rd!(X)`), signifying that it has read the value of X, without using it in any particular computation. At the same time, the source activity A can sense the corresponding event `read(X)` (abbreviated `rd(X)`).

Note the following rules, which hold when the actions `wr!` and `rd!` are applied to structures such as records and arrays and their components. The general idea is that when dealing with structures all of whose components exist in every occurrence of the structure, the special actions and events that involve the structure as a whole apply to all components, but the converse is not true. If R is a record, then the action wr!(R) and an assignment to R trigger the event wr(R.X), for each component R.X of R, and the action rd!(R) triggers the event rd(R.X). If A is an array, the action wr!(A) triggers the event wr(A(I)) for each component of A, and the action rd!(A) triggers the event rd(A(I)). An assignment to the entire array (e.g., A:=B), or to an array slice (e.g., A(1..3):=T), triggers the event wr(A(I)) for each index I in the assigned range but not vice versa; that is, an assignment to A(I) does not cause the event wr(A).

For unions, in which the components have an exclusive nature, actions on a component imply events related to the containing union data-item but not vice versa. Thus if U.F is a component of the union data-item U, then the action wr!(U.F) triggers the event wr(U), as does an assignment to U.F. The action rd!(U.F) triggers the event rd(U).

The written and read events are relevant to the *queue* data-item, too. This is discussed in Sec. 8.4.

8.2.2 Interface between "execution" components

The actions and events described earlier provide a way to monitor the behavior of the flow of information. An important issue related to the information elements that appear in controlling statecharts, mini-specs, and combinational assignments pertains to their origins and destinations. In particular, the statecharts themselves do not explicitly deal with the flow of information. The inputs and outputs of a statechart are presented in the activity-chart as flowing to/from the control activity associated with the statechart in question.

For example, refer to Fig. 4.3, the simplest version of the statechart describing the EWS_CONTROL. The operator commands EXECUTE, SET_UP, and RESET are input events to this statechart and are shown as flowing from an external activity into the control activity (as components of COMMANDS) in Fig. 2.5. Similarly, the event OUT_OF_RANGE, which is also used in this statechart, is an input that comes from the COMPARE activity.

Not all the elements used in the statecharts come from external sources. We have seen that orthogonal components may communicate via internal information elements. The events OPERATE and HALT, shown in Fig. 4.14, are generated by an orthogonal component and, as such, they do not appear in the external interface of the control activity in Fig. 2.5 at all.

In general, each element that appears in a behavioral description unit (i.e., a statechart, mini-spec, or combinational assignment) may be either used by or affected by this description unit. Some elements, such as the events HALT and OPERATE and the event TICK in the mini-spec of Sec. 7.4.1, are both used and affected by the same statechart or mini-spec and are thus considered internal to it.

If X appears in a trigger (along a statechart transition or in a reaction in a state or mini-spec), then we say that it is *used by* the statechart or activity. The same applies if X appears in a conditional expression in the *if* or *when* parts of an action. Data-items are also said to be used by a statechart or an activity if they appear on the right-hand side of assignment actions or combinational assignments.

Consider, for example, Fig. 8.3. The event E and the condition C are used by the statechart because they appear in the transition's trigger. If C is a compound condition (say, it is defined as C1 or I=J), then its components (in this case, C1, I, and J) are also used by the statechart. The data-items X and Z in Fig. 8.3 are also used because the former is tested and the latter participates in an assignment.

Similarly, if X is an event generated by an action (along a transition or in a static reaction or a mini-spec) in the statechart or in an activity, then it is *affected by* this behavioral unit. The same applies if X is a data-item or a condition that is assigned a value in an action (e.g., Y and K in Fig. 8.3), or in a combinational assignment (e.g., IN_RANGE of Sec. 7.4.3).

In a complete specification, we expect all elements that are used by a statechart or an activity (in its mini-spec or combinational assignment), but are not affected by it, to be inputs to the corresponding control activity or the activity itself, respectively. Similarly, elements that are affected by the statechart or the activity, but are not used internally, are expected to be outputs of the control activity or the activity.

We should remark that actions related to activities (e.g., st!(A) and sp!(A)), although they can be viewed as signals that flow out of the control activity, have no corresponding flow-lines in the activity-chart. The same goes for the events st(A) and sp(A), and the conditions ac(A) and hg(A), which can be viewed as signals that flow from A into the control activity.

8.3 Examples of Communication Control

We have seen several patterns by which activities communicate. For example, the data-item LEGAL_RANGE was assigned a value by the SET_UP activity, and this value was used later by the COMPARE function. In this scheme of shared data, the exact timing of the production and consumption of the values is not significant. On the other hand, we have

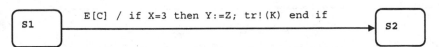

Figure 8.3 Elements used and affected by a statechart.

seen several cases in which events were used to detect an occurrence in which timing was important and an immediate response was required (e.g., the OUT_OF_RANGE notification and the RESET command).

We shall now see examples in which the communication involves synchronization aspects as well as data transfer.

8.3.1 Communication between periodic activities

In distributed computation models, the functionality is often divided among a number of periodic activities. Each of these has some mission to carry out, and upon completion it transfers control to some other activity. One activity might prepare data for processing and then notify the consuming activity when the data is ready. Figure 8.4 shows such a case from the EWS example, where we specify the activities PROCESS_SIGNAL and COMPARE. The checking that takes place in the latter is synchronized to the periodic rate at which signals are produced in the former. CHECK is a procedure-like activity that computes the IN_RANGE value for the current SAMPLE and then terminates.

In this example, like other similar ones, some assumptions are made about the processing time of the activities participating in the cycle.

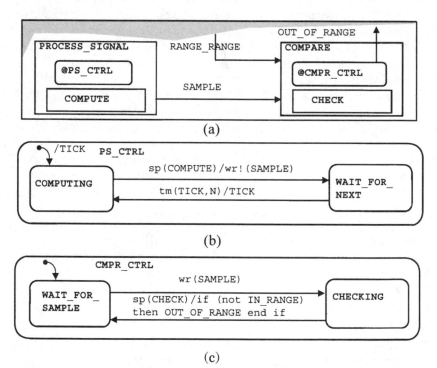

(a)

(b)

(c)

Figure 8.4 Communication between periodic activities. (a) The communicating activities. (b) The statechart of PROCESS_SIGNAL. (c) The statechart of COMPARE.

For instance, it is assumed that in every cycle the CHECK activity succeeds in completing its execution before the next SAMPLE is ready for processing; otherwise, some data may be lost.

In Fig. 8.4 we have shown only the top-level behavior; there is no explicit value assignment to SAMPLE, and no details about how it is used in the CHECK activity. The timing of the data transfer and how it influences the activity scheduling are expressed with the abstract write_data action and the written event. Actually, the read_data action and read event can be used in a dual manner to synchronize an activity execution with the time the data is consumed, so that a cycle of preparing new data can start.

8.3.2 Message passing

It is sometimes convenient to base the communication between activities on message passing. A good way to deal with this involves queues, which are described in the next section. However, in many cases, the mechanisms already discussed are sufficient. Dataless messages can be represented by events, while messages with data can be modeled by record data-items, whose departure from the source (or arrival at the target) can be sensed by the receiver using the written event.

As an example, assume we have a simple client/server setup, where the server waits in an idle state for a message that denotes a request for some service. The server is able to deal with three different kinds of messages, each with special data. This can be achieved using a union data structure whose components are the various message records, as follows.

First, we define a data-type MESSAGE as a record with two fields:

Field Name:	TYPE	Field Type:	Integer min=1 max=3
Field Name:	DATA	Field Type:	MSG_DATA

The first field, TYPE, holds the message type, one of three possible values, while the second holds the accompanying data. The user-defined type MSG_DATA is a union consisting of three fields, each corresponding to one of the message types:

Field Name:	D1	Field Type:	POSITION
Field Name:	D2	Field Type:	BITS
Field Name:	D3	Field Type:	KEY

Each message transfers some data represented by a different user-defined type. The client prepares and sends the message MSG (whose data-type is MESSAGE) by carrying out the following actions:

```
MSG.TYPE:=1; MSG.DATA.D1:=NEW_POSITION; wr!(MSG)
```

In Fig. 8.5 we see how the server may respond to the arrival of the message. Each of the three services activated in response to the respective message (i.e., service request) consumes its appropriate data.

In this example we did not discuss whether the server is guaranteed to be ready to respond when the request is sent, or how the client knows whether the request was fulfilled. Our language does *not* contain any built-in mechanism for identifying message senders so that replies can be automatically addressed. However, when this is required (e.g., for synchronization or confirmation purposes in a multiple-client environment), it can be implemented using explicit identification. Later, when multiple instances of generic charts are discussed, we shall see that an instance number can be used for this purpose.

8.4   Activities Communicating through Queues

Queuing facilities for messages are virtually indispensable in modeling multiprocessing environments, especially multiple client/server systems. We would like to be able to address situations in which an unlimited number of messages is sent to the same address, while the receiver is not always in a position to accept them. We also want to arrange things so that no message is consumed before one that was sent earlier. Moreover, we want it be possible for concurrently active components to write messages to the same address at the same moment and for concurrently active components to read different

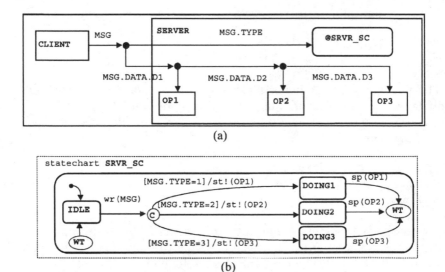

(a)

(b)

Figure 8.5   Server responding to three service requests.

messages from the same source, even at that very same moment. In our language set, we use *message queues* for this, simply called *queues* for short.

8.4.1 Queues and their operation

A queue is an ordered, unlimited collection of data-items, all of the same data-type. The queue is usually shared among several activities, which can employ special actions to add elements to the queue and read and remove elements from it. Our queues are of unrestricted length, which is in contrast to those used in some real-time kernels, which are defined with a maximal number of components.

A queue is itself a structured data-item, just like an array, and when defined in the Data Dictionary the data-type of its components must be specified. This data-type can be any basic predefined type (i.e., integer, real, etc.), or a user-defined type. There are no limitations on combining queues with other constructs, e.g., arrays, records/unions, or other queues. This means that we can define an array of queues, a record with a queue as a field thereof, or even a queue of queues. The usage of such compound constructs will be presented further shortly. A queue of records or unions, for example, is achieved by an intermediate definition of a user-defined type.

We supply several actions to manipulate a queue. The exact timing of these actions during the execution of a step is a delicate issue, which is discussed in Sec. 8.4.2.

The actions q_put(Q,D) (abbreviated put!(Q,D)) and q_urgent_ put(Q,D) (abbreviated uput!(Q,D)) add the value of the expression D (a data-item or condition) to the queue Q. The former action adds an element to the tail of the queue, while the latter adds it to the head of the queue, allowing messages with higher priority to precede all others. Both these operations cause the event wr(Q) to occur. The type of the expression D must be compatible with the data type of the elements of the queue, as in assignment actions.

The action that is dual to these two is q_get(Q,D,S), abbreviated get!(Q,D,S). It extracts the element residing at the head of the queue Q and places it in D, removing it from the queue in the process. The data type of D must be compatible with the data type of the elements in the Q. The third operand, the *status condition* S, is optional. It is set to true if the queue contained elements when the action was carried out, and to false if the operation failed to find data to extract.

The action q_peek(Q,D,S) (abbreviated peek!(Q,D,S)) is similar to get!, but it is not destructive; it copies the element at the head of the queue into D without removing it from the queue.

The actions get! and peek! may succeed or fail, the latter being the case if the queue is empty. If successful, D and S are assigned values, and the events rd(Q) and wr(D) occur. The event wr(S) always occurs, and if the values of D and S are changed from their previous values in the process, then ch(D) and ch(S) occur, too.

In addition to these actions, a queue can be totally cleared by the action q_flush(Q), abbreviated fl!(Q). It is also possible to examine the queue length by the operator q_length(Q), which returns the length of the queue prior to the step. More about this issue in the next section.

8.4.2　The semantics of queues

A queue is inherently sequential because the order in which the messages are put in the queue determines the order in which they are consumed (with the exception of the order-overriding action uput!). A problem arises when operations on the same queue occur in parallel components during the same step. Because there is an element of nondeterminism in the order of the operations, which depends on the tool implementing the execution of the model, the end result might not be fully determined. We now describe a carefully defined semantics, whose goal is to reduce this nondeterminism.

All get actions are performed when they are encountered. Actually, a get action immediately removes the element read from the head of the queue. However, the assignment to D in get!(Q,D,S) is performed only at the end of the step, unless the assigned variable is a context variable (i.e., $D instead of D, see Sec. 5.2.2). Several get actions in the same step read the elements from the queue sequentially, and each reads a different element one after the other in a nondeterministic order. Because get fails when the queue is empty, some of the get actions succeed and some fail. Using a context variable for the status condition (i.e., $S instead of S) makes it possible to check in the current step whether the operation succeeded.

In contrast to get actions, a put does not immediately affect the contents of the queue. All put actions are accumulated and are performed at the end of the step. This scheme reduces the chances of racing (see Sec. 6.3.2) because it prevents the interleaving of get and put actions in the same step. The order in which the put actions of the same step are performed at the end of the step is also nondeterministic, and it depends on the tool implementing the execution.

The clearing action flush also takes effect at the end of the step. When issued in the same step with some put actions on the same queue, flush will be the last to be carried out, and it will result in an empty queue. Of course, this situation is considered a racing condition.

Although the actual number of elements in the queue might change during a step, the returned value of the q_length operator is not updated continuously. Rather, it returns a unique value per step retrieved before all other queue operations of that step. The following example of its use is inappropriate, and when started on a nonempty queue, it will result in an infinite loop:

```
while q_length(Q)>0 loop
    get!(Q,$MSG,$S);
    if $S then
    . . . . .
    end if;
end loop
```

The following loop is more suitable for processing all messages in the queue:

```
for $I in 1 to q_length(Q) loop
    get!(Q,$MSG,$S);
    if $S then
    . . . . .
    else
      break
    end if;
end loop
```

The status condition $S is checked during the loop, because there may be several consumers reading from the queue in the same step.

Figure 8.6 illustrates the order in which operations on a queue are performed during a step.

8.4.3   Queues in an activity-chart

Queues can be associated with data-stores just as data-items of other types can be. To associate a queue with a data-store, both must have the same name. Figure 8.7 illustrates the combined use of data-stores and queues, and here, too, if the incident flow-lines are unlabeled, the queue Q is considered an output of the source activity, PRODUCER, and an input to the target activity, CONSUMER.

Note that P_MSG is not an output of PRODUCER and is therefore not written on the emerging flow-line. It is best to view the put!(Q, P_MSG) action as the assignment queue-head:=P_MSG. In terms of Sec. 8.2.2,

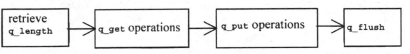

Figure 8.6   Operations on a queue during a step.

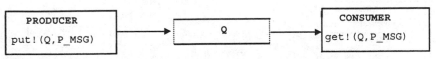

Figure 8.7   A queue associated with a data-store.

P_MSG is actually *used by* the put operation, and should thus flow into the PRODUCER activity, or, alternatively, it should be assigned internally. Moreover, P_MSG is not necessarily a variable data-item; it may be a compound expression or a constant that cannot even move along a flow-line. Dually, C_MSG is viewed as being *affected* by the CONSUMER activity, where actually it can be viewed as being assigned by C_MSG:=queue-head. Thus it is expected to be an output of CONSUMER, or used internally.

Sometimes a queue that transfers messages between activities is marked just as a label on a flow-line between the sender and the receiver. When messages flow among activities in both directions, two oppositely flowing lines can be used.

8.4.4 Example of activities communicating through queues

The special characteristics of queues make them suitable for modeling architectures consisting of several clients and servers. Before sending a new request, a client does not need to check whether its previous requests (and those of other clients) have already been granted and a server is available because all requests are kept in the queue until they are granted. However, the exclusive nature of the get operation guarantees that only one server will handle an individual request, although multiple servers may be available when the request arrives.

Let us now assume we have a multiple-EWS system, consisting of several EWS units of the kind described so far and connected to several printers. Any of the printers may serve any one of the units. See Fig. 8.8, which shows an activity-chart with four EWS units (the clients) connected via a queue PRINTING_Q to two printers (the servers). The queue, in addition to its appearance in the data-store, is defined in the Data Dictionary as a data-item whose type is queue of PRINT_REQST.

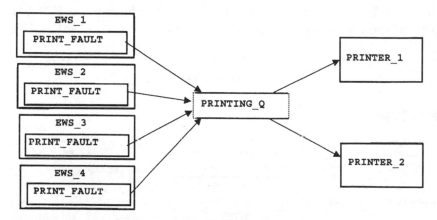

Figure 8.8 Multiple clients served by multiple servers via a queue.

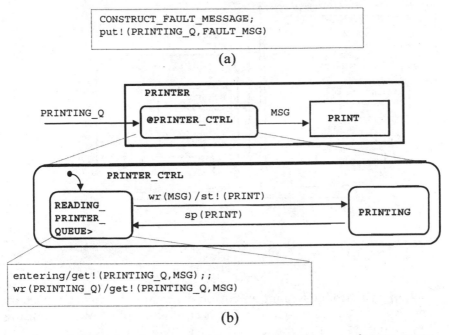

```
CONSTRUCT_FAULT_MESSAGE;
put!(PRINTING_Q,FAULT_MSG)
```

(a)

```
entering/get!(PRINTING_Q,MSG);;
wr(PRINTING_Q)/get!(PRINTING_Q,MSG)
```

(b)

Figure 8.9 Writing and reading messages from a queue. (*a*) Mini-spec of PRINT_FAULT activity. (*b*) Description of the PRINTER.

Each of the EWS units contains a PRINT_FAULT activity that converts the OUT_OF_RANGE_DATA into a printing request (FAULT_MSG of type PRINT_REQST) and sends it to the queue PRINTING_Q. A printer, when ready, reads the next request from the queue, if there is one, and performs the actual printing. See Fig. 8.9 for the mini-spec of the PRINT_FAULT activity and the internals of each PRINTER.

8.4.5   An address of a queue

The preceding example is of loosely coupled (asynchronous) communication. Because the sender does not wait for a reply, the receiver does not need to know the identity of its clients. When the server does not have any prior knowledge of its clients and tightly coupled (synchronous) communication is required; that is, the sender waits for a response, and the address for reply should be contained in the original request. This can be supported by referring directly to the queue data-item that actually holds the address to the queue. This implies that if Q1 and Q2 are both defined as queues of the same component type, then Q1:=Q2 is a legal action, after which Q1 will point to the same data that Q2 points to. Any put and get operation using either Q1 or Q2 will affect the common queue. We should point out that two queue data-items are considered equal only if they point to the same real queue; e.g., Q1=Q2 is true after the assignment Q1:=Q2. Otherwise, even if all of their contents are the same, the two are not equal.

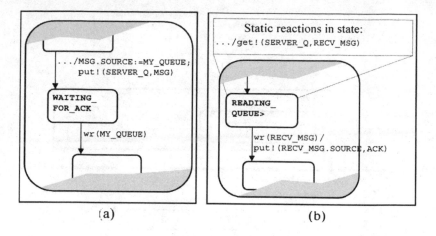

Figure 8.10 Using a queue address for synchronous communication. Behavior of (*a*) CLIENT and (*b*) SERVER.

When synchronous communication is required, each client may have its own queue through which it receives replies. When sending a message MSG, the client includes a field, say MSG.SOURCE, to which it assigns its queue address, say, MY_QUEUE, by the action MSG.SOURCE:=MY_QUEUE. Assume that the server reads the message into RECV_MSG, and acknowledges its receipt by sending a reply using the action put!(RECV_MSG.SOURCE,ACK). The client then waits for the event wr(MY_QUEUE) that results from this put, and can then proceed with its work. See Fig. 8.10.

9

The Structural View

Module-Charts

This chapter deals with the language of Module-charts. Module-charts describes the structural view—sometimes called the *architectural view*—of the system under development. This view deals with the system's actual structure, that is, its implementation, and should be contrasted with the conceptual model described by the other views. Module-charts is typically used in the high-level design stage of the project.

9.1 Structural Description: High-Level Design

The structural view captures the system's high-level design. A structural description of the system specifies the components that implement the capabilities described by the functional and behavioral views. These components may eventually materialize as hardware, software, or even as humans. As in the other views, they may be arranged in a hierarchy. The structural view also specifies the communication lines that connect the components. These communication lines can be described in terms of physical links or flowing information.

Let us now present the structural description of our EWS example. The subsystems constituting the implementation are as follows:

CCU (control and computation unit)	The central CPU, within which the main control of the system and the basic computations take place.
SIGNAL_PROCESSOR	The subsystem that processes the signal produced by the sensor and computes the value to be checked. It consists of an analog-to-digital unit and a high-speed processor that works at the required checking rate.
MONITOR	The subsystem that communicates with the operator. It consists of a KEYBOARD for commands and data entry, and a SCREEN for displaying messages.
ALARM_SYSTEM	The subsystem that produces the alarm, visually, audibly, or both.
PRINTER	The subsystem that receives the messages (text and formatting instructions) and prints them.

The environment systems are the OPERATOR and the SENSOR. By identifying these elements, we define the borders of the system; that is, we determine which facilities are part of the system (e.g., the PRINTER), and which are external (e.g., the SENSOR). Note that the environment components are common to the functional and structural view. We shall discuss this matter further in Chap. 10.

Sometimes, there is a clear correspondence between the top-level activities in the functional view and the top-level subsystems in the structural view. Often, a particular subsystem is responsible for carrying out a single activity from the functional description. Here, for example, the subsystem SIGNAL_PROCESSOR implements the algorithm specified in the activity PROCESS_SIGNAL. However, in many cases the structural decomposition is quite different from the functional decomposition. Thus a single subsystem in the structural view may be responsible for carrying out a number of different activities in the functional view, or an activity may be distributed among several top-level subsystems. In the EWS example, the CCU subsystem carries out both the EWS_CONTROL and COMPARE activities, whereas the DISPLAY_FAULT activity is divided into subactivities that are distributed among the ALARM_SYSTEM and MONITOR subsystems.

The communication between the subsystems of the EWS is discussed in Sec. 9.3.

9.2 Internal and External Modules

In our approach, the structural view is represented by the language of Module-charts and the associated entries in the Data Dictionary. The components, or subsystems, are called *modules* and are depicted as boxes (rectangles or rectilinear polygons). Names appear inside the boxes, adhering to the naming conventions of App. A.1. As in Activity-charts and Statecharts, decomposition is captured by multilevel encapsulation. The general terminology is also similar: we have *basic modules, submodules, parent modules, descendants,* and *ancestors.*

There are two kinds of internal modules: *execution modules,* drawn with solid lines, and *storage modules,* drawn with dashed sidelines like the data-stores in an activity-chart. The *external modules* represent the systems that are outside the top-level module and are drawn with dotted lines. An external module retains this line convention even if it really functions as storage, such as a disk or computer memory. Like external activities in an activity-chart, the external modules may correspond to real environment modules that are external to the entire system under description or to internal modules in other module-charts. This issue is discussed in Chap. 12. As in the case of box elements in other charts, sibling internal modules cannot have the same name. Several external modules, however, can bear the same name, in which case they are all occurrences of the same external module.

Figure 9.1 shows the structural decomposition of the EWS, including a storage module DISK, which stores the fault messages. We have left the arrows unlabeled; they will be discussed in the next section.

The following rules govern the allowed encapsulations in a module-chart:

- Execution modules may be submodules of other execution modules only.

- Storage modules may be submodules of other storage modules or of execution modules.

- External modules are always external to an execution module or storage module, and there is no hierarchy of external modules.

As in the other graphical languages, we use the Data Dictionary to specify additional information. Figure 9.2 shows the Data Dictionary entry of the SIGNAL_PROCESSOR. In it, we have used an attribute name/value pair to specify that the module is to be implemented in hardware, and the synonym field to identify the component in some

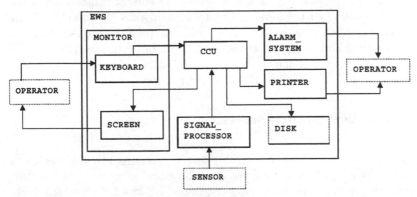

Figure 9.1 Structural decomposition of the EWS.

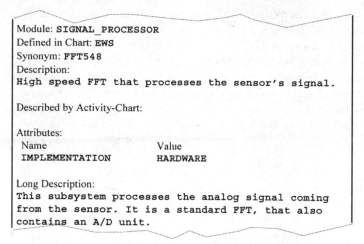

Module: **SIGNAL_PROCESSOR**
Defined in Chart: **EWS**
Synonym: **FFT548**
Description:
High speed FFT that processes the sensor's signal.

Described by Activity-Chart:

Attributes:
 Name   Value
 IMPLEMENTATION   **HARDWARE**

Long Description:
**This subsystem processes the analog signal coming
from the sensor. It is a standard FFT, that also
contains an A/D unit.**

Figure 9.2   A Data Dictionary entry of a module.

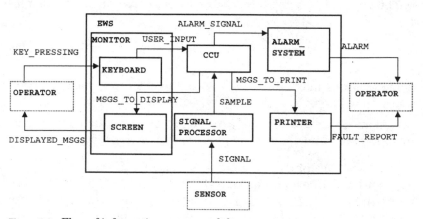

Figure 9.3   Flow of information among modules.

another hardware description. In addition to the standard fields, the Data Dictionary entry for a module contains a special field, Described by Activity-Chart, which is used to connect modules with their functional descriptions. This will be explained further in Chap. 10, where we discuss the connections between the functional and structural views. In Fig. 9.2 it is left empty.

9.3 Communication Lines between Modules

The communication between modules can be described to various levels of detail, from merely specifying the physical connections existing between the modules to specifying the details of the information items comprising the interfaces of the modules.

As in the other graphical languages, we draw labeled arrows between the modules. They are called *flow-lines,* as in activity-charts, or *m-flow-lines,* to emphasize that they connect modules. We do not use a different line style to distinguish lines that represent flow of information items from those that depict physical links.

As in activity-charts, lines attached to nonbasic modules carry special meaning. A flow-line emanating from a nonbasic module specifies that the information flowing along it can be produced by any of its descendant modules, and a flow-line leading to a nonbasic target module specifies that the information labeling it is available to any of its descendant modules.

9.3.1   Flow of information between modules

When a flow-line is used to denote information flowing between modules, the label is as in an activity-chart. That is, it can be a data-item, an event, a condition, or an information-flow that may contain several types. These elements are described in Chap. 3. As in activity-charts, the labels cannot contain compound elements. Also, recall that additional information about these elements (such as their physical implementation) can be specified in their Data Dictionary entries.

Figure 9.3 depicts the module-chart for our EWS example, with labels describing the information on the arrows.

Note that some of the elements appearing here appeared along the flow-lines of the corresponding activity-chart in Fig. 2.5, and some are information-flows that contain elements appearing therein. Here, USER_INPUT contains the information-flow COMMANDS, the data-item RANGE_LIMITS, and the condition SENSOR_CONNECTED. The precise relationship between the flows in activity-charts and module-charts is discussed in Chap. 10.

9.3.2   Physical links between modules

Arrows in a module-chart may also denote physical communication links, or *channels,* between modules. In this case, information-flows are used to name the links. The Data Dictionary entry for such a flow can be used to specify the type of link and the way the data is represented along it. The actual information elements that flow along the link can be specified in the Consists of field.

Figure 9.4 contains an alternative module-chart for the EWS example, showing the physical links. Some of them are really wires (or cables) of various types.

The interface with the user in the EWS is carried out by pressing buttons or by audio or visual outputs. Although these elements are not associated with physical links, they are also shown in the figure.

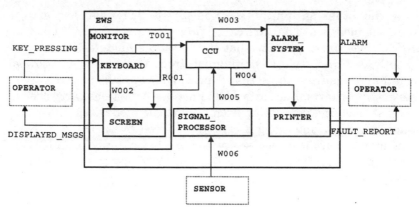

Figure 9.4 Physical links among modules.

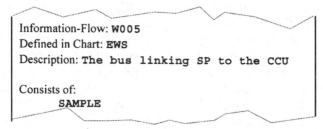

Figure 9.5 Information-flow describing a physical link.

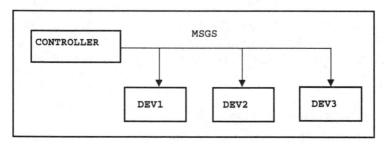

Figure 9.6 Communication link to several devices.

Figure 9.5 shows the Data Dictionary entry of the information-flow W005, which connects the SIGNAL_PROCESSOR and the CCU. The data-item SAMPLE flows inside this communication link.

9.4 Connectors and Compound Flow-Lines

Module-charts contain features that help in preparing clear and uncluttered charts, as do the two other types of charts. Connectors and compound flow-lines are allowed in module-charts exactly as they are in activity-charts. See Chap. 2.

Joint connectors are often used to depict a flow-line that links several modules. An example is shown in Fig. 9.6, where several peripheral devices listen out for messages arriving along a communication link that emanates from the central controlling unit.

10

Connections between the Functional and Structural Views

In Chap. 2 we discussed the functional view, described via the language of Activity-charts, and in Chap. 9 we discussed the structural view, described via Module-charts. The former depicts the system's decomposition into functional components, or activities, and the latter depicts its decomposition into structural components, or modules. This chapter discusses the connections between these two views and the way the connections are captured in our languages.

10.1 Relating the Functional and Structural Models

The functional view provides a decomposition of the system under development into its functional components, that is, its capabilities and processes. The structural view, on the other hand, provides a decomposition of the system into the actual subsystems that will be part of the final system, and which implement its functionality. The subsystems may be physical in nature, as were most of the modules in our description of the EWS example in Chap. 9, or logical in nature. For example, an MMI subsystem, which carries out all functions related to the man-machine interface of some system, would be considered a logical subsystem of that system.

We now describe the three types of connections between the functional and structural views: one is to describe the functionality of a module by an activity-chart (Sec. 10.1.1); the second is to allocate specific activities in an activity-chart to be implemented in a module (Sec. 10.1.2), and the third is to map activities in the functional description of one module to activities in that of some other module (Sec. 10.1.3). The way these three kinds of connections are specified in our languages is described in Secs. 10.2, 10.3, and 10.4, respectively.

10.1.1   Functional description of a module

Our discussion of the functional view of the EWS in Chap. 2 centered around providing a functional description of the entire system, that is, the EWS module. However, there are a number of reasons for developing separate functional descriptions for some or all of the various submodules identified in the structural view:

- A module might represent an autonomous subsystem that is to be developed separately and then combined with the whole system (often with a relatively humble interface). For example, we may want to describe the SIGNAL_PROCESSOR of the EWS as a separate component. It may be used in other systems, and its independent description could be valuable for other purposes.

- A separate functional description of a submodule is sometimes a necessary prerequisite to its detailed design and implementation. Note that the description of the submodule's functionality may depend on a good understanding of the entire system specification, in which case a top-down approach is appropriate. For example, prior to the implementation of the CCU—the control and computation unit of the EWS—we might want to develop a separate description of its functionality. However, we can determine its specification only after identifying relevant functions in the entire EWS.

- It might be beneficial to obtain a good understanding of the functionality of a subsystem by identifying its capabilities to help carry out the functional specification of the entire system. In this case, a bottom-up approach is best. For example, we may prefer to first analyze the functionality of the MONITOR module, identifying the activities it will perform (such as GET_INPUT and DISPLAY_MESSAGE), and use these later, in the description of the processes that take place in the overall system. We shall discuss this approach further in Sec. 10.1.3.

In conclusion, we may wish to attach functional descriptions (i.e., activity-charts) to modules on different levels of the structural decomposition. See Fig. 10.1.

10.1.2   Allocating activities to modules

The structural decomposition and the identification of the flow of information between modules is part of the design stage of a system's development. But the design must be related to the system's functionality.

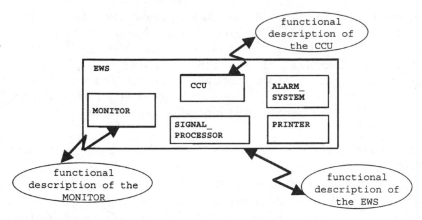

Figure 10.1 Functional descriptions attached to different modules.

That is, the functions identified in the functional view must be specified as being carried out by certain modules in the structural view. To
capture this association, each of the functions must be allocated to one
or more modules. In the EWS, for example, the SIGNAL_PROCESSOR
performs the activity PROCESS_SIGNAL. This is a straightforward case
of such an allocation. A more delicate case is the SET_UP activity, which
contains subactivities that interact with the operator, as well as activities that carry out calculations. SET_UP should probably be divided
among several modules with appropriate capabilities. Interaction
would be carried out by the MONITOR, while the control of SET_UP and
its calculation would be implemented by the CCU.

The allocation of activities to modules is the main activity carried out
during top-level design. Indeed, some methodologies provide heuristic
criteria for allocating activities to modules, for example by analyzing
cohesion and coupling (Gomma 1993; Yourdon and Constantine 1979).
This allocation actually determines the flow of information among the
modules. Information that flows between two activities that are carried out by two modules will flow also between those modules. It is possible to examine alternatives for the allocation, using the amount of
implied communication among the modules to decide which is best.

The allocation of activities to modules is also used in requirement
traceability analysis. A functional requirement that was part of the
original requirements of the system and was translated into an activity in the functional view will be automatically associated with the
module that carries out that activity.

The allocation of activities to modules also allows restructuring
of the functional description to define the implementation structure.
One of the main criticisms of function-based decomposition methods such as Structured Analysis is that there is a troublesome discontinuity between the specification and design descriptions. This gap is

overcome to some extent in object-based methods, where both specification and design use the same components (objects) and the design is, in general, a refinement of the specification. This means that if the functional decomposition was carried out using an object-based approach, the mapping between activities and modules can be made easy: the decomposition into modules will use (or at least it will start with) the same components as the functional description.

10.1.3 Mapping activities to a module's activities

Sometimes it is not sufficient to allocate activities described on the system level to their implementing modules. We might want to be more concrete about the activities within the module's specification (as a subsystem) that are responsible for implementing the system activities. For example, the COMPARE activity is performed by the CCU, so there should be an activity within the CCU's functional description that implements the comparison. We could thus include an activity in the CCU's functional description, called CMP, which would be responsible for this. In such a case, we would map activities appearing on the system level to those appearing on the subsystem level.

This type of connection is even more useful in a bottom-up development process, where we first analyze the capabilities of each of the subsystems by developing their functional descriptions and later use them to construct the functional description of the entire system by detailing the scenarios in which these functions participate. Actually, the two views can be developed in parallel: while identifying the possible scenarios that occur during system operation, the required functions are defined and are specified as part of the appropriate subsystem. This approach is suggested by the ECSAM methodology, described in Lavi and Winokur (1989) and in Chap. 15 below. It is somewhat similar to an object-oriented analysis method in which the operations each object can perform are identified in parallel to the development of the scenarios (use cases) that use them. In Sec. 10.5 we illustrate this approach using the EWS.

In the following sections we show how our languages support the three connections discussed in the last three subsections.

10.2   Activity-Chart Describing a Module

The activity-chart EWS_ACTIVITIES, shown in Fig. 2.5, constitutes the functional description of the entire EWS system. In the structural view, the system appears as the top-level module of the module-chart EWS of Fig. 9.1. We may thus say that the *activity-chart* EWS_ACTIVITIES *describes* the functionality of the *module* EWS .

This connection between a module and its describing activity-chart is specified in the Data Dictionary entity of the module, in the field `Described by Activity-Chart` (see Fig. 10.2).

Notice that the connection is between an activity-chart and a module (and not between an activity-chart and a module-chart, or between an activity and a module). In our example, the module thus related is a top-level module, but this is not mandatory. It is possible to associate an activity-chart with any module in a module-chart. One reasonable way of proceeding (having already described the structural view of the system by a module-chart) would be to first describe the functionality of the entire system, that is, to construct a functional view for the top-level module, and then describe the detailed functionality of specific lower-level modules. Thus, in our example, we may now want to specify the activity-chart `CCU_AC` for the module `CCU`. The situation is illustrated in Fig. 10.3. (More about this issue in Secs. 10.4 and 10.5 and in Chap. 12.)

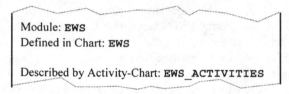

Module: **EWS**
Defined in Chart: **EWS**

Described by Activity-Chart: **EWS_ACTIVITIES**

Figure 10.2 A module described by an activity-chart.

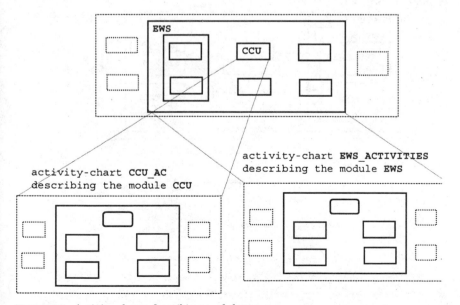

Figure 10.3 Activity-charts describing modules.

There must be a correspondence between the functional and structural decompositions of a module in terms of the environment and the interface with it. Because the top-level activity in the describing activity-chart represents the "functional image" of the module, we expect the external activities that interact with this top-level activity to correspond to the environment of the module described by the module-chart. When an external activity has been given a name, it must be the name of some module from the relevant environment. Indeed, as we saw in Fig. 2.5, the external activities in the chart EWS_ACTIVITIES were OPERATOR and SENSOR, the same as the modules external to the EWS module in the module-chart EWS. In this case, they are environment modules because EWS is the top-level module. However, in Fig. 10.4, the external activities in the activity-chart CCU_AC for the CCU module will be MONITOR, SIGNAL_PROCESSOR, ALARM_SYSTEM, and PRINTER, because they are the modules external to the module CCU, with which it interacts.

Notice that we included MONITOR as an external activity in CCU_AC but not its submodules KEYBOARD and SCREEN, although in the module-chart the CCU is connected to them through the communication lines. This is because the CCU is not supposed to "know" the internal structure of the modules with which it communicates.

Because the external activities in an activity-chart that describes a module correspond to modules, they have no entity of their own in the Data Dictionary, and they are viewed as pointers to the modules they

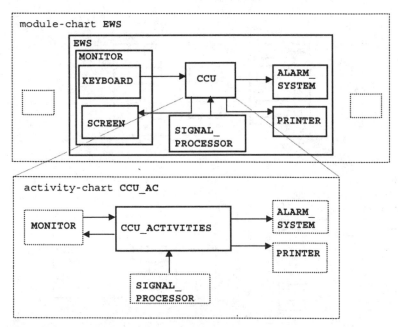

Figure 10.4 External activities corresponding to modules.

represent. Not only must the external elements of a module and its corresponding activity-chart match, but so must the information flowing in and out of them. To get a feeling for this requirement, compare Fig. 2.5 with Fig. 9.3. The former shows the information flowing to and from EWS_ACTIVITIES, and the latter shows the same for the EWS module in the module-chart. Most of the flows connect identically named external elements. However, notice that COMMANDS, RANGE_LIMITS, and SENSOR_CONNECTED were drawn in the activity-chart as flowing from OPERATOR, while in the module-chart they arrive from KEYBOARD (as components of USER_INPUT), and not from OPERATOR. This inconsistency arises from the fact that when we constructed the activity-chart we did not include the activity named GET_INPUT, for simplification. This activity is performed continuously in the MONITOR, whose role is to translate the KEY_PRESSING of the OPERATOR into COMMANDS and other information elements contained in USER_INPUT. To correct this problem, thus making the views consistent, we must add the GET_INPUT activity to the functional description. The revised version of the activity-chart EWS_ACTIVITIES of Fig. 2.5 that describes the module EWS is given in Fig. 10.5.

When constructing an activity-chart that describes a module, the names of the particular modules that produce or consume the externally flowing information may not be interesting. In such cases, the external activities can remain unnamed, as we illustrate in some of the following examples. However, as stated earlier, if an external activity is named, that name must correspond to a module in the corresponding module-chart.

10.3   Activities Implemented by Modules

Now that we are familiar with the general connection, whereby an activity-chart describes the functionality of a module in the module-chart, we can discuss how the components of each of these charts are related.

The relationship is this: all internal activities and control activities that appear in the activity-chart that describes a certain module are implemented by that module, and all the data-stores that appear in the chart reside in that module. In our EWS example, all activities in the EWS_ACTIVITIES chart (e.g., GET_INPUT, SET_UP, PROCESS_SIGNAL, etc.; see Fig. 10.5) are implemented by the EWS module, and the data-store LEGAL_RANGE resides in the EWS module.

When the module described by the activity-chart is eventually decomposed into submodules, we may be more concrete and allocate the relevant activities and data-stores to the submodules. This is done in the field Implemented by Module of the activity entity in the Data Dictionary, or in the field Resides in Module of the Data Dictionary

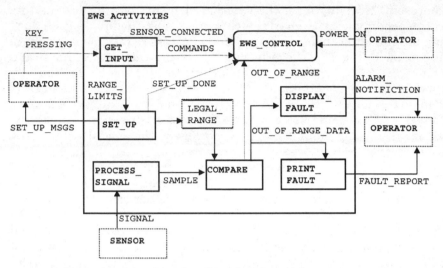

Figure 10.5 Revised activity-chart describing the EWS module.

entity for the data-store. For example, the PROCESS_SIGNAL activity is implemented by the module SIGNAL_PROCESSOR, and we have written this information in the Data Dictionary entity of the activity, as shown in Fig. 10.6. Similarly, the fact that LEGAL_RANGE resides in CCU appears in the Data Dictionary entity of the data-store.

Activities can be implemented by execution modules only (not storage or external modules), and data-stores can reside in any internal module, that is, in either execution or storage modules.

Several activities and data-stores can be allocated to a single module via the implemented by module or resides in module relation. For example, the activities COMPARE and EWS_CONTROL, as well as the data-store LEGAL_RANGE, are all allocated to the CCU module. However, a single activity or data-store cannot be distributed among several modules. In our example, the activities SET_UP, DISPLAY_FAULT, and PRINT_FAULT are each carried out by several modules. We could, of course, assign them to sufficiently high-level modules to cover this distribution, but this might lead to allocations that are too general to be useful. It is often better to further decompose such activities into subactivities that can each be allocated to a single module. This allocation will obviously be more informative. Thus, for example, SET_UP will be decomposed into PROMPT_RANGE, DISPLAY_SU_ERROR, VALIDATE_RANGE, and the control activity SET_UP_STATES. The role of the first two is to display messages, and they are implemented by the MONITOR module, while the other two are implemented by the CCU module. See Fig. 10.7.

The association of activities and data-stores with modules must be consistent with the module hierarchy and the activity hierarchy. As discussed earlier, all components of the top-level activity must be implemented in the module described by the activity-chart. Similarly, all subactivities and data-stores of an activity A that is implemented by a module M must be themselves implemented by M or its submodules. In other words, descendants of A cannot be allocated to modules outside of M. In the EWS example, we would not be allowed to specify that the SET_UP activity is implemented by the CCU and, at the same time, that its subactivity DISPLAY_SU_ERROR is implemented by the MONITOR module, because MONITOR is not contained in the CCU.

In Sec. 10.2 we discussed the consistency between the interface of the described module and the flows to the top-level activity. A similar consistency requirement applies to the flow of information on all levels. If two activities in the activity-chart are implemented by two different modules, we expect the information elements flowing between

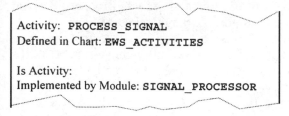

Figure 10.6   An activity implemented by a module.

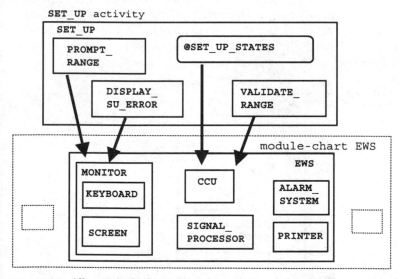

Figure 10.7   Allocation of subactivities of SET_UP to modules.

the activities to also flow between these modules. For example, compare Figs. 9.4 and 10.5. We allocated the PROCESS_SIGNAL activity to the SIGNAL_PROCESSOR module and the COMPARE activity to the CCU. In both charts the data-item SAMPLE flows between the corresponding boxes.

10.4 Activities Associated with a Module's Activities

This section deals with the possibility of mapping activities from the functional description of the entire system to activities from the functional description of its subsystems. The next example illustrates how this is actually done.

Figure 10.8 contains the activity-chart MONITOR_AC that describes the functionality of the module MONITOR. This module performs two functions, GET_INPUT and DISPLAY_MESSAGE, which are described, together with their inputs and outputs, in the activity-chart. (Some of the external activities are left unnamed in the figure because the sources and targets of the flowing data are not relevant here.)

Thus there are two activity-charts: EWS_ACTIVITIES for the entire system (EWS) and MONITOR_AC for one of the subsystems (MONITOR). In addition to allocating activities of the former chart to the EWS modules, we can also specify which activities in the latter chart correspond to these higher-level activities. In this example, we say in the Data Dictionary entity of the subactivity DISPLAY_SU_ERROR of SET_UP that it is activity DISPLAY_MESSAGE, implemented by module MONITOR. See Fig. 10.9. Similarly, the subactivity PROMPT_RANGE of SET_UP will also correspond to the activity DISPLAY_MESSAGE, using the field Is Activity. Attaching both activities to the same activity DISPLAY_MESSAGE means that the two will actually be implemented by the same function.

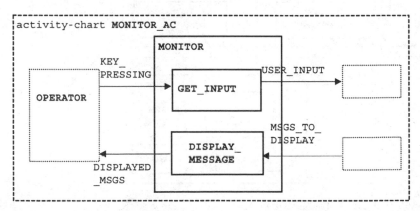

Figure 10.8 Activity-chart of MONITOR.

Activity: **DISPLAY_SU_ERROR**
Defined in Chart: **SET_UP**

Is Activity: **DISPLAY__MESSAGE**
Implemented by Module: **MONITOR**

Figure 10.9 Mapping of activities by the is activity relation.

We also attach the activity GET_INPUT from the EWS_ACTIVITIES activity-chart to the activity GET_INPUT in MONITOR_AC. Although we use the same name for both activities, the field Is Activity must be specified. We say that PROMPT_RANGE in SET_UP is an *occurrence of the activity* DISPLAY_MESSAGE in the MONITOR module. The DISPLAY_MESSAGE activity is called the *principal activity* of PROMPT_RANGE.

Note that the field Is Activity is meaningful only when the Implemented by Module field is not empty. Moreover, the activity referred to must be one of the activities in the activity-chart that describes the implementing module.

In a similar way, a data-store may be associated with another data-store in the description of the submodules. The relevant field is Is Data-Store, which is completely analogous to Is Activity in the Data Dictionary entity for an activity. The terms used are the same: if a data-store P is defined as is data-store Q, then P is called an *occurrence of the data-store* Q, and Q is the *principal data-store* of P.

10.5 Object-Oriented Analysis with Module-Charts

Chapter 2 discussed an object-based approach to decomposition. This approach often fails to address one of the main goals of the specification phase because the decomposition alone makes it difficult to see the system's global behavior. Object-oriented approaches recommend that during requirement analysis, the behavioral scenarios (use cases) that might occur throughout the system should be identified, not just the objects and their operations. Here we show how the combination of module-charts and activity-charts and the Is Activity relation described earlier can be used to provide full specifications.

We shall use a module-chart to describe the system's objects. The operations of each object will be described as activities in the activity-chart that describes the module (object). The activity-chart that describes the top-level module (i.e., the entire system) will be used to describe the behavioral scenarios as sequences of object operations. An activity with its controlling statechart and subactivities will represent a set of related scenarios, while the subactivities are mapped to the object operations by the `Is Activity` relation. Figure 10.10 illustrates this scheme.

The module-chart `EWS_OBJS` in Fig. 10.11 shows the decomposition of the `EWS` into objects and is similar to the one described in Sec. 2.1.3.

The operations of the `RANGE` object are described in the activity-chart `RANGE_OPS`, shown in Fig. 10.12. The Data Dictionary entry for the module `RANGE` contains the fact that it is `described by activity-chart RANGE_OPS`.

The activity-chart that describes the functionality of the entire system—the top-level module `EWS` in the figure—consists of the possible scenarios. The `SET_UP` scenario is the activity shown in Fig. 10.13; it consists of subactivities mapped to operations of the objects `RANGE` and `MMI_HANDLER`.

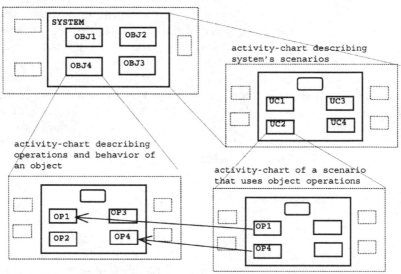

Figure 10.10 An object-oriented analysis model.

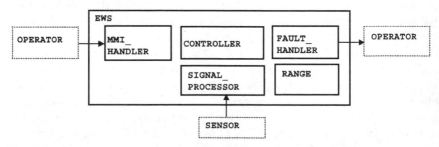

Figure 10.11 A module-chart based on object decomposition.

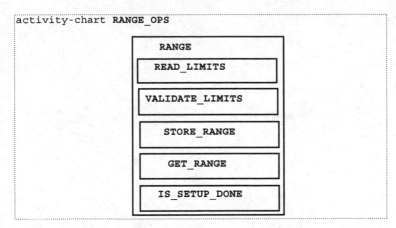

Figure 10.12   An activity-chart specifying the operations of RANGE.

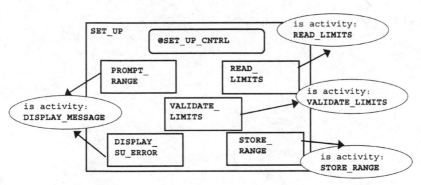

Figure 10.13   An activity-chart describing the SET_UP scenario.

11

Splitting Up Charts

The three graphical languages described in this book allow the decomposition of elements: each activity, state, or module is either basic or is described by a set of subelements. Other modeling notations and tools also allow multilevel descriptions, but many of them require that each level be described in a separate chart. Our languages allow multiple levels in the same chart but also allow the description to span several charts. In this chapter we discuss the possibility of presenting different levels of decomposition in separate charts. We deal mainly with linking the graphical information. The visibility of elements belonging to different charts is discussed in Chap. 13.

It is worth distinguishing separate charts depicting different levels of the decomposition from generic charts that are considered reusable components of a model. This chapter deals with the former; the latter are described in Chap. 14.

11.1 Separating a Chart into Multiple Pages

The charts drawn in earlier chapters contained a top-level box, representing the element being described. This box was then decomposed into lower-level boxes, with each level being drawn inside the higher one. See, for example, Figs. 2.3, 4.11, and 9.1. Often, however, it is convenient to break down the drawing into a number of charts, each containing one or more levels of decomposition. For example, instead of chart A of Fig. 11.1a we might want to draw the two separate charts of Fig. 11.1b. Although there are now two physically distinct charts, A and A2, logically there is just one, and the information in chart A2 is treated as if it were drawn inside the box named A2 in A. Thus there is a single *logical chart* that consists of two *physical charts,* which are also called *pages*.

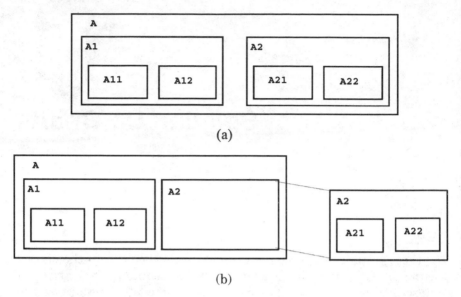

(a)

(b)

Figure 11.1   Splitting up a chart into pages.

Here are some of the reasons for dividing a chart into pages. They are similar to the reasons for breaking down a large piece of software into functions and subroutines.

- *Overly detailed charts.*   A complex chart that contains too many details is difficult to read and comprehend. Breaking it down into several pages has a "decluttering" effect. Because this is the primary reason for dividing charts, we often term the separation of charts into pages as *decluttering.*

- *Information relevant to different people.*   Often, different pieces of information in a chart are relevant to different observers. Here, the breakup is according to the responsibilities or interests of different people. We might call this *person-oriented information hiding;* that is, each person gets to see only the information relevant to the parts of the system he or she is working on. This is a widely acclaimed principle of system development, and decomposing charts into pages can help support it. Also, such a division can help overcome difficulties that arise when different people update parts of the same chart, or when one updates it while another analyzes it.

- *Information relevant to different levels.*   Here, the idea is to support information hiding in the classical sense, that is, to make sure each level of the specification contains only the elements relevant to it.

- *Information from different configuration management units.*   Here, the splitting is done according to different versions or releases (or both) of the system under development, or according to different ownership and read/write/modify privileges.

- *Hybrid process of building the charts.*   Some charts are built partly by a top-down process and partly by a bottom-up one. Breaking down charts can be used to draw the low-level components on separate pages and incorporate them as the internal descriptions of components in charts of higher levels. This introduces flexibility into the chart-building process.   .

- *Easing modification.*   Splitting up the model into many charts can simplify the logistics of modification. Subcharts represented by separate pages can be replaced easily by others with the same interface. This makes it easy to present specification alternatives simply by changing the contents of black boxes.

Although chart decluttering can be beneficial, sometimes it is not recommended. We have in mind situations in which the system does not lend itself to neat structuring or where despite the availability of a good structuring there is a tight interrelationship between the low-level elements in different parts of the structure. In such cases, decluttered charts may be harder to comprehend. For example, it is sometimes easier to follow the behavioral aspects of a complex model when these elements are concentrated in a single statechart. The same goes for presenting and comprehending the flow of information in an activity-chart down to the basic low-level activity that actually produces and consumes the data elements.

11.2   Offpage Charts

We now discuss the mechanism used to split a chart into several pages. The contents of a box element (activity, state, or module) may be drawn in a separate chart. The box element is called an *instance box,* and the associated chart is called an *offpage chart* or a *definition chart.* The relationship between the two is sometimes termed the *box-is-chart* relation. The chart of the instance box is sometimes referred to as the *instance chart.*

To represent the relation between an instance box A and a definition chart B, we label the instance box by A@B, which means that this is box A but its internals are to be described in chart B. If we want to use the same name for the box and its definition chart, we may simply omit the first of the two names. Thus a box labeled @A means that the box and its definition chart are both named A (which is therefore like labeling it A@A).

In our EWS example, the functional decomposition of the SET_UP activity of Chap. 2 may be described in a separate chart. Figure 11.2*a* shows this activity named @SET_UP, meaning that its contents are

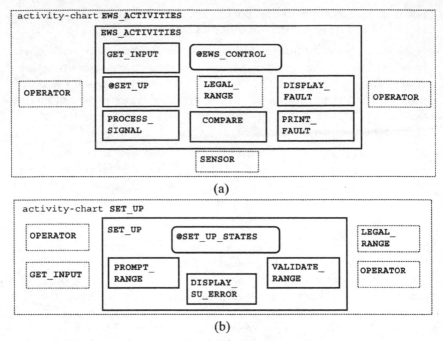

Figure 11.2 An instance activity and its definition (offpage) chart.

defined in a chart named SET_UP, and Fig. 11.2*b* shows the corresponding definition chart with its further decomposition. As explained earlier, no name precedes the @ symbol, so the box name is the same as the definition chart name, and we may, for example, use the action start(SET_UP) in the controlling statechart EWS_CONTROL. Had we labeled the box SU@SET_UP, that action would have had to take the form start(SU).

Note that the notation used to associate a box with its offpage chart is the same as that used to associate a control activity with its describing statechart. See Fig. 11.2*a*; the control activity labeled @EWS_CONTROL is described by a statechart named EWS_CONTROL.

When a box is described by an offpage chart, say, A@B, the definition chart B must have a unique top-level box, and the instance box A may have no subboxes. Of course, the subboxes appearing in the top-level box in B are considered *logical subboxes* of A, but A has no *physical subboxes*. This terminology is used for parents, too. Boxes may thus have *logical* and *physical parents*.

Referring again to Fig. 11.2, the PROMPT_RANGE activity is considered a subactivity of the instance activity SET_UP, and therefore it is also a logical descendant of EWS_ACTIVITIES. The physical parent of PROMPT_RANGE is the top-level activity SET_UP in the activity-chart with the same name. Because the top-level box is considered an "image" of the instance box, we have named the two identically in our example. However, it is possible—although not recommended—to have three different names, one each for the instance box, the definition chart, and the top-level box.

The external activities that are presented in the definition chart are the boxes that surround the SET_UP activity in the instance chart (EWS_ACTIVITIES) with which SET_UP communicates. We shall return to this issue in the following section and in Chap. 12, where the entire model is discussed.

Both the instance box and the top-level box of the definition chart have associated entries in the Data Dictionary, and the information appearing therein must be consistent. More specifically, the following fields, if not empty, must contain the same information: Termination Type and Implemented by Module in an activity entry and Described by Activity-Chart in a module entry. For all other fields, such as Static Reactions and Active Activities in a state entry and Attributes for all elements, the information in the entries for the instance box and the top-level box of the definition chart is accumulated and viewed as applying to the common entity.

We do not allow multiple instances of a common definition chart. In other words, two instance boxes cannot be described by the same definition chart. When the need arises for multiple instances of the same chart, the generic chart mechanism of Chap. 14 should be used.

11.3 Connecting Offpage Charts by Matching Flows

One advantage of having multiple levels in the same chart is the ease of viewing arrows (flow-lines in activity-charts and module-charts, and state transitions in statecharts), in that sources and targets are seen together. When charts are decluttered into separate pages, this will necessarily be less convenient. In any case, we need to have reasonable mechanisms for combining arrows over pages. We supply two. The first, discussed in this present section, concerns matching flows and can be used only in activity-charts and module-charts. The second concerns diagram connectors and is described in Sec. 11.4. Although diagram connectors can be used in all three types of charts, we describe their use for statecharts only, because the first method is preferred for the two other types of charts.

Here is how to link flow-lines between pages in activity-charts and module-charts. The arrows leading to and from the borderline of the instance box are matched with the arrows exiting or entering external boxes in the definition chart. The actual matching is carried out by identifying common information elements included in the labels.

Let us examine an example. In Fig. 11.3 part a is the original chart and b describes its partition into two charts, by extracting the contents of A1 and relegating them to a new activity-chart. The flow-lines in activity-chart A that depict the interface of activity A1 are all connected to the borderline of the instance box, including those that are related to

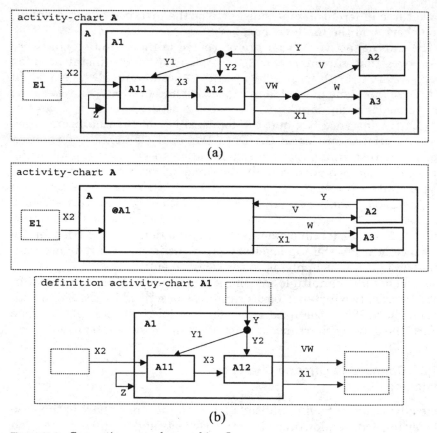

Figure 11.3 Connecting pages by matching flows.

the internal activities of A1. In the definition chart of A1, all flow-lines
are labeled with the flowing elements and are connected to their actual
sources and targets inside A1.

Note that the matching is carried out according to the flowing elements and not the written labels. For example, in the definition chart
A1, the flow-line emanating from A12 is labeled VW, an information
flow consisting of V and W. This line is matched with the two separate
flows labeled V and W in the instance chart.

Note also that the external boxes in the definition chart of Fig.
11.3*b* are unnamed. This is done mainly to emphasize the fact that
arrows are linked by matching the flowing elements and not by the
sources and targets. However, the names may be added if it is important to represent these sources and targets explicitly. This indeed
might be the case in a top-down development effort because the sources
and targets are already determined in the instance chart.

Another point worth making is that there is no correspondence
between sources and targets of the flows in the definition and
instance charts. For example, V and W of Fig. 11.3, when considered as

the compound information item VW, have a single external target in the definition chart, whereas in the instance chart they lead to two separate boxes. This illustrates the fact that unnamed external boxes are really just place holders, or external agents that are connected to arrows that lead to or from the outside. (In a bottom-up development effort, this is particularly helpful; we might not want to specify the actual external elements when developing the definition chart because we might not yet know about them.) If the external boxes in the definition chart *are* named, the names must be consistent with those of the corresponding sources and targets in the instance chart.

For example, Fig. 11.4 shows the SET_UP definition chart with its external interface. Comparing it with Fig. 10.5, we see that the boxes in this external interface correspond to the various boxes with which the SET_UP activity communicates. In the case of decluttering an activity-chart, the external activities in the definition chart may correspond to the following kinds of elements in the instance chart: regular internal activities, control activities, external activities, and data-stores. In particular, the data-store LEGAL_RANGE is also depicted as an external activity in the definition chart. In a similar way, when decluttering a module-chart, external modules in the defining chart may correspond to execution modules, storage modules, or external modules in the instance chart.

Clearly, each input or output of the top-level box in the definition chart must also appear in the instance chart, either as a direct flow to the instance box or as a flow-line connected to one of its ancestors. We also expect each flow-line connected to the instance box to appear in the definition chart that contains the particular source or target, even when it is specified as being consumed or produced by all subelements of the instance. For example, comparing Fig. 11.3*b* with Fig. 11.3*a*, we see that although X1 is an output of A1, it also appears in the definition chart. The reason for this is that when drawing the interface of the instance, it is considered as the interface to a "black box." That is, drawing an input line means "one or more of the components consume this input, and the actual consumer(s) will be specified in the definition chart." The reasoning is similar for outputs.

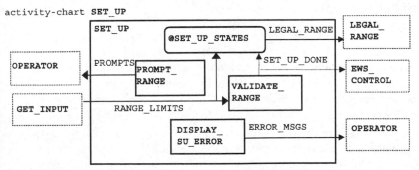

Figure 11.4 SET_UP definition chart.

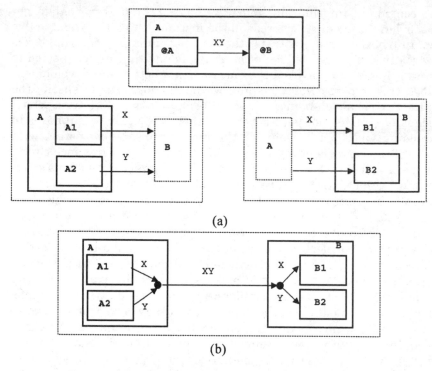

Figure 11.5 Compound flow-lines distributed over several pages.

In Sec. 2.5.4 we introduced the notion of a compound flow-line; we talked about the logical flows between activities (or modules) that consist of several flow-line segments linked with connectors. Now here, although using a different construction method, we have compound lines that are distributed over several pages. Figure 11.5a shows an example that contains two compound flow-lines: X, flowing from A1 to B1, and Y, flowing from A2 to B2. An equivalent construct is shown in Fig. 11.5b.

11.4   Connecting Offpage Statecharts Using Connectors

The method presented above for connecting offpage charts to the description in the instance chart cannot be applied in the case of statecharts because they are not connected via flows. For them we use an alternative mechanism that is based on diagram connectors. In earlier chapters we already used diagram connectors to combine several arrow segments into a single logical compound arrow. See, for example, Fig. 4.21, in which three compound transitions between states were constructed from two segments each, using diagram connectors. Because these connectors appear in the same chart, or page, we refer to them as *inpage diagram connectors.* When they are used to connect arrows on separate pages, as is the case here, we call them *offpage diagram connectors.* In the instance chart (i.e., the chart that contains the instance box) the connectors are drawn inside the instance box, and in the definition chart they are drawn outside the top-level box.

Like inpage connectors, offpage diagram connectors may be labeled either with numbers or with an alphanumeric string that starts with a letter and might contain underscores. A useful convention is to label the connector with the name of the source or the target of the arrow in the instance chart. Another possibility is to use the name of the trigger of the transition.

Each connector in the instance chart must have a matching connector in the definition chart, with consistent directionality of the arrow. See Fig. 11.6*b,* in which one arrow enters the GO connector in the instance chart and one exits the GO connector in the definition chart. A connector is not allowed to have both entering and exiting arrows. We allow several offpage connectors in an instance box, all with the same label, and follow a similar convention for connectors in the definition chart. Such multiple occurrences in one chart must all have the same arrow directionality. The same label can also be used for offpage connectors in separate instances. However, we do not allow an offpage connector in an instance box to have the same label as an inpage connector on the same page, because that might be confusing.

When imagining the compound arrows constructed from arrow segments leading to and from connectors, the offpage connectors are treated like junction connectors (as in the inpage case; see Chap. 4). Consequently, the triggers on these segments are combined by *and,* and all the actions on them are performed.

When connecting the statechart pages logically, the only transitions that have to be connected are those that cross the boundary of instance states. Transitions that enter or exit an instance state without crossing its borderline will typically not appear in the definition chart at all. The reason is that such entering transitions will enter substates in the definition chart via the default connectors, and the exiting transitions will exit the state regardless of the internal configuration. This rule is consistent with the idea of a structured specification, in that the reasons for entering and exiting the state are not to be known inside the state. Exceptions to this rule include exits that do not necessarily apply on the top level, that is, to all internal states, but only to some of them. In such cases, it is appropriate to describe the outgoing transitions in the definition chart as well as in the instance chart.

Figure 11.6 contains an example: part *a* shows the chart before decluttering, and part *b* after it. Notice that in Fig. 11.6*b,* transitions that cross the borderline of state ON are connected by connectors, while those

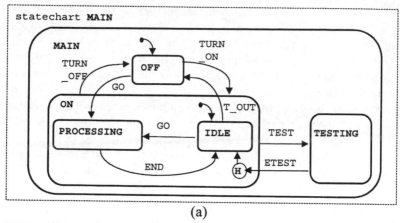

(a)

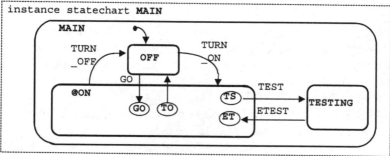

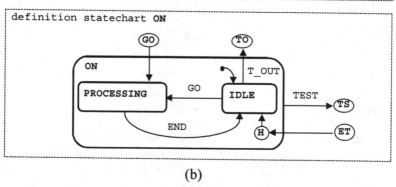

(b)

Figure 11.6 Transitions between pages of a statechart.

that emanate from that borderline (i.e., TEST and TURN_OFF) are drawn with or without the connector, depending on the particular case. The fact that TURN_OFF is an event that triggers an exit from every state is important information on the upper level. On the other hand, the decision about which states the event TEST acts on was made on the lower level. In Fig. 11.6b, the trigger labels appear in at least one page, depending on the specifier's preference, but not necessarily in both.

12

Putting Things Together

In the preceding chapters we discussed different kinds of charts and elements, and their interrelationships. A full-fledged model of a system may consist of many charts, each containing many elements. Now, although we have not yet described all the features of our languages, we pause here to take a bird's eye view and discuss how charts are connected to build a full model. Later, when we introduce additional features, such as generic charts, we will also address the issue of their location in the entire model. Do not be misled, however; when modeling a system, it is not necessary to specify all parts of the full structure as presented here.

This chapter also deals with entities external to the model—environment systems and testbenches. It discusses their role and how they relate to the other elements of the model.

Charts that make up the model share elements among themselves. Therefore, the picture is incomplete without the material of Chap. 13, in which we discuss the scope of elements and their visibility with regard to the various components of the model. We also introduce there another component of a model, the *global definition set*, which contains information that is visible to the entire model.

12.1 Relationships among the Three Kinds of Charts

We now describe the full picture of our EWS example, as it emerges from the various pieces described in earlier chapters. The fact that our exposition follows a certain order is not meant to imply any specific order recommended in developing the model.

The interface of the EWS with its environment and its structural decomposition appear in the module-chart EWS of Fig. 1.7, which is also shown on the left-hand side of Fig. 12.1. The entire system is depicted by the top-level module therein, named EWS. The activity-chart EWS_ACTIVITIES, whose contents is shown in Fig. 1.4, describes the functionality of this top-level module. The top-level activity in that chart, EWS_ACTIVITIES, corresponds to the EWS module, so the interfaces of the two must be the same. See Chap. 10.

Control activities appearing in an activity-chart are described by statecharts. See Chaps. 6, 7, and 8. Thus in Fig. 12.1 we see that the control activity of the activity EWS_ACTIVITIES is described by the statechart EWS_CONTROL of Fig. 1.6. Similarly, the control activity of SET_UP is described by the statechart of Fig. 7.3.

We refer the reader to App. B, which contains the entire EWS model.

As we saw in Chap. 10, an activity-chart can be attached to any module in the module-chart as its functional description. The control activities in these activity-charts are also described by statecharts. For our EWS example, this results in the structure shown in Fig. 12.2.

Figure 12.2 captures only the relationships between the three types of charts that describe the three views. However, as explained in Chap. 11, each of these logical charts can be decomposed into several physical charts, thus creating a more complex network of charts. These additional connections are based on the three types of relationships described therein: one, a module described by an activity-chart, is specified in the module entry in the Data Dictionary, and the other two, that between a control activity and its describing statechart, and

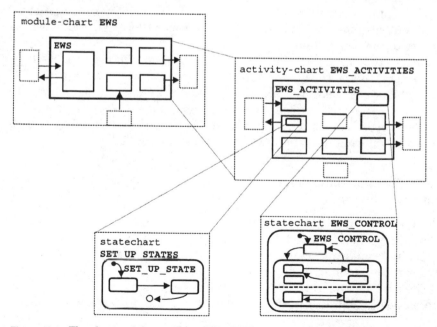

Figure 12.1 The charts of three views of the EWS.

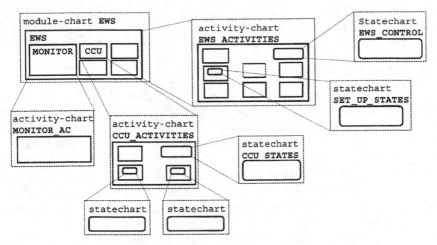

Figure 12.2 Charts in multilevel specification of the EWS.

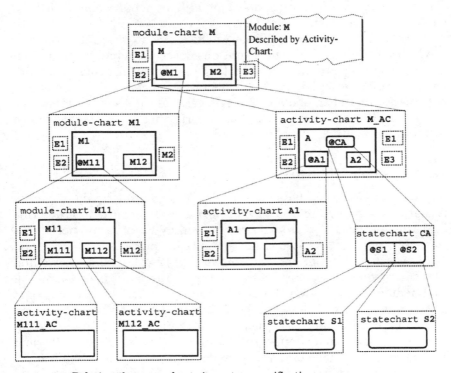

Figure 12.3 Relations between charts in system specification.

the offpage (decluttering) relationship, are depicted graphically, using the @ symbol.

A schematic example of a structure built up from many of these relationships is shown in Fig. 12.3. Notice that this particular figure contains only one logical module-chart, consisting of the three physical charts M, M1, and M11, but three logical activity-charts, namely, M_AC, M111_AC, and M112_AC.

12.2 A Chart in a Model

Regarding the terms *logical chart* and *physical chart,* from here on, we mostly use *chart* to mean physical chart. Each (physical) chart plays a role in the whole specification according to its relationships with other charts. The top-level box of the chart is its subject. For example, the activity-chart EWS_ACTIVITIES of Fig. 10.5 describes the functionality of the EWS module. Its top-level activity is EWS_ACTIVITIES, which is therefore its subject. In our examples we almost always use the same name for the chart and its top-level activity, although this is not mandatory.

Charts will always be identified by name. Chart names must be unique throughout the entire model, even those of different types. Thus we may not have a module-chart and an activity-chart with the same name in a single model.

Like other elements in the model, a chart has an associated entry in the Data Dictionary. This entry contains descriptive information, such as short and long descriptions and attributes. It may also contain administrative information, such as the owner of the chart and its creation date, version number, and access privileges. We shall see later that this entry is also used to define a chart as generic, that is, as one that can be instantiated multiple times in the model.

12.3 Hierarchy of Charts

The relations between boxes and charts induce a *hierarchy of charts.* A chart is considered to be a *parent chart* of all the charts that describe its boxes by the offpage chart relation, by the relation between a control activity and its statechart, and by the module described by activity-chart relation. Referring to Fig. 12.3, for example, we find that the module-chart M is the *root* of the hierarchy; it is the parent of the module-chart M1 and the activity-chart M_AC. The activity-chart M_AC, in turn, is the parent of the activity-chart A1 and the statechart CA, and the statechart CA is the parent of statecharts S1 and S2. As in other cases, here, too, we use the terminology *subchart, ancestor,* and *descendant.* Thus, for example, the module-chart M1 is a subchart of M, and all the charts in Fig. 12.3, except for M itself, are descendants of M.

The chart hierarchy is sometimes called the *static structure of charts.* The structure for the example of Fig. 12.3 is shown in tree form in Fig. 12.4. The chart hierarchy serves as a sort of table of contents for the specification.

The uniqueness rules discussed in earlier chapters (e.g., that each chart can be a definition chart of a single box only) imply that each chart

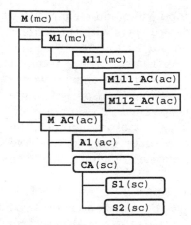

Figure 12.4   Hierarchy of charts.

has (at most) one parent. In addition, cyclic definitions are not allowed, so that the hierarchy of charts will indeed be either a tree (as in Fig. 12.4) or a forest of trees. Now, in a typical full specification there is usually a module-chart that describes the system context and sometimes the top levels of the structural decomposition, too, and all the other charts are its descendants. This renders that module-chart the root chart, so that the chart hierarchy is a single tree. However, in many cases, especially if the specification is carried out in a bottom-up manner and is not yet complete or when using methodologies that do not call for a single module-chart for the context description, there might be no such root, and the structure will therefore be a forest. Moreover, we shall see later that generic charts, those that can be instantiated multiple times in the model, have no parents and are considered roots in the chart hierarchy, so that here, too, the structure will be a forest. A tree in the chart hierarchy is sometimes called a *cluster*; in Fig. 12.4, the entire structure consists of a single cluster.

12.4   Entities External to the System under Description

The model that specifies the system under development operates in the context of the environment systems. We now discuss these systems and other external entities that are connected to the system model and might interact with it.

12.4.1   Environment modules or activities

A number of times we stated that the external boxes in a chart represent either boxes in the parent chart or parts of the real environment of the model. The EWS example, as presented throughout this book, models the context of the system by the top-level module-chart EWS. This is the root of the chart hierarchy, and, as always with the context module-chart, all of its external boxes (in our case, OPERATOR and SENSOR) are *environment modules* and are not part of the system. In a typical model, all other module-charts are offpage charts, whose external modules are occurrences of modules from their parent chart. For example, if the MONITOR's structure is specified in a separate off-page module-chart, this chart will contain two external modules, the CCU and the OPERATOR, which are simply occurrences of the two modules that appear in its parent chart, the module-chart EWS. See Fig. 12.5.

In Fig. 12.5, we also show the activity-chart EWS_ACTIVITIES, which describes the top-level module EWS (see Sec. 10.2), and which, as such, is a subchart of the EWS module-chart. Its external activities OPERATOR and SENSOR are simply occurrences of the corresponding environment modules from the parent module-chart. Other offpage activity-charts participating in the functional description, such as the SET_UP chart in Fig. 11.2, also contain external boxes that are linked to other activities and data-stores from the parent chart (e.g., GET_INPUT, LEGAL_RANGE, and OPERATOR). However, a model does not necessarily contain a module-chart. One can construct the functional view only, starting with a root activity-chart that will contain the environment systems, too.

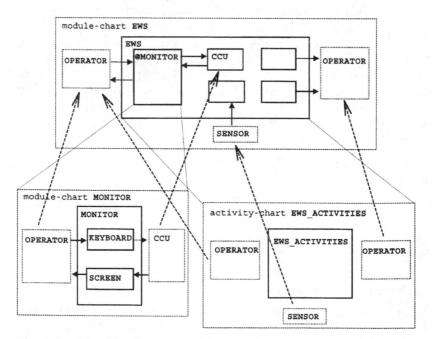

Figure 12.5 External and environment boxes.

An environment box—module or activity—has an entry in the Data Dictionary, but an external box that points to another box has no entry of its own. The Data Dictionary entry of an environment box may contain descriptions and attributes, but not behavioral information. For instance, a mini-spec cannot be associated with an environment activity. In fact, when modeled as external entities, the environment systems cannot be associated with functional and behavioral descriptions in our languages at all. It is impossible to associate an activity-chart or a statechart with an environment module or activity. Often there is only limited and imprecise knowledge about the external entities. However, in some cases there are assumptions about the behavior of the interface signals that are significant to the design of the system, and the designer might want to express them explicitly. This can be done by including the relevant environment systems as part of the model and representing them as internal modules or activities. It helps to give them some user-defined marks to indicate that they are beyond the scope of the system under development. This technique can also be used when the designer wants to simulate the system in its environment and wants to use the modeling languages to describe the external systems. It is often convenient to specify environment behavior in a statistical manner, for which purpose one can use the random functions listed in App. A.3.

The ECSAM methodology, which essentially employs our modeling languages (Lavi and Winokur 1989), has been extended recently to construct what its authors call *a black box external model* by including the environment systems in the model, as we suggest here (Lavi and Kudish 1996).

Sometimes it is easier to use a conventional programming language to simulate the external systems, particularly when these systems have already been implemented in software. In general, any existing implementation can be used for simulation and prototyping purposes. The value of supporting tools based on our languages can be enhanced if they can be made to provide means for linking the model execution facilities to an external existing environment.[1]

12.4.2 Testbenches

Other external entities that interact with a typical model are the tests developed to check its behavior. These tests are valuable even beyond their primary purpose, which is to check whether the model matches some preliminary requirements and behaves as expected. Sometimes the model is built as a reference model, that is, it is to be compared with its implementation. In such a case, the model is developed for

---

[1]STATEMATE indeed provides such means.

prototyping purposes, and the real system is developed later, independently, with the intention that it behave similarly. Hence, tests that are developed to check the model can be used later to check the implementation. Extensive testing of the model is even more justified when it is automatically transformed to yield an implementation. In this case, if the model fulfills the requirements and is found to be correct by the tests, then the synthesized implementation is correct, too.

One approach to testing the model is based on generating test scenarios according to some patterns and rules, by a special-purpose test driver (written as an external program or with the aid of our modeling languages). The outputs of the modeled system are then collected by some monitoring function, and the collected data can be analyzed and checked in order to learn about the system's behavior and performance and to detect undesired reactions.

Another approach uses auxiliary charts (mainly statecharts) to express and verify temporal requirements that are related to the model, such as safety and liveness properties (Manna and Pnueli 1992). These special charts are called *testbenches,* or sometimes *watchdogs,* and we now illustrate how they are used.

Assume that we want to be convinced that the EWS model satisfies the *causality property* that an alarm is issued only after an out-of-range situation has been detected. This requirement is expressed in terms of our model as follows: the activity DISPLAY_FAULT operates (is started) only after the event OUT_OF_RANGE has occurred. We can now construct a testbench statechart, ALARM_CAUSALITY, shown in Fig. 12.6, that will run in parallel with the system model and will "watch" the model execution under different scenarios of external changes. Whenever the requirement is violated by some scenario, the testbench will enter the state ERROR.

This testbench checks for the kind of causality categorized as a *safety property* in the literature on program verification. Safety properties often take the form *B never occurs after A* (Manna and Pnueli 1992). In such a case we look for a scenario that violates the property (i.e., one

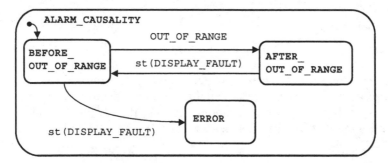

Figure 12.6 The testbench statechart ALARM_CAUSALITY.

in which B occurs after A) to prove that the model does *not* satisfy the requirement. A similar technique can be used to check whether the model satisfies what is called a *liveness property*. One variation of liveness states that *after A occurs, B can occur*. To convince ourselves that this requirement is satisfied, we draw a testbench in which a scenario of B after A leads to a success state.

A supporting tool (such as STATEMATE) can be instructed to try out many scenarios, perhaps even all of them exhaustively, to find one that satisfies or violates such requirements.

Testbench statecharts are not an integral part of the model and the hierarchy of its charts. Due to their special role, they are allowed to refer to the model's elements without necessarily obeying the scoping rules discussed in Chap. 13. For example, in Fig. 12.6, the testbench chart ALARM_CAUSALITY refers to the activity DISPLAY_FAULT, although this violates the visibility rules defined in Chap. 7 for activities.

In terms of the scoping rules, the difference between environment modeling and using testbenches is analogous to two different ways of testing a hardware board: the former has a well-defined interface and is therefore like connecting to a board via the connector's pins, and the latter is less disciplined and therefore more like monitoring a signal with a probe.

13

Scope and Resolution of Elements

Charts are the building blocks of a model. These blocks are not isolated entities, but are linked together by information that might flow between them and by elements they might share. In particular, some of the elements defined in one chart can be used in others. Clearly, however, in large projects there are many elements that need not be known outside a limited portion of the specification.

Hence issues of scope—dealing with the questions of where elements are defined, where they are recognized, and where they may be used—are important. This chapter discusses these issues, and the way we deal with them is strongly related to the hierarchy of charts, which was discussed in Chap. 12.

This chapter also introduces a new component of our languages, the *global definition set* (GDS), which contains information that is visible throughout the entire model.

13.1 Visibility of Elements and Information Hiding

Decomposing specifications into many charts raises issues of visibility and the scoping of elements. Consider Fig. 13.1. The activity MAIN has two subactivities, A and B, between which X flows, and each is described in a separate chart. Obviously, we want X to be recognized in both charts because it is part of their external interface. The X in both charts is thus the same X. On the other hand, we would like the two Ys appearing in these charts to be different when each is internal to the chart in which it appears. These two charts may actually have been prepared by different teams. In fact, the two Ys could be of very different types, say, a data-item in A and an event in B. Thus X represents the case of an element that has to be *visible* to several charts, and the Ys represent cases of elements that are to be *hidden* inside specific charts.

These notions of *visibility* and *information hiding* are important in any kind of structured development. Some elements are allowed to be known only in specific parts of the model, and others might be *global,* that is, known throughout it. Often, it is important to give subteams the freedom to name their elements as they wish, regardless of the possible existence of identical names elsewhere in the model, and to produce reports and carry out analysis on particular portions thereof. To accommodate these possibilities, we associate a *scope* with each element. The scope of an element is a set of charts in which the element is known and can be used. As in modern programming languages, we have a notion of where the element is *defined* and a set of scoping rules that determine where it is visible.

13.2   Defining, Referencing, and Resolving Elements

Each element in the model belongs to a specific chart. We say that it is *defined in* that chart. Graphical elements (boxes, arrows, and connectors) are defined in the chart in which they are drawn, besides the special case of external boxes. Textual elements (information elements and actions) are defined in the chart that is specified in the element's Data Dictionary entry. See Sec. 13.4.

Elements defined in one chart may be used in others. For example, we may define the data-item X of Fig. 13.1 in the higher-level chart MAIN by writing MAIN in the field Defined in Chart of its Data Dictionary entry, as shown in Fig. 13.2. Because X is used along a flow-

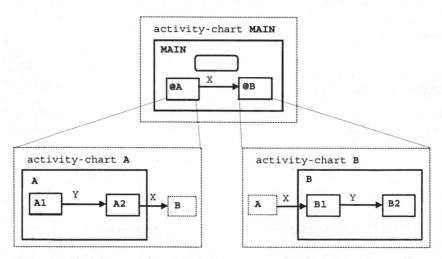

Figure 13.1   Visibility vs. information hiding.

Data-Item: **X**
Defined in Chart: **MAIN**

Figure 13.2 An element defined in a chart.

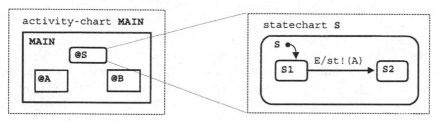

Figure 13.3 A reference activity.

line between the subactivities A and B, it also appears along flow-lines in the charts for A and B. In these two charts, in which X is used but not defined, we say that X is a *reference element*.

Another example of a reference element appears in Fig. 13.3. Here, the activity A is defined in the activity-chart MAIN, by virtue of its being drawn there. On the other hand, because it is started in the statechart S, which describes the control activity of MAIN, activity A is a reference element in S, where it is used but not defined.

Each reference element must be matched with, or *resolved to,* an element in some other chart. The latter is said to be the *resolution* of the former. In the aforementioned examples, the reference data-items X of Fig. 13.1 in both charts A and B are resolved to the data-item X defined in the chart MAIN, and, similarly, the reference activity A of Fig. 13.3 in the statechart S is resolved to the activity A in MAIN.

Often, it is useful to be able to refer to elements that have not yet been defined. In the terminology just introduced, this amounts to having a reference element that cannot be resolved to any element. Such a situation might occur in intermediate stages of the specification process. A simple example is the use of an external event as a trigger in a statechart before the activity-chart that defines that event is constructed. Another example appears in Fig. 13.4, which is similar to Fig. 13.3. The difference is that here the activity K, which is started in statechart S, has not yet been defined in MAIN. This could have been intentional (K is not ready yet), or it could indicate an error. Thus K is an *unresolved reference element* in chart S.

The specific rules for visibility and resolution differ for different types of elements. They are discussed in detail for graphical elements in Sec. 13.3 and for textual elements in Sec. 13.4.

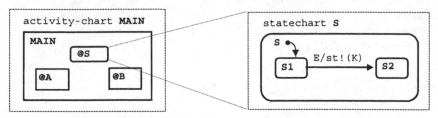

Figure 13.4 An unresolved reference activity.

Having scopes associated with elements makes it possible to use the same name for different elements, and there are rules that determine when this is allowed. Elements with the same name can be distinguished by attaching the chart name (i.e., the one in which they are defined) to their own name. The format is `chart-name:element-name`. However, this use is not always allowed, and the rules for referring to elements in this way are related to the scoping rules. Such practice is useful for testbenches (see Chap. 12), where the scoping rules do not hold, and any element of the model can be referred to freely.

The rules for uniqueness of names and for referencing are discussed in the following sections.

13.3   The Scope of Charts and Graphical Elements

Charts involve several kinds of graphical elements—boxes, arrows, and connectors. These elements, with the exception of external boxes (which are discussed later), are defined in the chart in which they are drawn. Arrows have no names and cannot be referred to in other charts. Also, the only connectors that have names are diagram connectors, and their naming and reference rules were discussed in Chap. 11. This leaves us with having to discuss the scoping and reference rules for charts and boxes only.

13.3.1   Referring to charts and box elements

Charts are global in the entire model. Their names are unique, even for different types of charts, and they are recognized everywhere. So far, we saw that charts are referred to in other charts in two ways: in the names of boxes (to point to offpage charts) and in the Data Dictionary (to specify that a module is described by an activity-chart). We shall see later that generic charts are referred to in a similar way. As for other elements of the model, references to charts are resolved to charts of appropriate type. If such charts do not exist yet in the model, we say, as for other element types, that the reference charts are *unresolved*.

The box elements of our languages are activities and data-stores, which are defined in activity-charts, states, which are defined in state-charts, and modules, which are defined in module-charts. As we have seen in earlier chapters, the box elements are named in the graphics, and the name of the box must be unique among its siblings boxes. When the name is not unique in the chart, the box can be referred to by its pathname, preceded by its ancestor(s), (e.g., A.B.C; see App. A.1). If there is a synonym for the box, defined in its Data Dictionary entity, then that synonym must be unique among the names and synonyms of the boxes defined in the same chart. A box can be referred to by its name or its synonym.

We now describe the rules for referencing a box element in a chart other than the one in which it is defined. Any cases that are not discussed, such as referencing a state in an activity-chart, are not allowed.

13.3.2 Referring to activities in statecharts

Activities can be referred to in statecharts in actions (e.g., st!(A)), in events (e.g., sp(A)), and in conditions (e.g., ac(A)). These actions, events, and conditions may appear as parts of labels along transitions, as parts of static reactions, and in the definitions of other elements in the Data Dictionary. In addition, activities may be referred to in a state's Data Dictionary entity in the field Activities in State. See Chap. 7.

As discussed in Chap. 7, in a (logical) statechart reference is allowed only to activities that are siblings of the control activity described by the statechart. This is the only way to refer to activities in a state-chart. As an example, in Fig. 13.5, the activity A in the chart MAIN is referred to in the statechart S2, which belongs to the logical state-chart S that controls the activity MAIN.

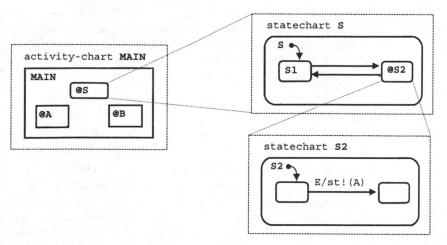

Figure 13.5 Referring to an activity in a statechart.

Notice that the activities that can be referred to in a given statechart SC must belong to a very particular activity-chart, namely, the parent activity-chart of SC, that is, the one containing the control activity described by SC. Therefore, there is no need to attach a chart name to the name of a referenced activity, and, indeed, such an attachment is not allowed.

If a statechart refers to an activity name that does not appear in the parent activity-chart, as in Fig. 13.4, that reference remains unresolved. This is true even if there is an activity with the same name elsewhere in the model.

13.3.3   Referring to states in statecharts

States can be referred to in statecharts in events (e.g., en(S)) and conditions (e.g., in(S)). These events and conditions can be used along transitions, as part of static reactions, and in Data Dictionary definitions of other elements. See Chap. 5.

The visibility rule is that a state can be referred to in any state that belongs to the same logical statechart. In other words, any state that is defined in a page that is a descendant of some statechart SC is visible to all charts that are descendants of SC. States defined in other charts that are not part of the logical statechart of SC are not visible.

States in the same page are referred to by name or pathname (if the name is nonunique in the page), while states in other pages are preceded by the appropriate chart name (i.e., chart-name:state-name). As an example, consider Fig. 13.6. In the statechart S2, the state OFF that appears in the label E[in(OFF)] is understood to be the state OFF in the orthogonal component S22, which appears in the same statechart, although there is a state named OFF in the chart S1, too. On the other hand, to refer to S2:ON in the label in chart S1, the state name is preceded by the chart name S2, and although the name Q is unique in the entire logical chart, the chart name is also added to it when it is used in another chart.

A reference to a state name that does not appear in any chart of the same logical statechart remains unresolved.

13.3.4   External activities or modules

External activities and modules are considered to be "real" elements, (e.g., they have their own entities in the Data Dictionary) only when they are defined explicitly in the Data Dictionary as environment activities or modules. An unnamed external box is just a graphical object, like a connector, that signifies some anonymous external source or target. A named external box that is not defined as an environment box serves as a reference to another box. Like other reference elements, an attempt is made to resolve such a

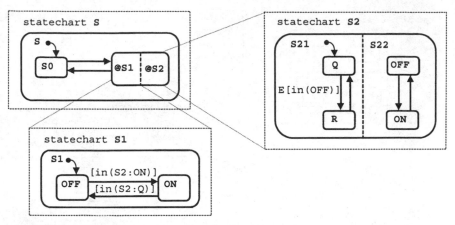

Figure 13.6 Referring to states in a statechart.

box to a matching element—in this case, a box from the parent chart. The matching box in the parent chart has the same name, and it can be an internal box (i.e., a module, activity, or data-store) or an external box.

Consider the example in Fig. 13.7. Activity-chart M1_AC contains a number of external activities: E1 is resolved to the environment module E1, and M2 is resolved to the internal module M2, but M31 does not match any module in M (although M contains a module named M31). This is because the matching boxes are allowed to be found only among the siblings of M1 (e.g., M3) or the siblings of M1's ancestors (e.g., E1). Similarly, in activity-chart A, the external activity D is resolved to the data-store D in M1_AC, and E1 is resolved to E1 in M "via" E1 in M1_AC.

A named external box in a root chart (i.e., one with no parent), or a box to which no box in the parent can be matched, is considered to be an unresolved external box. For example, if the external module E2 in the root chart M is not explicitly defined as an environment module, it is considered unresolved. Also, K in the activity-chart A and M31 in M1_AC are unresolved external boxes, because no matching boxes for them are found.

13.3.5 Referring to modules and activities in activity-charts

Modules can be referred to in an activity-chart in the field Implemented by (respectively, Resides in) of the Data Dictionary entity of an activity (respectively, a data-store). See Fig. 10.6. Any module, from any module-chart, can be referred to in these fields. Recall, however, that the rules of Chap. 10 concerning the consistency of the hierarchies of modules and activities must be followed.

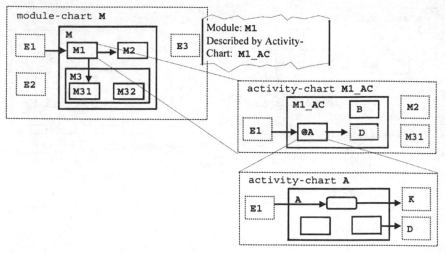

Figure 13.7   Resolution of external boxes.

Because module names are not unique, our languages allow module names to be referred to from different charts. In cases of possible ambiguity, the chart name should be attached to the module name.

Activity names and data-store names are entered in the related fields Is Activity and Is Data-Store, respectively. As explained in Sec. 10.4, an element name in these fields is meaningful only when the implementing module is specified. The activity or data-store entered must be from the activity-chart that describes the implementing module. See Fig. 13.8. Consequently, there is no need to specify the chart name of the referred to element, and, indeed, attaching this name is not allowed.

13.4   The Scope of Textual Elements

Textual elements (i.e., events, conditions, data-items, user-defined types, information-flows, and actions) are defined via the Data Dictionary. The chart in which the element is defined is specified by the modeler in the field Defined in Chart. See Fig. 13.2. This should be contrasted with graphical elements, for which the definition charts are determined by where they are drawn.

13.4.1   Visibility of textual elements

A textual element that is defined in a particular chart is recognized in and can be used in other charts. The visibility rules for textual elements are very similar to those employed in programming languages that support nesting and block structure. A textual element is clearly visible in the chart in which it is defined. It is also visible in all the descendant charts in the chart hierarchy defined in Chap. 12. An exception is when the element is *masked by* another textual element with the same name, as discussed shortly.

Let us take an example. The event OUT_OF_RANGE, defined in the activity-chart EWS_ACTIVITIES, is used in the statechart EWS_CONTROL on a transition; see, for example, Fig. 4.3. To use our terminology, the reference to OUT_OF_RANGE in EWS_CONTROL is resolved to the event OUT_OF_RANGE that is defined in EWS_ACTIVITIES. Because the statechart EWS_CONTROL is a subchart of the activity-chart EWS_ACTIVITIES (see Fig. 12.2), the textual elements defined in the latter are visible in the former and can therefore be used therein.

Figure 13.9 illustrates masking. The data-item X flows between activities A and B in the activity-chart MAIN. Assume that it is also defined there. The offpage chart C, which defines an internal activity of MAIN, uses an element with the same name, X (in the example, X is actually an event in C). According to the visibility rule, the data-item X of MAIN could have been used in the subchart C, but because an event X is defined in C, the data-item X is no longer recognized there. Moreover, the same applies to C's subchart C1, in which we may refer only to the event X of C and not to the data-item X of MAIN. In such a case, we say that the data-item MAIN:X is *masked by* the event C:X.

13.4.2 Naming textual elements

The name and synonym of a textual element are given in its Data Dictionary entity. Within a chart, all such names and synonyms must be unique. Hence, if an event named E has already been defined in

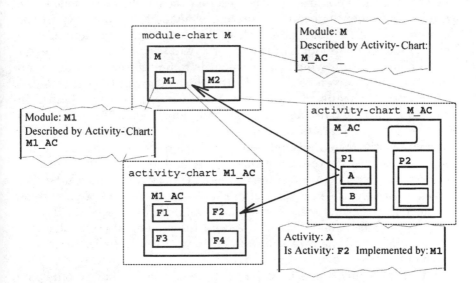

Figure 13.8 Referring to activities in Is Activity field.

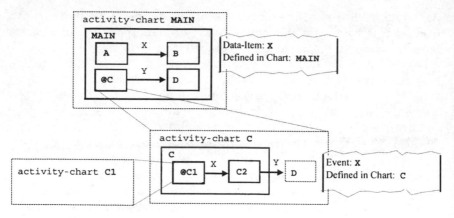

Figure 13.9 Masking a textual element.

some chart A, the name E cannot be used to define, say, a condition in the same chart. It may be used, however, in some other (physical) chart, to name an event, a condition, or any other textual element. As for naming graphical elements, the name E can be used anywhere, even in the chart A itself.

The possibility of using the same name for different elements is convenient and useful, especially in big projects when different teams use the same names in different scopes. However, despite the presence of rules for resolving references and detecting masking situations, this option should be exercised with care, as it may cause confusion.

Special attention must be paid when the same element is used in several charts to ensure that the different occurrences are resolved to the same element. Because a textual element is visible only in the descendants of its defining chart, an element should be defined in a chart that is high enough in the hierarchy to be the common ancestor of all charts within which the element is to be referenced. For example, consider the event E in Fig. 13.10, which is generated in state S1. If we want E to cause a transition in state S2, it must be defined in the statechart S or in one of its ancestor charts, even if it is not used there, because elements that are defined in S1 are not visible in S2, and vice versa. When E is defined in S, both references to it in S1 and S2 are resolved to the definition in S, and the two are therefore understood to refer to the same element. This example should be contrasted with the case illustrated in Fig. 13.1, where we used the same name Y in the two charts A and B for two different elements flowing between subactivities. Because we want these elements to be distinct, we should define them in separate entities in the Data Dictionary in each of the two charts.

A textual element can be referred to in the same chart or in some other chart by its name or synonym. We do not allow the format `chart-name:element-name` for textual elements because the chart name would be either redundant (if the chart is the one containing the resolution) or illegal (if another chart is referenced, thus referring to an "invisible" element or one that is out of scope). For example, in Fig. 13.10 we are not allowed to replace the event E in the statechart S2 by S1:E because, according to the visibility rules, elements defined in S1 are not visible in S2. Note that this rule does not apply to testbenches, where all elements of the model are visible.

13.4.3   More about resolution of textual elements

Reference elements are always resolved to elements of the same type. Thus if we were to define a condition named E, not an event, in the statechart S of Fig. 13.10, the two references to E in S1 and S2 would not be resolved to this condition because they are used as events.

If a textual element is referred to without having been defined explicitly in the Data Dictionary and there is no corresponding element in the ancestor charts, the element remains unresolved. Typically, this happens in intermediate stages of the specification. Sometimes the type of an unresolved element is not clear from its usage. A good example is when an element appears as a label on a flow-line, in which case it can be an event, a condition, a data-item, or an information-flow. However, elements appearing in transition labels, for example, have uniquely determined types, as do those appearing in expressions that define other textual elements. (An exception is the case of an action that can possibly turn out to be an event, such as E in Fig. 13.10.)

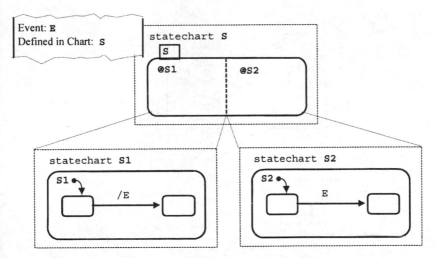

Figure 13.10   Connecting elements from different charts.

Being unresolved does not prevent elements from being visible, and hence from being used, in descendant charts. Thus elements from such descendant charts can be resolved to unresolved elements. For example, assume that in Fig. 13.1 we do not explicitly define the element X. It will nevertheless be considered a reference element in the three charts appearing in the figure. It will be unresolved in chart MAIN, but in the other two charts it will be resolved to an unresolved element X in MAIN. As in other cases, however, this kind of resolution will be carried out only if the types of the elements match. For example, in Fig. 13.11, E is not explicitly defined in chart MAIN, and therefore it is an unresolved reference element. Judging only from its usage in MAIN, it may be an information-flow, a condition, a data-item, or an event, but in this case it is considered to be an event because it is used as an event in the subchart S.

13.5   Global Definition Sets

The visibility rules imply that textual elements that have to be global to the entire model should be defined in the root of the chart hierarchy, which is the common ancestor of all charts in the model. The resolution scheme described earlier, which is based on the hierarchy of the functional components, is compatible with the functional decomposition method. In this method, every accessed data variable—event, condition, and data-item—is either local (i.e., it belongs to the functional component) or is part of the external interface (i.e., it appears on a flow-line and, as such, belongs to an ancestor functional component). Textual elements that are employed as abbreviations (i.e., information-flows and actions) are usually defined in the charts in which they are used. Therefore, the only "real" global information that has to be

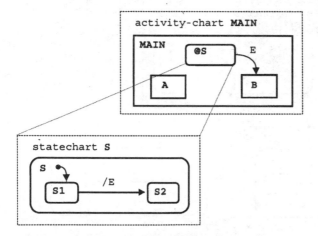

Figure 13.11 Compatible usage of textual elements.

```
User-Defined Type: TIME
Defined in Chart/GDS: TIME_DEFS
Data-Type: record
        Field Name: HOURS     Field Type: integer min=0 max=23
        Field Name: MINUTES Field Type: integer min=0 max=59
        Field Name: SECONDS Field Type: integer min=0 max=59

Data-Item: MINUTE
Defined in Chart/GDS: TIME_DEFS
Defined as: constant
Definition: 60

Data-Item: HOUR
Defined in Chart/GDS: TIME_DEFS
Defined as: constant
Definition: 3600
```

Figure 13.12 Elements defined in a global definition set.

shared throughout the entire model in an unstructured manner (and can even be moved between models) is that of constant definitions and user-defined types.

Our languages provide a special type of model component, the *global definition set* (GDS), for capturing such global definitions. This type of component is part of the Data Dictionary, and it is similar in many ways to a chart. There may be several GDSs in a model, each containing definitions of user-defined types as well as constant data-items and conditions. Figure 13.12 shows several Data Dictionary entities that belong to a GDS named TIME_DEFS. A GDS that contains definitions related to time, as in this example, is relevant to many application domains.

As mentioned, elements appearing in a GDS are visible in the entire model. For example, a data-item definition in any chart of a model that contains the GDS TIME_DEFS can be of type TIME. In particular, definitions in one GDS can use definitions in another GDS, but this should not be done in a circular fashion.

There are no hierarchical relationships among the GDSs in a model or between them and the charts of the model itself.

Global definition sets have a special role in the context of generic charts, as will be seen in Chap. 14.

14

Generic Charts

Chapter 11 discussed the possibility of describing the contents of a box element in a separate offpage chart. An offpage chart can describe only a single box. In this chapter we introduce generic charts, which are reusable components that may have multiple instances in a model. In other words, a generic chart can be used to describe the contents of several similar boxes.

Generic charts are linked to the rest of the model via parameters; no other elements (besides the definitions in global definition sets) are recognized by both generic charts and other portions of the model.

In this chapter we describe how generic charts and their formal parameters are defined, how they are instantiated in the model, and how the actual elements are bound to their formal parameters.

14.1 Reusability of Specification Components

Many kinds of systems give rise to cases requiring a number of similar components. For example, assume that the EWS monitors several sensors, each with its own processing function, and all with the same pattern, as shown in Fig. 7.12. The new activity-chart with the multiple sensors is shown in Fig. 14.1a. The function PROCESS_SIGNALS contains five similar activities, PS1 through PS5, which process SIGNAL_1 through SIGNAL_5, respectively. Each PSi is described by a separate Data Dictionary entry, similar to the one shown for PS1 in Fig. 14.1b. The output of the function dealing with the ith sensor is sent to the COMPARE function via the ith component of the array SAMPLES. The functions vary in the sampling interval, SAMPLE_INTERVAL_i, and in the constant factor K_i that multiplies the sampled signal.

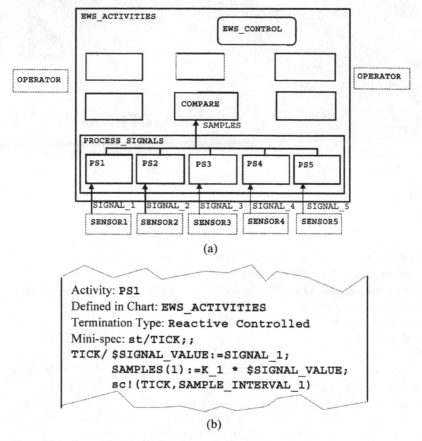

(a)

Activity: **PS1**
Defined in Chart: **EWS_ACTIVITIES**
Termination Type: **Reactive Controlled**
Mini-spec: **st/TICK;;**
TICK/ $SIGNAL_VALUE:=SIGNAL_1;
**   SAMPLES(1):=K_1 * $SIGNAL_VALUE;**
**   sc!(TICK,SAMPLE_INTERVAL_1)**

(b)

Figure 14.1   Processing multiple sensors in the EWS.

It is quite obvious that this solution is not efficient. In addition, it does not make it clear to a viewer that the components are essentially identical. There should be a way to specify a repetition of the same component many times, as in electronic and software design, defining the detailed contents only once and using the component generically wherever needed. For this purpose our languages provide the mechanism of *generic charts.*

We saw that when used the various components can differ in the details of their connections with the outside world (i.e., in the data elements through which they exchange information), as well as in the internal settings that determine the nature of each specific instance. Both will be handled by *parameters.*

The generic chart mechanism can be used to model electronic designs with repeating components, and software systems that contain multiple objects of the same class.

14.2   Definition and Instances of Generic Charts

In a sense, generic charts are similar to offpage charts: in both cases we draw an empty box and point to another chart that describes its contents. Here, however, we can specify repetition; indeed, sometimes we draw an offpage chart first, later realize that we really want to repeat the specified portion, and switch to a generic chart. The similarities and differences between these two mechanisms are discussed next.

14.2.1   Notation and basic rules of generics

A chart can be defined as a generic chart in its Data Dictionary entry, and it can then have multiple *instances* in the model. An instance of a generic chart is sometimes called a *generic instance,* to distinguish it from an *offpage instance.* To apply this to the EWS example, we define an activity-chart PROCESS_SIGNAL and specify it as generic. Its top-level activity PROCESS_SIGNAL has a Data Dictionary entry. This is shown in Fig. 14.2a. We then specify instances of this generic activity-chart (PS1 through PS5) inside PROCESS_SIGNALS, using the symbol <, as in PS1<PROCESS_SIGNAL. See Fig. 14.2b.

While this example was of a generic activity-chart, we can also have generic module-charts and generic statecharts. The former can be useful when the system is built of similar modules, such as multiple signal processors, and the latter are often used to describe similar orthogonal components, as we shall see shortly.

Because generic charts usually appear in different contexts, the external boxes in a generic chart are not allowed to point to any particular boxes in the model and are very often left unnamed. In Fig. 14.2a, the SIGNAL comes from some "generic" SENSOR, while the activity's output flows to an unknown target, which is why the external box is left unnamed.

Regarding names, the box name can really be omitted in an instance (and we can thus write, say, <GEN), as is usually done for offpage instances. However, here this is not recommended, and it is only possible when the instance is unique on that level of decomposition. More commonly, instance activities have their own individual names, as in PS1, PS2, etc. The name of the generic chart should not appear when we refer to the instance, so we write expressions such as the start action st!(PS1).

The instance box must be basic, that is, it may not contain subboxes. Moreover, it cannot contain any behavioral information, and this applies to all three kinds of charts: instance states in a statechart cannot have static reactions and attached activities, instance activities in an activity-chart cannot have mini-specs and combinational assignments, and instance modules in a module-chart cannot be described by

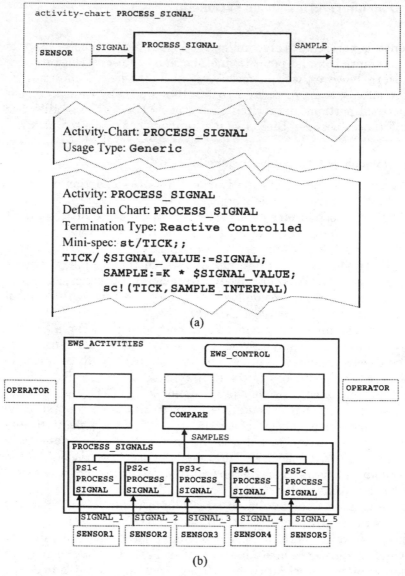

Figure 14.2 (*a*) A generic activity-chart and (*b*) its instances.

an activity-chart. All such information is inherited by the instances from their describing generic charts.

In modeling a generic chart, one may include instances of offpage charts, as illustrated in Fig. 14.3. Note that this reference to the offpage chart COMPUTE in the generic chart PROCESS_SIGNAL implies that there will be multiple occurrences of COMPUTE in the full expansion of the model, but each of them will belong to a different scope.

A generic chart may also contain instances of other generic charts, but care must be taken to avoid cyclic instantiation thereof.

The notion of resolution is applied to charts just as it is applied to other elements in the model; that is, a reference to a chart appearing in an instance name will be resolved to a chart of appropriate type whose definition in the Data Dictionary matches the reference. Therefore, if an ordinary activity, for example, is named A>GEN, GEN must be defined as a generic activity-chart. Similarly, a chart defined as generic cannot be used as an offpage chart or as an activity-chart describing a module. This means that if GEN is a generic chart, no box · can be named A@GEN, and GEN cannot appear in the Data Dictionary entry of any module in the field Described by Activity-Chart. A model containing instances of charts that do not yet exist is incomplete, and in such a case the same chart cannot appear both as a generic and an offpage instance. For example, A1>A and A2@A is an inconsistent situation, even when A is not yet defined; any completion of such a model would be illegal.

14.2.2 Generic charts in the chart hierarchy

In Chap. 12 we discussed the hierarchy of charts. We saw that this hierarchy is based on several kinds of relationships between a box and a chart: an instance of an offpage chart, a control activity described by a statechart, and a module described by an activity-chart. The hierarchy of charts in Fig. 14.4 is derived from the components of the EWS model appearing in Fig. 12.2.

The hierarchy of charts defines the visibility scope of textual elements and has a dominant role in the resolution algorithm. Generic charts have no parent charts; each generic chart is the root of a tree that it induces in the chart hierarchy. The tree itself is defined as in the ordinary case. Therefore, according to the visibility rules and the resolution algorithm (see Chap. 13), generic charts do not recognize elements from other clusters. Instead, they share elements with the rest of the model via parameters, as we shall see. In addition, like all portions of the model, generic charts can see the data in the global definition sets, and they may thus use the definitions of constants and user-defined types appearing there.

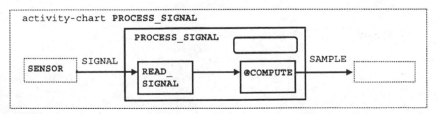

Figure 14.3 A generic chart containing an offpage chart.

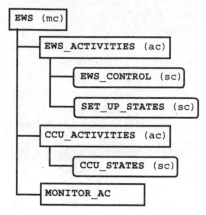

Figure 14.4 The hierarchy of charts for the EWS model.

The external boxes in a generic chart cannot be resolved to other boxes in the model because there is no parent chart to which they can refer. As mentioned earlier, they are usually left unnamed.

Because the chart hierarchy is determined by making an offpage chart an offspring of the chart in which it is referred to, this structure is actually a kind of "table of contents" for the model that shows where charts are used. When generic charts are involved, the chart hierarchy is expanded to a *chart usage hierarchy*[1]; the generic charts appear under the chart in which they are used (instantiated), just as offpage charts do, but the special symbol < is used to distinguish them from the others and to emphasize the fact that they do not participate in the resolution algorithm. Note that a generic chart can appear along several branches of the hierarchical structure as a leaf. Because a generic chart may have many instances in the same chart, it can be useful to provide the number of instances near the chart name.

As an example, let us assume that the chart EWS_ACTIVITIES contains five instances of the generic chart PROCESS_SIGNAL, as described earlier, and that this generic chart contains an instance of the offpage activity-chart COMPUTE. Figure 14.5 contains the tree of Fig. 14.4 enhanced with these additional components. Note that this usage hierarchy contains two separate trees.

14.3   Parameters of Generic Charts

Parameters are used to characterize the particular instances of a generic chart and to link it to its environment. Parameters are the

---

[1]In STATEMATE the chart usage hierarchy is called the *model tree*.

main means by which an instance of a generic chart is able to share data with the rest of the model.

14.3.1 Formal parameters of a generic chart

Each generic chart has a set of *formal parameters*. These are either *ports* (i.e., channels, through which information flows in and out of the component) or *constant parameters* (i.e., values used to characterize the particular instance at hand). The parameters are defined explicitly by the specifier in the Data Dictionary entry of the generic chart. They are given by their name, element type (event, condition, data-item, or activity), and mode (`constant` or one of the three port modes: `in`, `out`, and `in/out`). Each formal parameter has a Data Dictionary entry in which more information about the element can be added, such as its structure and data-type.

The generic chart `PROCESS_SIGNAL` described earlier has an `in` port `SIGNAL`, and an `out` port `SAMPLE`. In addition there are two `constant` parameters, `SAMPLE_INTERVAL` and `K`, that make it possible to set some values differently for each individual instance; the first influences the sampling rate of the sensor, and the second is used to calibrate the sampled value. The Data Dictionary entries of the generic chart, including its parameters, are shown in Fig. 14.6.

Port parameters can be of any data-type and structure. Array parameters can be defined with or without an index range. The index range

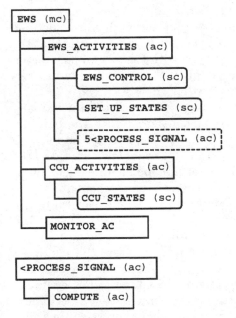

Figure 14.5 The chart usage hierarchy of the enhanced EWS.

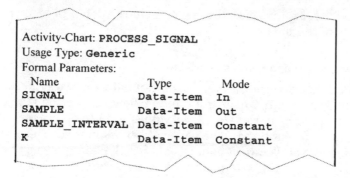

Activity-Chart: **PROCESS_SIGNAL**
Usage Type: **Generic**
Formal Parameters:

Name	Type	Mode
SIGNAL	**Data-Item**	**In**
SAMPLE	**Data-Item**	**Out**
SAMPLE_INTERVAL	**Data-Item**	**Constant**
K	**Data-Item**	**Constant**

Figure 14.6 Definition of formal parameters of a generic chart.

definition can use literal or named constants, constant parameters, or it can be based on an index range (e.g., parameter A is `array 1 to length_of(A) of integer`, which defines an array parameter whose upper range index is equal to the length of the actual binding). When the array parameter is defined without an index range, the index limits are inherited from the actual binding, a notion defined in the next section.

A generic chart that communicates with its environment via a queue will have a queue `in/out` parameter. The example shown in Fig. 8.8, in which four EWS instances communicate with two printers, can be modified so that it uses generic charts for the EWS and the printer, and each of these has a queue parameter.

Record and union parameters must be defined with a user-defined type that has the desired structure. This follows from the rule that the actual bindings must be consistent in type with the formal parameter, and two records/unions are consistent only if they have the same user-defined type. This issue is discussed further shortly.

The formal parameters are used inside the generic cluster like any other element, but their usage must be consistent with the parameter's mode: the value of an `in` parameter is expected to be used by the component, while that of an `out` parameter should be affected by the component. The value of an `in` parameter may be modified, as long as the modified value is not used later on outside the component.

Constant parameters can be used in places where constants are allowed: constant parameters can appear, for example, in the definition of an array index range, but they cannot label a flow-line or be assigned a value in an assignment action. Very often, the instances of a generic chart are arranged in an array, and an integer constant parameter is used to identify the individual instances. For example, in models of client/server architectures when multiple similar clients send messages to a server via a queue, each client can be an instance of a generic chart that identifies itself by its index.

Statecharts (but not activity-charts or module-charts) may have parameters of type activity. An activity parameter is considered to be an `in/out` port, the idea being that the component can send a control signal to an activity (e.g., `st!(A)` or `sp!(A)`), and can sense its status (e.g., by `sp(A)` or `ac(A)`). For example, assume that in the processing unit of a mission-critical system there are several components that perform a similar function. (Such redundancy is often incorporated to enhance reliability.) Each of these components has the same behavioral pattern, which is specified by the generic statechart `ACT_CNTRL` of Fig. 14.7. The formal parameters include the input events that trigger transitions, and the activity `A`, which is activated by the statechart. This pattern can control any activity that is bound to the formal parameter when the chart is later instantiated. The input events consist of control commands (`GO`, `HALT`, and `RESET`) and an indication of an error in the input device. The `out` parameter `FAULT` is used to report the status of the particular instance. A sample usage of this generic statechart is illustrated in Fig. 14.7.

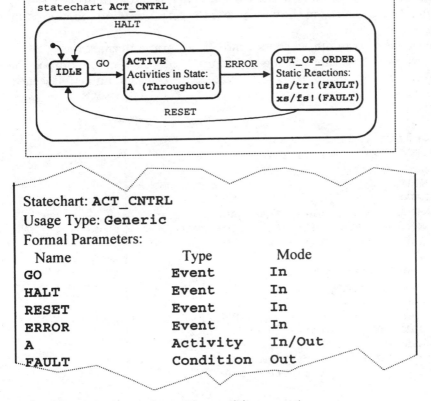

Figure 14.7   A generic statechart with an activity parameter.

14.3.2 Actual bindings of parameters

For each instance of a generic chart there is a binding of actual elements to the formal parameters. Ports can be bound to variables or aliases; in fact, any data element that labels a flow-line (with the exception of an information-flow) can be bound. The port binding is analogous to connecting components ports with signal lines in an electronic scheme. Every change in the actual element will be available immediately to the instance, and every change inside the instance will be sensed outside by the connected elements. Constant parameters are bound to constant values, that is, literal constants, named constants, or operators that yield constant values, such as those that relate to the index range of arrays (e.g., length_of(A)).

The binding information is supplied in the Data Dictionary entry of the instance. Figure 14.8 shows the parameter bindings for the instances PS1 and PS2 of the generic chart PROCESS_SIGNAL, whose formal parameters were defined in Fig. 14.6. The different bindings to the constant parameter SAMPLE_INTERVAL determine different sampling rates in each component. HIGH_RATE and LOW_RATE are two named constants; they can be defined, for example, in a global definition set. The in and out ports are bound to the actual data-items—the signal that comes from the sensor and the corresponding component in the array of SAMPLES.

As another example, we instantiate the generic statechart ACT_CNTRL of Fig. 14.7 three times in the statechart PROC_CNTRL. The purpose of the containing statechart is to activate three copies of an activity, each

```
Activity: PS1<PROCESS_SIGNAL
Defined in Chart: EWS_ACTIVITIES
Actual Bindings:
  Name                 Type          Binding
SIGNAL                 Data-Item     SIGNAL_1
SAMPLE                 Data-Item     SAMPLES(1)
SAMPLE_INTERVAL        Data-Item     HIGH_RATE
K                      Data-Item     0.5

Activity: PS2<PROCESS_SIGNAL
Defined in Chart: EWS_ACTIVITIES
Actual Bindings:
  Name                 Type          Binding
SIGNAL                 Data-Item     SIGNAL_2
SAMPLE                 Data-Item     SAMPLES(2)
SAMPLE_INTERVAL        Data-Item     LOW_RATE
K                      Data-Item     1.0
```

Figure 14.8 Activity instances and actual parameter bindings.

processing a signal from a different sensor. The statechart also continuously monitors the status of these activities, and when all of them fail it issues a fault alarm. See Fig. 14.9, which shows the activity-chart that contains PROC_CNTRL, the statechart itself, and the Data Dictionary entries of the state instances. These entries contain the actual parameter bindings; in particular, they contain the binding to the activity parameter.

The actual binding must have the same type and structure as the formal parameter. In particular, in the case of data-items the following rules hold:

- When the formal parameter is of a user-defined type, the actual binding should also be of this user-defined type.

- Arrays must be of the same length and must have the same component types. If the index range of an array formal parameter is not specified, the index range values are inherited from the actual binding.

- Queues must have the same component types.

- Formal parameters cannot be defined directly as records and unions, because these structures are considered to be consistent only if they have the same user-defined type.

Note that because generic charts are the roots of the separate trees in the chart hierarchy, only elements appearing in global definition sets are commonly visible by them and to the charts of their instances. Therefore, user-defined types and constants that are used in the definition of the formal parameters must belong to some global definition set.

Finally, the bindings to ports must be consistent with the flow of information that appears in the activity-chart or module-chart of the instance. The binding to an in port should flow into the instance and the binding to an out port must be an output of the instance. This has indeed been adhered to in the example, as can be seen by inspecting Figs. 14.2*b* and 14.8.

14.4   Referring to Elements in Instances

An element that belongs to a generic chart will have an occurrence in the model for each instance of the chart. As explained earlier, instances of generic charts share elements with the rest of the model only via the parameters. In other words, it is impossible to refer to elements appearing in instances of charts outside the generic cluster, and therefore references to these elements do not appear in expressions of the model. However, testbenches, which do not obey *any* visibility rules (see Sec. 12.4.2), should be allowed to refer to elements in generic instances for purposes of analysis. In addition, external tools, such as

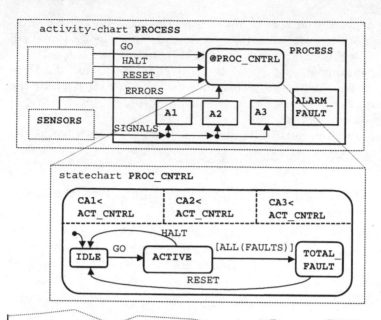

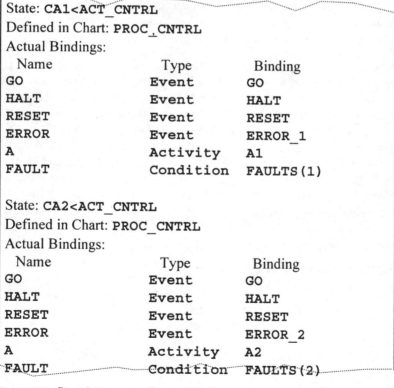

State: **CA1<ACT_CNTRL**
Defined in Chart: **PROC_CNTRL**
Actual Bindings:

Name	Type	Binding
GO	Event	GO
HALT	Event	HALT
RESET	Event	RESET
ERROR	Event	ERROR_1
A	Activity	A1
FAULT	Condition	FAULTS(1)

State: **CA2<ACT_CNTRL**
Defined in Chart: **PROC_CNTRL**
Actual Bindings:

Name	Type	Binding
GO	Event	GO
HALT	Event	HALT
RESET	Event	RESET
ERROR	Event	ERROR_2
A	Activity	A2
FAULT	Condition	FAULTS(2)

Figure 14.9 State instances and actual bindings.

simulators and prototype generators, should also allow references to these elements. For example, such tools should be able to present the value of each instance of an element, and we must provide a way to do so.

Going back to the example in Fig. 14.2, the TICK event is local to the generic chart PROCESS_SIGNAL. It has five occurrences in PROCESS_SIGNALS, one in each instance PS1 through PS5. Each occurrence can be identified by its instance name (e.g., PS1^TICK, which means "the element TICK in the instance PS1"). When the element name is not unique in the generic cluster, the chart name should be added to the element name. For example, if there is another TICK event in the subchart COMPUTE of Fig. 14.5, PS1^COMPUTE:TICK is how we would refer to the occurrence of COMPUTE:TICK in PS1, which is different from PS1^PROCESS_SIGNAL:TICK. The situation becomes more complicated when generic instances are nested within other generic charts, resulting in a chain of instance names (e.g., PS1^CMP3^X, which is "the element X in the generic instance CMP3 in the generic instance PS1"). Box names that might not be unique in their charts are identified in these references by unique pathnames. See App. A.1.

15

Related Approaches

In the preceding chapters we described the STATEMATE approach for modeling reactive systems. Other authors have also proposed methods for this purpose. Some have been presented as modeling languages, some as methodologies, and some as development standards. By and large, they address the same development stages and the same kind of systems that we do.

This chapter discusses a number of these methods. They are compared to the STATEMATE approach, and when appropriate we show how they can be used in conjunction with STATEMATE.

15.1   An Overview of Specification Methods

In this chapter we review methods that deal with reactive systems and cover the early stages of development, that is, specification and top-level design. We should add that by *methods* we mean methodologies, modeling languages, or standards.

A methodology is usually proposed together with a particular modeling language that matches its concepts. Similarly, modeling languages are more fitting for use with some methodologies than with others. The borderline between a methodology and a modeling language is thus not clear, and people often do not distinguish between the two. Our interest is mainly in methods that are heavily based on diagrammatic modeling.

We also discuss development standards. Standards are used in organizations, and are often imposed on modelers and system developers. In some sense they are similar to methodologies: They define processes of development, the various steps these processes involve, and their deliverables (such as special documents in predefined formats). Some standards are strict and very well defined, but some are more flexible.

The flexible ones—unlike most methodologies—do not dictate any particular modeling language, although they may talk about the concepts that should be dealt with when adhering to the standard and the resulting elements and relationships that should be described during the specification.

It is interesting to survey some of the highlights of methodologies for reactive systems. Our purpose is to represent the trends, and not to give a full history survey. Moreover, we concentrate only on methods that we found meaningful in comparison with STATEMATE.

Two variations of modeling methods based on the Structured Analysis paradigm (SA; see, for example, DeMarco 1978) were developed by Ward and Mellor (1986) and by Hatley and Pirbhai (1987). These authors added real-time provisions to the data-flow diagrams of the basic SA approach. The resulting extensions are usually referred to as *RTSA methods* (for real-time Structured Analysis).

A consolidation of these two methods into a new notation called ESML (Extended Systems Modeling Language) has been proposed by Bruyn et al. (1988). We discuss the Ward/Mellor and Hatley/Pirbhai methods in Sec. 15.2.

Around the same time, several other methods were developed for modeling reactive systems, taking a variety of approaches to the description of concurrent processes and their communication. Some examples are the Jackson System Development (JSD) method (Jackson 1983; Cameron 1989), Alford's Software Engineering Requirement Methodology/Distributed Computer Design System (SREM/DCDS) method (Alford 1985), and the CCITT Specification and Description Language (SDL) (International Telecommunication Union 1995). The last of these, SDL, was developed mainly for telecommunication systems, and it has evolved over the years into an object-based version. It is discussed in more detail in Sec. 15.4, which deals with other object-based methods.

Since the late 1980s, there has been an increasing interest in object-based and object-oriented techniques. This trend started in the programming community with the advent of object-oriented programming languages but has moved up to the earlier stages of specification and design, too. This is a natural process, because people want to avoid discontinuity between early and later stages of system development and to allow more natural traceability between them.

Several object-oriented methodologies and modeling languages have been proposed in the last few years, and some are aimed at reactive systems. We discuss three. The first is Real-time Object-Oriented Modeling (ROOM), an executable modeling language supported by the computerized tool ObjectTime (Selic et al. 1994). The second is Unified Modeling Language (UML) (Rational 1997), a broad and general approach, combining elements from the Booch method (Booch 1994), the Object-Modeling Technique (OMT) (Rumbaugh et al. 1991), and scenario-like use-cases (Jacobson 1992), with Statecharts at its heart. The third is a UML-consistent executable language set called XOM (Executable Object Modeling), which was co-developed by one of us and is supported by a computerized tool, Rhapsody (Harel and Gery 1997).

Many methods, including some of those already mentioned, are the result of wide efforts, sometimes spanning a number of large companies. They were aimed at easing the task of developing complex systems in a particular industry or across several industries. For example, the Embedded Computer Systems Analysis and Modeling (ECSAM) methodology (Lavi and Winokur 1989) has been evolving since the early 1980s to address the needs of the Israel Aircraft Industries (IAI) in its system development projects. It uses the STATEMATE languages for modeling.

During the past 20 years or so many standards have been written and approved by various organizations, providing guidelines and criteria to be used in system development activities. Some of these are documented in Dorfman and Thayer (1990a). One of the best known standards is the U.S. Department of Defense Military Standard 2167A (*Military Standard* 1988) and its successor MIL-STD-498 (*Military Standard* 1994). Like most other standards, DOD-STD-2167A does not require the use of a particular modeling language. In Sec. 15.5 we show how our languages can be used to apply this particular standard.

The remainder of this chapter is devoted to briefly describing the aforementioned methods. We compare them with our own approach, and when relevant show how they can be used in conjunction with STATEMATE.

15.2 Methods Based on Structured Analysis

In the early 1980s, two methods were proposed, extending the classical structured analysis of DeMarco (1978) with means for modeling reactive, real-time systems, in the form of timing and control information. The two approaches are very similar and have the same expressive power. We shall concentrate on the parts of these methods that address the functional and behavioral views as defined in this book. Both methods contain portions that deal with the architecture of a system, too, but as far as we know, these aspects are rarely used, and the popular implementations of these methods do not cover them.

15.2.1 Ward and Mellor

The Ward/Mellor method was initiated by a group at Yourdon, Inc., principally by P. Ward and S. Mellor, and was described in detail in their 1986 book (Ward and Mellor 1996). We base our discussion on that book, concentrating on what the authors call *the transformation schema*.

The transformation schema contains diagrams based on the data-flow diagrams of DeMarco (1978). The diagrams of Ward and Mellor (1986) contain nodes for *data transformations* and for *control transformations* connected by edges depicting different types of flows between them. See Fig. 15.1*a*.

The *control transformations* are denoted by dashed circles. They map input event flows into output event flows. Among these are events whose effect is to *enable, disable,* or *trigger* a data transformation. The control transformations are described by state transition diagrams or tables. See Fig. 15.1*b* for a state transition diagram describing the control transformation in the transformation schema of Fig. 15.1*a*.

A *data transformation* may be stated procedurally in pseudocode or in any appropriate graphical or tabular language. The method also allows nonprocedural specification of relationships between the inputs and the outputs.

The notation for specifying data is a modified version of DeMarco's. Figure 15.2 presents the symbols used to define data compositions.

Ward and Mellor (1986) offer a way of executing the transformation scheme, which is based on the description of the execution of the Petri nets described by Peterson (1981).

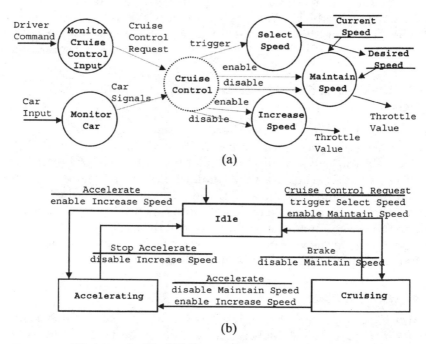

Figure 15.1 Diagrams in Ward/Mellor notation. (*a*) Transformation schema. (*b*) State transition diagram.

Symbol	Read as
=	is composed of
+	together with
[...|...|...]	select one of
m{ ... }n	at least **m** but no more than **n** iterations of

Figure 15.2 Data composition notation in the Ward/Mellor method.

15.2.2 Hatley and Pirbhai

The development of the Hatley/Pirbhai method was started by D. Hatley of Lear-Siegler, Inc., in collaboration with some engineers at Boeing. The method is described in detail in Hatley and Pirbhai (1987). Our discussion of the method is based on that book.

The Hatley/Pirbhai method prescribes that the system's requirements be captured by two related models: the *process model* and the *control model*.

The *process model* consists of a hierarchical structure of data-flow diagrams, each of which consists of processes describing the functions of the system, interconnected by data flows. A primitive process is described by a *process spec* (PSPEC). PSPECs are usually written in structured English, but they can also employ tables, diagrams, and equations. Each data flow is specified in *the requirement dictionary*.

The *control model* uses *control-flow diagrams* (which are very similar to the data-flow diagrams of the process model) to show the flow of control signals between the processes. Each nonprimitive process can be described by a pair consisting of a data-flow diagram and a control-flow diagram. The behavior of the process is described by *control specifications* (CSPECs), which are represented by a bar on the control-flow diagram, to show their input and output signals (their role is very similar to that of control activities in our Activity-charts). See Fig. 15.3*a*. The control specifications themselves may be presented in several ways: conventional state transition diagrams or tables, *decision tables* that describe functions between discrete inputs and outputs, or *process activation tables* that connect signal values with activation and deactivation of processes in a specified order. Figure 15.3*b* shows a process activation table.

Timing requirements can be added, too, specifying repetition rates of output signals in the requirement dictionary and input-to-output response times in tables or in timing diagrams.

The method does not include rigorous definitions of the languages used in PSPECs and CSPECs or in the timing requirements. However, the authors provide what they call balancing rules, which enable verification of a model's consistency.

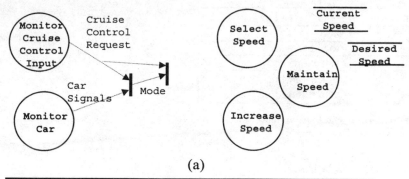

(a)

INPUT		PROCESS		
Mode	Cruise Control Request	Select Speed	Increase Speed	Maintain Speed
idle	Off	0	0	0
	On	1	0	0
accelerating	Off	0	1	0
	On	0	1	0
cruising	Off	0	0	1
	On	0	0	1

(b)

Figure 15.3 Components of the Hatley/Pirbhai notation. (*a*) Control-flow diagram. (*b*) Process activation table.

15.2.3   Evaluation and comparison with STATEMATE

The Ward/Mellor and Hatley/Pirbhai methods are quite similar and have very similar expressive power. There are, however, some differences between them, especially with regard to the activation of processes. Both methods allow the use of a variety of languages for describing primitive processes, and both allow the use of different kinds of grammars and tables for this purpose. To implement these methods one must supply a rigorous syntax and semantics for whatever languages are used for this purpose.

As far as the relationship of these methods to ours is concerned, we note that all components of their languages have equivalents in ours. As both these methods use conventional state transition diagrams for control specification, they cannot take advantage of the features present in Statecharts, especially hierarchy, concurrency, history, and timing.

A significant deficiency of Ward/Mellor and Hatley/Pirbhai is their inability to deal with multiple similar components. There is no mechanism to deal with instances of a generic component, a feature that is essential for object-based modeling.

We refer the reader to the 1989 survey of Wood and Wood, which compares and evaluates the three approaches: those of Ward/Mellor, and of Hatley/Pirbhai, and ours (as well as a related forth one, ESML). This survey is quite illuminating, and it emphasizes the differences between the methods, particularly those relevant to modeling behavior. Davis' 1990 book contains interesting discussions and comparisons of these and other modeling approaches, too.

15.3   ECSAM

The Embedded Computer Systems Analysis and Modeling (ECSAM) methodology was developed at the Israel Aircraft Industries (IAI) for the analysis and design of computer-based systems (Lavi and Winokur 1989; Lavi et al. 1992). The method has evolved since the early 1980s, and it is used by several projects at the IAI. For modeling, it employs the languages described in this book. Some of the features of the structural view and its connection with the functional view that were described in Chaps. 9 and 10 were actually added to our languages to support the special needs of the ECSAM method.

According to ECSAM, a system is specified by two models—the *conceptual model* and the *design model*. Here we describe the conceptual model only. It consists of the following three views: the *logical modules view*, the *operating modes view*, and the *dynamic processes view*.

The *logical modules view* describes the partitioning of the system into logical subsystems (modules), the external information that flows between the system and its environment, and the information that flows between the subsystems. These are presented by module-charts, as described in Chap. 9. The logical modules view also defines the capabilities (activities) performed by each of the logical subsystems. This is done by linking an activity-chart that describes the module to each of the modules constituting the system, as explained in Sec. 10.2. In Fig. 15.4 the module-chart SYSTEM contains the system's logical modules. The capabilities of the logical module M3 are described by the activity-chart M3_ACTIVITIES.

The *operating modes view* describes the main operating modes of the system and the transitions between them. This view is described by a statechart that is linked to the control activity of the entire system. In Fig. 15.4, the system's modes are described in the statechart MODES, which is connected to the control activity of the activity PROCESSES.

The *dynamic processes view* describes the behavioral processes that occur in the system in its various operating modes. This view is presented by a set of activity-charts. One activity-chart, which describes the system on the top level, details the processes (as activities) and connects them by the throughout construct to the states representing the

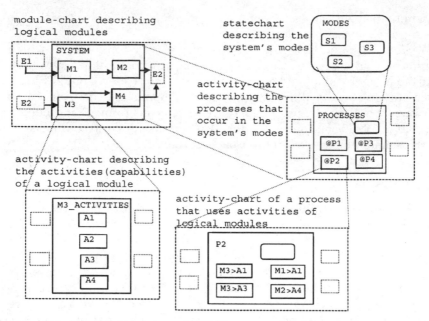

Figure 15.4 Relationships between ECSAM conceptual model components.

system modes (see Sec. 7.3.3). See the activity-chart PROCESSES in Fig. 15.4.

Each of the processes is then described by an off-page activity-chart containing the activities that constitute the process (e.g., see P2 in Fig. 15.4). These activities are associated with the capabilities of the logical modules by the is activity relation, as explained in Sec. 10.4. For example, in Fig. 15.4 the activity named M3>A1 is an occurrence of activity A1 in module M3. The dynamics of the process is described by its control activity using a statechart.

In addition to defining these three views, the ECSAM method outlines roughly a dozen analysis steps that are to be applied to the system and to each of its subsystems. These can be found in Lavi et al. (1992).

15.4   Methods Based on Objects

We now discuss some methods that involve object-oriented concepts, such as abstract data types, object decomposition using class-instantiation techniques, and inheritance.

15.4.1   SDL

There have been several versions of Specification and Description Language (SDL) since its inception in 1976 as the Z.100 recommendation of CCITT. SDL was developed by the International Telecommunication Union mainly for telecommunication systems. Our review here is based on SDL-92 (International Telecommunication Union 1992), which extends SDL-88 by adding means for object-oriented modeling.

SDL is a rich language. It offers two different syntactic forms: a *graphic representation* (SDL/GR) and a textual *phrase representation* (SDL/PR), which are equivalent and are based on the same abstract grammar. The following example uses the graphical version.

A *system* in SDL is decomposed into *blocks* connected to each other and to the environment by *channels* that convey *signals*. The blocks are either further decomposed into other blocks or contain *processes*. A process in SDL is a kind of state machine that communicates with other processes or with the environment; processes are used to describe the behavior of the system.

A process, like any state machine, consists of *states,* in which it may consume signals. The *transition* between states is a sequence of *actions,* such as performing a *task* (assignment statement or informal text), making a *decision,* causing the *output of a signal,* setting a *timer,* calling a *procedure,* or creating an *instance of a process type.* See Fig. 15.5.

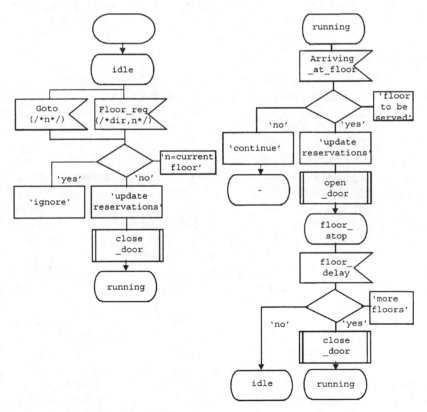

Figure 15.5 A process in SDL.

There are several ways in SDL to make the specifications more compact and easier to read. They include *referenced definitions, macros,* and *packages.* In particular, *types* of components are defined in packages that can be *used* in different contexts (e.g., in Ada), wherever the components are instantiated.

As a language, SDL is defined very rigorously. The recommendation document is very detailed (International Telecommunications Union 1995). It gives a formal definition—semantics included—for each entity and construct of the language. The processes—the dynamic components of the specification—are executable, with well-defined semantics.

As to the relationship to our languages, there are a many similarities, due to the similar evolution of both. They both support function-based and object-based decomposition. Their expressive power is quite similar. SDL, like our languages (and unlike the methods based on structured analysis, described in Sec. 5.2), has an instantiation mechanism, which is necessary in object-based modeling. SDL went one step further in support of object technology by including an inheritance (type specialization) mechanism. In contrast, our approach was to construct a separate language set and a separate tool specifically for object-oriented modeling; see Sec. 15.4.4.

15.4.2 ROOM

The Real-Time Object-Oriented Modeling (ROOM) language and methodology originated at the Telos Group at Bell-Northern Research in the late 1980s (Selic et al. 1994). This group started the development of the ObjectTime toolset, which supports the construction and execution of ROOM models.

The ROOM language is based on an object paradigm in which a system is viewed as a set of concurrently active objects, communicating by message passing. ROOM refers to these objects as *actors.* Each actor is an independent machine whose interface to its environment is defined by *ports.* Actors exchange messages through these ports. Each port has an associated *protocol* that restricts the type of messages that may flow through the port. Actors can be organized into a structure by connecting their ports via channels that are called *bindings.* A ROOM actor can itself be organized with an internal structure of component actors. See Fig. 15.6.

The behavior of an actor can be described by an extended state machine called a *ROOMchart,* which in the words of Selic et al. (1994) was "inspired by the Statechart formalism." Several features of Statecharts are included in ROOMcharts, such as state hierarchy (referred to as *composite states*), transitions exiting from the containing state (*group transitions*), condition connectors (*choicepoints*), and history entrances. On the other hand, ROOMcharts do not have

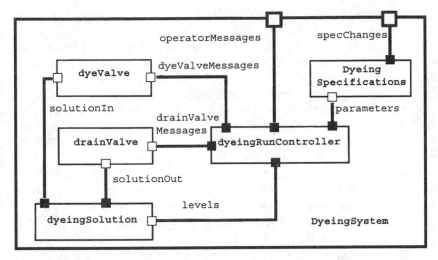

Figure 15.6   An actor in a ROOM model.

orthogonality; that is, they do not admit the and-state feature, a decision that is explained in Appendix C of Selic et al. (1994).

ROOM incorporates a conventional programming language into models (e.g., the ObjecTime implementation uses C++) to represent actions and data structures in low-level detailed descriptions.

ROOM models are based on class definitions for actors, protocols, and data objects. Class hierarchies are supported for each entity type, with different inheritance rules.

ROOM's concepts have a rigorous semantics, and its models are executable. The supporting tool, ObjecTime, includes a compiler that translates models into high-level source code that runs in a special run-time environment.

An interesting recent development is the newly announced commercial alliance between Rational Corporation (and their Rose toolset) and ObjecTime. This might effectively cause the ROOM method and the current ObjecTime tool to be dismissed and their development discontinued in favor of a UML-based approach.

15.4.3   UML

Unified Modeling Language (UML) is a large-scale effort to unify three of the many object-oriented methodologies that appeared in the late 1980s. These are the so-called Booch method (Booch 1994), the Object Modeling Technique (OMT) (Rumbaugh 1991), and Object-Oriented Software Engineering (OOSE) (Jacobsen 1992). The first two are general modeling methods that incorporate an object-based structural model, with *classes, object instances, relationships, aggregation, inheritance,* etc., and use variants of the Statecharts language for modeling behavior. OOSE, on the other hand, is based on *use-cases*.

The unifying effort resulting in UML began in 1994 and is organized by Rational Corporation. It is led by the principal authors of the three aforementioned methods, G. Booch, J. Rumbaugh, and I. Jacobson. Many other people from several organizations participated in putting UML together, especially in the more recent effort on version 1.1, which was aimed at getting the earlier version 0.8 to be better defined. These include the people responsible for the ROOM method and its underlying tool ObjectTime (see Sec. 15.4.2) as well as the team responsible for i-Logix's object-oriented approach with its underlying tool, Rhapsody (see Sec. 15.4.4) represented by Eran Gery from I-Logix, Inc. and David Harel. UML version 1.1 was submitted as a proposal to the Object Management Group (OMG) Analysis and Design Task Force's RFP-1 for adoption as a standard. A decision by the OMG to adopt UML 1.1 as a standard was made in late 1997.

The UML involves many different kinds of diagrams. *Use-case diagrams* show the interaction of external entities with the system. These diagrams present the functional requirements of the system; they are similar in appearance to those in OOSE. *Class diagrams* are more or less the standard object models from the Booch method, OMT, and several other object-oriented methods. They show the collection of static model elements, their contents, and relationships. *Statechart diagrams* are based on the usual Statecharts, as defined here, with modifications that cater to object orientation. *Activity diagrams* are behavioral flow-chart–like diagrams. *Sequence diagrams* are a variant of MSCs (message sequence charts) found in many object-oriented writings. They show object interactions arranged in a time sequence. *Collaboration diagrams* also show object interactions, but they are organized around objects, and they show the relationships among them.

Detailed documents specifying the meta-model, notation, and semantics of UML can be found by following the links in www.rational.com/uml/ (Rational 1997). It is worth mentioning that one of the basic premises of UML is to leave many of the details vague enough to permit different implementations. This means that one can expect any number of tools to be built in the future, all claiming, correctly, to implement UML, although there might be quite significant differences between them.

15.4.4   XOM and Rhapsody

The Rhapsody tool is the first executable implementation of the core of the UML. It started out in the form of a carefully defined set of diagrammatic languages for modeling object-oriented systems with Statecharts at its heart, called XOM (Executable Object Modeling); see the conference version of Harel and Gery (1997). Joint work with the UML team has resulted in modifications to both approaches, so that although the XOM language set of Harel and Gery (1997) does not cover all aspects of UML, it is fully compatible with it. In fact, this language set constitutes, in essence, the core executable portion of UML, and it comes complete with a fully worked-out behavioral semantics.

The XOM approach is supported by Rhapsody, a tool that enables model execution and full-code synthesis into object-oriented programming languages such as C++. The philosophy driving the development of Rhapsody is similar to the one that drove the development of STATEMATE, except that Rhapsody is used exclusively for object-oriented modeling, and it is intended more for software than for systems in general.

The XOM and Rhapsody approach involves two constructive modeling languages, *object-model diagrams* and *Statecharts,* and a reflective language, *message sequence charts* (MSCs, also called *sequence diagrams*). A language is *constructive* if it contributes to the dynamic semantics of the model. That is, its constructs contain information needed in executing the model or in translating it into executable code. Other languages are *reflective* and can be used by the system modeler to capture parts of the thinking that go into building the model— behavior included—or to derive and present views of the model to aid in analysis and to check for consistency against the constructive parts of the model. Object-model diagrams specify the structure of the system by identifying classes of objects (i.e., object types) and their multiplicities, object relationships and roles, subtyping, and inheritance. Especially noteworthy in object-model diagrams is the provision for specifying composite objects, which capture a strong form of aggregation; they are depicted by encapsulation, as in Activity-charts; see Fig. 15.7.

The behavior of an object is specified by a statechart that is associated with its class; see Fig. 15.8. Statecharts employ two mechanisms for interobject interaction, *events* and *operations*. An object can generate an event, which is queued, to be later consumed by the target object's statechart, and an object can also directly invoke an operation of another object, thus causing its statechart to carry out an appropriate method and perhaps return a value. One upshot of the hierarchical modeling of composite structure is that these interactions can be arranged to take on the form of either direct communication or broadcast. Statecharts can also create and destroy object instances and can delegate events to their components.

15.5   MIL-STD-498 (DOD-STD-2167A)

The system software development standard DOD-STD-2167A (*Military Standard* 1988) was used for many years by the contractors who developed software for the U.S. Department of Defense. A few years ago it was combined with the automated information system documentation

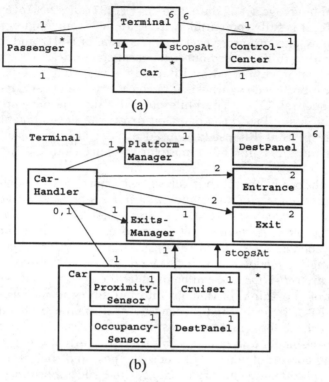

Figure 15.7 Object-model diagrams in a Rhapsody model. (a) High-level object-model diagram for a rail car. (b) Detailed diagram for composite objects.

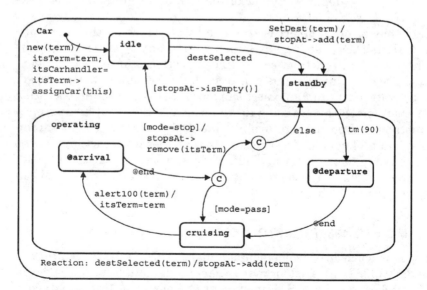

Figure 15.8 Statechart in a Rhapsody model.

standard DOD-STD-7935A to form the military standard MIL-STD-498 (*Military Standard* 1994). These standards detail the activities included in the software development process and provide a set of *data item descriptions* (DIDs), which form the requirements for documenting the development process.

Our languages, and hence the STATEMATE toolset, can be used to accomplish many of the specification and design activities required by these standards. The standards recommend using the DIDs as a checklist of items to be covered in the planning or engineering activity during the development and as a template for recording the results of this activity. Here we show how the concepts and terminology used in each DID of these standards map to the concepts and elements of our languages.

When conceptualizing the operational aspects of the system, a DID called the *operational concept description* (OCD) is used. The purpose of this phase is to obtain consensus among the acquirer, the developer, and the user on the operation of the system under development. Activity-charts and statecharts are used to describe the behavior of the system, and STATEMATE tools can be used to automatically generate a prototype of it.

During the system requirements phase the *system / subsystem specification* (SSS) and the *interface requirements specification* (IRS) are used. In this phase, an activity-chart describing the entire system (which is a module) is prepared, and the system capabilities are presented by the activities contained in it. The external and internal interfaces are represented by the flow-lines and their labeling data elements. These elements, in turn, are characterized in the Data Dictionary according to the requirements appearing in the DIDs. The system's states and modes, with their hierarchy, are described by a statechart, which is linked to the control activity of the top-level activity of the system.

During the system design phase the *system / subsystem design description* (SSDD) and the *interface design description* (IDD) are used. In this phase, the system components, which are the *computer software configuration items* (CSCIs) and *hardware configuration items* (HWCIs), are identified by a hierarchical module-chart, in which each component is represented by a module. The interfaces between the system components are described by the flow-lines between the modules. Each interface entity is a data element (information-flow, data-item, condition, or event) defined with all the required characteristics in the Data Dictionary.

During the software requirements phase the *software requirements specification* (SRS) and the *interface requirements specification* (IRS) are used. In this phase, a *computer software configuration item* (CSCI) is specified by an activity-chart whose activities present the CSCI's capabilities. The external and internal interfaces are described by the

TABLE 15.1   **Mapping of MIL-STD-498 Documents to STATEMATE Concepts**

Development Phase	Applicable IDDs	Modeling Constructs in the STATEMATE Languages
System requirements analysis	OCD	Activity-charts and statecharts describing the system behavior
	SSS IRS	Activity-chart and Data Dictionary describing the system capabilities and external interfaces. Statechart describing the system modes.
System design	SSDD IDD	Module-chart and Data Dictionary describing the CSCIs and HWCIs, and the interface data elements between these components
Software requirements analysis	SRS IRS	Activity-charts and Data Dictionary describing the CSCI's capabilities and the internal and external data elements
Software design	SDD IDD	Module-charts and Data Dictionary describing the CSCI's components (software units) and the interface data elements

flow-lines in this activity-chart, labeled by data elements that are defined in the Data Dictionary.

During the software (top-level) design phase the *software design description* (SDD) is used. In this phase, a CSCI is described by a module-chart. The CSCI components (software units) are defined as modules, which may be arranged in a hierarchy. The interface between these units is described by flow-lines between the modules labeled with the corresponding interface entities, accompanied by definitions in the Data Dictionary.

Table 15.1 presents STATEMATE modeling constructs that are used in each development phase according the standard.

An important facet of this connection between the military standard and the STATEMATE modeling languages is the fact that the same model can be used for all the development phases, with each phase refining the model and adding new parts. This assures good traceability between the phases, and makes it possible to document the traceability information together with the other specification details.

The STATEMATE system contains tools that support the production of the documents required by MIL-STD-498. Using these tools ensures that the documents are consistent. A description of this capability exists in the STATEMATE documentation provided by I-Logix.

16

Transition to Design

The main thrust of this book has been the careful description of a set of languages for modeling complex reactive systems. A model built with these languages can be used during the system development process in various ways, depending on the development method adopted. We shall call such a model the STATEMATE model, and as explained briefly in Chap. 1, it is commonly used in the specification phase.

Now that we have finished describing and illustrating the modeling languages themselves, we would like to come full circle and return to the issue of positioning the resulting specification models within the entire development process. In most development schemes, the design phase comes after the specification and leads to the implementation. Because different implementation technologies give rise to different concerns and different criteria for the quality of the design, the methods used in the transition from specification to design will differ, too.

This chapter concentrates on using the STATEMATE model for specification and on the main ways for carrying out the transition from the specification model to the design.

16.1 STATEMATE Models in the Development Process

There have been a number of proposals for defining the life-cycle process of system development. Among these are the classical waterfall model (Boehm 1976; Royce 1970), the rapid throwaway prototyping approach (Gomma and Scott 1981), the evolutionary prototyping (Gomma 1986; McCracken and Jackson 1986), and the spiral model (Boehm 1988). In general, such development processes start with requirements analysis, during which the system's specification is constructed. Although specifications—and therefore the models describing them—are treated differently in the various approaches, the subsequent phase is almost always design, which is an essential prerequisite to implementation.

A STATEMATE model can be used in the specification phase of most of the development processes. Nevertheless, it is important to understand the model's role in the overall process and how the information contained in it can be used in subsequent phases, mainly the design phase. We now show how STATEMATE models can be used in various ways during specification.

16.1.1   Models as prototypes

One common approach in developing complex systems is to use the specification model for prototyping. Because a STATEMATE model is executable, it lends itself nicely to this purpose. In fact, executable specifications—termed *operational* by Zave (1984)—are the basis of the "rapid throwaway prototyping" approach of Gomma and Scott (1981). The structure of prototyping models in this case is problem-oriented, not implementation-oriented, and the system's external behavior is studied by executing the model. The observed behavior must then be preserved during transition to design, a topic we take up in Sec. 16.2.2.

When the system is to interface with humans, developers can use special tools to build images of screen windows in computer systems or mock-ups of the control panels that will eventually make up the actual interface. If and when the interface of the model with its environment (i.e., the input/output data) is defined as it will be in the implementation, this information can be transferred to the design phase. Other portions of the model are not directly used in the design, and most of the design has to be started from scratch.

16.1.2   Design using specification models

The second approach calls for using the specification model directly to obtain a design. In other words, STATEMATE modeling is used as a high-level implementation language. Because the model can then be translated automatically into the target implementation by code synthesis, this process can be viewed as true compilation.

In this approach, the principal structure of the implementation is determined in the specification phase. This is one of its disadvantages, because the specifier must consider issues that are not relevant to this phase. However, the main advantage is continuity, which is hailed as one of the main virtues of object-oriented development methods. If an object-oriented approach is indeed taken, objects from the problem domain are refined and appear in their new guise in the implementation structure. Work that was carried out in the first phase is not lost. There are better means for traceability, and the resulting systems are therefore easier to maintain. The transition to design is thus more reliable, depending mainly on the reliability of the code-synthesizer.

16.1.3   Restructuring for design

A "middle of the road" approach (i.e., not exactly full prototyping and not exactly designing during the specification, but a little bit of both) is restructuring the specification for design. There are two issues that raise the need for a new model for design purposes, and hence for such restructuring to take place:

- Specification is carried out in the problem domain, and design in the implementation domain.
- There are many different kinds of implementation frameworks, which requires using different design languages.

Restructuring requires the system developer to allocate elements of the model to elements of the design. Thus the STATEMATE specification model is not discarded. Rather, new constructs are prepared for the system's design, and the constructs of the STATEMATE languages are mapped into them.

We should remark that although design is often carried out in a language external to the STATEMATE framework, some parts of the design can be carried out within STATEMATE, using module-charts and their connections with other parts of the STATEMATE model. See Chaps. 9 and 10.

16.2   Mapping Models to Design Structures

We now discuss "real" transition to design, that is, restructuring the specification model and mapping it into the design structures, as introduced in Sec. 16.1.3.

Specification structures must be mapped into a particular configuration of implementation resources. Ideally, we would like automatic transformations that preserve external behavior but change the mechanisms that produce that behavior. This is usually not the case, so we will more commonly use heuristics that recognize structures in the specification model and transfer them to the design model. In general, this transition to design involves a number of concepts regarding the usage of design criteria for obtaining a mapping and the evaluation of the resulting mapping. Some of these are common to the different target environments, and some are more specific to particular implementation technologies.

16.2.1   Design criteria

Different architectures are used for different target implementation technologies, and each case involves different design considerations.

Moreover, the level of design can vary, too: one could decide to work on a high level of system design, in which there is a division into subsystems, or on lower levels, in which there is a mapping into the actual constructs of the final software or hardware.

In high-level design, especially in real-time embedded systems, there will often be both software and hardware components. In such cases, the first stage in the mapping to design involves allocating the functional requirements described by the system-level specification model to software and hardware components. This is done by the systems engineer, according to a variety of criteria: the basic nature of the function (e.g., certain things can only be done with hardware, such as sensing information from the physical world), desired performance, existing components, etc.

The decomposition itself can be carried out in STATEMATE mapping from activity-charts to module-charts (using the "implemented by module" relationship), as discussed in Chap. 10. One such case, used in MIL-STD-498, was described in Chap. 15, that is, the division of a system into its software and hardware components (the CSCI and HWCI of the standard, respectively).

When we carry out this design decomposition, some additional issues have to be dealt with these concern requirements management, deriving interfaces from the allocation, and traceability concerns. Many of these are discussed in articles appearing in the two first chapters of Thayer and Dorfman (1990), and some of them can also be carried out within the STATEMATE languages.

If a system is pure software (or if we are in later levels of software/ hardware design), we will reach the need to map into software components. This, too, depends on the target technology. There are essentially three general issues here. One is the fact that since we have an orderly, complete and consistent specification model, we are in a position to identify patterns of similarity in the functional components. This makes it possible to make decisions regarding the mapping of, say, similar functions that appear in different processes of the behavioral specification into a single software function with parameters or to a class with several instances or subclasses.

The second issue is that of an object-oriented target implementation, an extremely popular and beneficial approach in recent years. While objects are very useful in the implementation stage, some systems are better thought of at the early stages of development in nonobject ways. In such cases, the issue is to transfer requirements based on functional decomposition into an object-oriented implementation. This is discussed in several places; see, for example, Ward (1989) and Gomma (1993). Some of the methods are based on Ward/Mellor or Hatley/ Pirbhai specifications, but they hold also for function-based STATEMATE models. Other possibilities involve generating scenarios (or the more general use-cases) from the STATEMATE model and to proceed from there as in object-oriented design. Of course, if the modeling itself is carried out—already in the specification stage—in an object-oriented fashion, the mapping to an object-oriented design will be straightforward. The generic-charts construct of our languages (see Chap. 14) can help with this because a generic chart is a natural candidate to be a class in the implementation.

The third issue is that of specific kinds of applications, such as hard, real-time systems. For these, there are usually more singular criteria and specialized considerations of performance. Some techniques and components available in specific implementation environments are concurrent tasks, synchronization and communication mechanisms, and timers of the particular real-time kernel. Good coverage of the design process for real-time systems, starting from the specification is given by Gomma (1993).

In principle, many of the special criteria can be embodied in algorithms for carrying out the mapping. The automatic code generation can be based on them, with some user guidance (employing various compilation profiles) about such questions as to whether an activity should be translated into a function or a task, whether to use a polling method for some particular input or interrupt, and so on.

This guided translation into code has proved itself very well in the arena of pure hardware (e.g., ASIC). Chip designers use VHDL and Verilog, high-level design languages similar to programming languages, to express their designs (Smith 1996). (This code can be later automatically transformed into chip schemes by commercial tools.) The designers can write the code manually; alternatively, they can develop STATEMATE models, which are translated into VHDL and Verilog by automated tools (such as the translator developed by I-Logix). There are also compilation profiles to guide the translation. These profiles are based on the designer's knowledge and the criteria he or she applies in the particular case at hand. The profiles contain high-level instructions, such as putting several model components in the same design entity and defining the port signals, and low-level decisions, such as how the signals will be implemented (e.g., the polarity of conditions).

16.2.2 Evaluation of the mapping

Once a mapping from the model to the design has been constructed, it should be checked for completeness and consistency, from both structural and behavioral points of view. The formality of our languages obviously make such tests possible in principle, and indeed the STATEMATE tool supports a broad variety of them.

First, we have to make sure that all the requirements have been covered, for example, that all the functions in the specification model have been mapped to structures in the design. Conversely, we must show that all parts of the design have some source in the specification model. The better and more detailed these links are between the specification model and the design, the easier it is to carry out forward and backward traceability, which is crucial for convenient maintenance of the system under development.

We also have to check the structural consistency of the mapping. This includes several things, such as consistency of the hierarchy and of the interfaces. For example, if an activity A was mapped to some design structure M, and a subactivity B of A was mapped to N, then N must be a substructure of M in an appropriate sense. Similarly, if a data-item X was specified as flowing from an activity A to an activity B, there must be a way for X (or its mapped image) to flow from the design structure implementing A to that implementing B.

The behavioral aspects are far more problematic. We mentioned that behavior must be preserved by the mapping. Put simply, we want things we know about the behavior of the model (e.g., those discovered by executing it or by running the synthesized code) to hold for the implementation, too. Of course, we could run the implemented system and check that the scenarios match. However, it is necessary to emphasize that running or executing models and designs usually cannot guarantee full behavioral consistency because the number of possible scenarios will often be infinite or at best unreasonably large. As Dijkstra once put it, testing and debugging cannot be used to demonstrate the absence of errors, only their presence.

What is needed for air-tight confidence in the system's desired behavior is true program or system *verification*. Because verification is a whole science in itself, we shall not dwell on it here, except to make a few general comments. Good basic books on verification include Francez (1991) and Loeckx and Seiber (1984).

When we use the term *verification,* we mean rigorous mathematical proofs of correctness. In our framework, this means proving that the mapping indeed preserves behavior under all circumstances. Even this needs to be more carefully stated. For example, we might want to know that the values of certain variables are preserved in the transition to design or that certain kinds of sequences of events that take place in executing the model will also take place in the implementation.

The three basic facts about verification in our framework are as follows (see Chap. 5 of Harel, 1992a):

- The general verification problem is noncomputable. This means that we cannot hope for a verification tool that will be able to routinely prove the correctness of any mapping.

- In principle, a correct mapping can be proved correct in an appropriate mathematical setup, so that this direction of work is definitely worth pursuing.

- In recent years there have been major advances in techniques and automated tools for verifying systems. Hardware industries are beginning to use them on real systems, and the feeling is that software and embedded systems will not be long in following this lead. These modern verification methods are based on specifying properties in temporal logic and on model-checking techniques. A large amount of material can be found in Manna and Pnueli (1992).

Names and Expressions

This appendix presents the syntax rules for names and expressions in the languages described in the book.

A.1 Names

A.1.1 Reserved words

```
ac active all and any
break
ch changed
dc deep_clear downto
else en end entered entering ex exited exiting
false for fs fl
get
hanging hc hg history_clear
if in
length_of lindex loop
make_false make_true
nand nor not ns nxor
or
put peek
q_put q_urgent_put q_get q_peek q_flush q_length
rd read read_data resume rindex rs
schedule sd sp st start started stop stopped
suspend
then timeout tm to tr true
uput
wr write_data written when while
xor xs
```

A.1.2 Textual element names

- A legal name of a textual element is a sequence of alphanumeric characters, excluding blanks, and possibly including _ (underscore). It must begin with a letter.

- The maximal length of a name is 31 characters.

- Names are not case-sensitive.

- Synonyms contain at most 16 characters.

- A name cannot be a reserved word.

- A name cannot be the same as the name of a predefined function.

- User-defined types cannot have the following names: `integer`, `real`, `bit`, `array`, `queue`, `record`, `union`, `bit_array`, `string`, `condition`, `single`.

- When referring to a textual element in an expression (e.g., in a transition label), names can be spread out over multiple lines and \ (back slash) must be written before the "new-line" inside the name.

- A textual element can be referred to outside the model prefixed by the chart name in which it is defined: `chart-name:element-name` (e.g., `MAIN:X`).

A.1.3   Box element names

- A legal name of a box element is a sequence of alphanumeric characters, excluding blanks, and possibly including _ (underscore). It must begin with a letter.

- The maximal length of a name is 31 characters.

- The names are not case-sensitive.

- Synonyms contain at most 16 characters.

- The name cannot be a reserved word.

- A box element can be referred to by pathname, i.e., preceded by its parents's name: `...grandparent-name.parent-name.box-name` (e.g., `A.B.C`) and optionally also with the chart-name in which it is defined: `chart-name:pathname` (e.g., `MAIN:A.B`).

- The pathname of a top level box is: `.box-name` (e.g., `.TOP`)

- When referring to a box element in an expression (e.g., in a transition label), names can be spread out over multiple lines, and \ (back slash) must be written before the "new-line" inside the name.

A.1.4   Names of elements in generic instances

- An element in a generic instance is referred to by: `instance-name^unique-element-name-in-instance`.

- An instance name can have several levels of nesting (instance in instance in instance, etc.), in which case, several ^ signs are used.

- An instance name (box name) on each level of the nesting and the element name in the instance must be unique. Therefore, each may contain a chart name.   For example, `A:K^L^B:M^C:X`.

A.2   Expressions

A.2.1   Event Expressions

Atomic event and array of events   An *atomic event* is one of the following:

- Named single (nonarray) event.
- E(K), the *k*th component of an event array E; K is any integer expression.

An *array of events* (also referred to as an *event array*) is one of the following:

- Named event array.
- Array slice, E(K..L), of an event array E; K and L are integer expressions.

Events related to other elements   The following operators, which are related to various types of elements, produce a single (nonarray) event.

Event	Abbreviation	Occurs when	Note
entered(S)	en(S)	State S is entered	Used only in statecharts
exited(S)	ex(S)	State S is exited	Used only in statecharts
entering	ns	Current state is being entered	Used only as trigger of reaction in state
exiting	xs	Current state is being exited	Used only as trigger of reaction in state
started(A)	st(A)	Activity A is started	Used only in statecharts
started	st	Current activity is started	Used only as trigger in reactive activity
stopped(A)	sp(A)	Activity A is stopped	Used only in statecharts
changed(X)	ch(X)	The value of X is changed	X is data-item or condition expression or array (including array slice); can be structured, or a queue
true(C)	tr(C)	The value of condition C is changed to true	C is condition expression (not array)
false(C)	fs(C)	The value of condition C is changed to false	C is condition expression (not array)
read(X)	rd(X)	X is read by action rd!, or from a queue, by peak! or get!	X is primitive (not alias) data-item or condition; X can be array (not slice), array component (not bit-array component), structured and queue

Event	Abbreviation	Occurs when	Note
written(X)	wr(X)	X is written by action wr!, by assignment, or by put! in queue	X is primitive (not alias) data-item or condition; X can be array (not slice), array component (not bit-array component), structured or queue
timeout(E,N)	tm(E,N)	N clock units passed from last time event E occurred	E is event expression (not array); N is numeric expression
all(E)		All components of event array E occurred	E is event array
any(E)		At least one component of event array E occurred	E is event array

Compound events

The following operations use only single (nonarray) events and conditions and produce a single event.

Event	Occurs when
E[C]	E occurred and the condition C is true
[C]	Condition C is true
not E	E did not occur
E1 and E2	E1 and E2 occurred simultaneously
E1 or E2	E1, E2, or both, occurred

The list presenting operations is in descending order of precedence. Parentheses can be used to alter the evaluation order.

A.2.2   Condition expressions

Atomic condition and array of conditions   An *atomic condition* is one of the following:

- Literal constant: true, false (not case-sensitive).

- Named single (nonarray) condition (can be of user-defined type).

- C(K), the *k*th component of a condition "indexable" array C; K is any integer expression.

- R.C, a field expression of type condition in a record or union R, for example, A.B.C, where C is a field of type condition in the field B (with a record structure) in the record A.

An *array of conditions* (also referred to as *condition array*) is one of the following:

- Literal constant: {C1,C2,...,K*CN,...,*CL}; each Ci is a literal constant condition, and K is a literal constant integer.
- Named condition array (can be of user-defined type).
- R.C, a field expression in a record or union of a type condition array.
- Array slice, C(K..L), of a condition indexable array C (defined next); K and L are integer expressions.

An *indexable condition array* is one of the following:

- Named condition array (can be of user-defined type)
- R.C, a field expression in a record or union of a type condition array.
- A component of an array, whose type is a condition array, for example: RRC(I), where RRC is an array of condition arrays. RRC(I) is an array of conditions, and RRC(I)(K) is a condition.

Conditions related to other elements   The following operators, which are related to various types of elements, produce a single (nonarray) condition.

Condition	Abbreviation	True when	Note
in(S)		System is in state S	Used only in statecharts
active(A)	ac(A)	Activity A is active	Used only in statecharts
hanging(A)	hg(A)	Activity A is suspended	Used only in statecharts
X1 R X2		The values of X1 and X2 satisfy the relation R	X1 and X2 are data-item or condition expressions; When numeric, R may be $=, /=, >, <, =<, =>$; When strings, arrays, structured, or queues, R may be $=, /=$
all(C)		All components of condition array C are true	C is a condition array
any(C)		At least one component of condition array C is true	C is a condition array

Compound conditions   The following *logical operations* use only single (nonarray) conditions and produce a single condition.

Condition	True when
not C	C is not true
C1 and C2	Both C1 and C2 are true
C1 or C2	C1 or C2 or both are true

The list presents the operations in descending order of precedence. Parentheses can be used to alter the evaluation order.

Logical operations have lower precedence than comparison relations.

A.2.3   Data-item expressions

Data-item expressions are converted to the required type when needed:

- Bit-arrays shorter than 32 bits to integer and vice versa.
- Bit to integer.
- Integer to real.

Therefore, *integer expression* means also expression of type bit and bit-array (with length less than 32); *numeric expression* means real expression and integer expression, including bit-array expressions (with length less than 32).

Atomic, array, and structured data-items   An *atomic numeric data-item* is one of the following:

- Literal constant:
  integer: decimal integer (of value less than 2**31)
  bit-array: 0X. . .(hexadecimal); 0B. . . (binary); 0O. . . (octal)
  real: dec.dec[(E|e)[+|-] dec] (dec=decimal integer).
- Named real, integer bit-array, or bit (can be of user-defined type).
- Named data-item defined as numeric expression.
- D(K), the kth component of a numeric indexable array or bit-array D, where K is any integer expression.
- R.C, a field expression in a record or union of numeric type. For example: A.B.C, where C is a field of numeric type in the field B (whose type is record), in the record A.

An *atomic string data-item* is one of the following:

- Constant literal: sequence of characters enclosed by single quotation marks (e.g. `` `ABC' ``); maximal length is 79 characters.
- Named string (can be of user-defined type).
- Named data-item defined as string expression.
- S(K), the kth component of a string indexable array S, where K is any integer expression.
- R.C, a field expression in record/union of string type.

An *array of data-items* is one of the following:

- Literal constant: {D1,D2,...,K*DN,...,*DL}, where each Di is a numeric or string literal constant data-item, and K is a literal constant integer.
- Named bit-array, array of any type, or user-defined array type.
- R.D, a field expression in a record/union, whose type is a data-item, array, or bit-array.
- Array slice, D(K..L), of an indexable data-item array or bit-array D, where K and L are integer expressions.
- A component of an array, whose type is a data-item, array, or bit-array.
- Named data-item defined as an array or bit-array expression.

An *"indexable" data-item array* is one of the following:

- Named bit-array, array of any type, or user-defined array type.
- R.D, a field expression in a record/union, whose type is a data-item, array, or bit-array.
- A component of an array, whose type is a data-item, array, or bit-array.

A *structured data-item, record,* or *union,* is one of the following:

- Named data-item defined as record or union (can be a structured user-defined type).
- R.S, a field expression in a record/union of a type structured data-item.
- A component of an array, whose type is a structured data-item.

Queue data-items are data-items, array components, or record or union fields defined in the Data Dictionary as having the structure queue (directly or via a user-defined type).

Data-items related to other elements   The following operators are applicable to strings, arrays, and bit-array data-items and to user-defined types that are defined as string, array, or bit-array. The result is a constant integer.

Operator	Meaning
length_of(A)	Length of array, bit-array and string A (data-item or user-defined type)
rindex(A)	Right index of array or bit-array A (data-item or user-defined type)
lindex(A)	Left index of array or bit-array A (data-item or user-defined type)

The following operator is applicable to queues:

Operator	Meaning
q_length(Q)	Current number of elements in queue Q

Compound data-item expressions
Numeric operations.   The following operations are relevant to integer, bit, bit-arrays (of length less than 32), and real operands; the result is numeric:

```
+EXP, -EXP
EXP1**EXP2
EXP1*EXP2, EXP1/EXP2
EXP1+EXP2, EXP1-EXP2
```

The list presents the operations in descending order of precedence. Parentheses can be used to alter the evaluation order.

Numeric operations have higher precedence than comparison relations and logical operations.

Bitwise operations.   The following operations are relevant to integer, bit, and bit-array operands; the result is a bit-array:

```
not EXP1
EXP1 & EXP2 (denotes concatenation)
EXP1 and EXP2, EXP1 nand EXP2
EXP1 or EXP2, EXP1 nor EXP2
EXP1 xor EXP2, EXP1 nxor EXP2
```

The list presents the operations in descending order of precedence. Parentheses can be used to alter the evaluation order.

Bitwise operations other than the not operation have lower precedence than comparison relations and numeric operations. The not operation has higher precedence.

A.2.4   Action expressions

Actions manipulating other elements

Action	Abbreviation	Does	Note
E		Generates the event E	E is primitive single event (not array)
make_true(C)	tr!(C)	Assigns true to condition C	C is primitive single condition (not array)
make_false(C)	fs!(C)	Assigns false to condition C	C is primitive single condition (not array)
X:=EXP		Assigns the value of EXP to X	X is primitive or alias data-item, array or bit-array, condition or array condition (including slices)
start(A)	st!(A)	Activates activity A	Used only in statecharts
stop(A)	sp!(A)	Stops activity A	Used only in statecharts
stop		Stops the current activity	Used only in mini-spec of reactive activity
suspend(A)	sd!(A)	Suspends activity A	Used only in statecharts
resume(A)	rs!(A)	Resumes activity A	Used only in statecharts
read_data(X)	rd!(X)	Reads data-item or condition X	X is primitive (not alias) data-item or condition, or array (including slices); bit-array components or slices are not allowed
write_data(X)	wr!(X)	Writes to data-item or condition X	X is primitive (not alias) data-item or condition, or array (including slices); bit-array components or slices are not allowed
history_clear(S)	hc!(S)	Forgets history information of stat S	Used only in statecharts
deep_clear(S)	dc!(S)	Forgets history information of descendants of state S	Used only in statecharts
schedule(K,N)	sc!(K,N)	Performs action K delayed by N clock units	N is numeric expression
q_put(Q,X)	put!	Adds data-item or condition X to tail of queue Q	X's type is compatible with type of queue components

(Continued)

Actions manipulating other elements (*Continued*).

Action	Abbreviation	Does	Note
q_urgent_put(Q,X)	uput!	Adds data-item or condition X to head of queue Q	X's type is compatible with type of queue components
q_get(Q,X,S)	get!	Moves head of the queue Q into data-item or condition X; returns status S	X's type is compatible with type of queue components; condition S is optional
q_peek(Q,X,S)	peek!	Copies head of queue Q to data-item or condition X; returns status S	X's type is compatible with type of queue components; condition S is optional
q_flush(Q)	fl!	Clears queue Q	

Compound, conditional, and iterative actions Action expressions may contain context variables: $legal-name, of no more than 16 characters (see Sec. A.1). Context variables are allowed for any type of data-item or condition.

Action expression	Note
AN1;AN2	The actions are performed sequentially; the ; is optional at the end of the list
if C then AN1 else AN2 end if	C is a condition expression; the else part is optional
when E then AN1 else AN2 end when	E is an event expression; the else part is optional
for $I in K to|downto L loop AN end loop	$I is a context variable; K and L are integer expressions; AN is an action expression
while C loop AN end loop	C is a condition expression; AN is an action expression
break	Causes the containing loop action to terminate

A.2.5   Data-type expressions

Data-types of a record or union's fields can be defined (textually) in the Data Dictionary entry of the record or union using the following syntax. Note that fields of a structured type (record and union) cannot be defined directly but only via user-defined types.

The keywords and the element identifiers are not case-sensitive. N below is a constant integer expression, that is, literal integer constant, named integer constant, or operation returning a constant value.

Square brackets denote an optional segment.

Basic types

```
integer
integer length=N
integer min=N1 max=N2
real
string [length=N]
bit
bit-array [N1 to N2]
condition
<user-defined type> (identifier)
```

Compound types

```
array [N1 to N2] [of <basic type>]
queue [of <basic type>]
```

A.3   Predefined Functions

A *predefined function call* has the following syntax:

```
returned-value := function(arg1,arg2,...)
```

To describe the arguments's type and the returned value in the following table, we use the following abbreviations: I=Integer, R=Real, S=String, W=Bit-array, B=Bit.

Conversion of the arguments's type is carried out when needed.

A.3.1   Arithmetic functions

Function	Arguments	Returns	Meaning
MAX	Mixed R and I	Input's type	Maximum value
MIN	Mixed R and I	Input's type	Minimum value
TRUNC	R	I	Truncated value
ROUND	R	I	Rounded value
ABS	I or R	Input's type	Absolute value
MOD	I1, I2	I	I1 modulus I2

A.3.2   Trigonometric functions

Function	Arguments	Returns	Meaning
SIN	R	R	Trigonometric sine
COS	R	R	Trigonometric cosine
TAN	R	R	Trigonometric tangent

A.3.3   Random functions

Function	Arguments	Returns	Meaning
RAND_EXPONENTIAL	R	R	Random exponential
RAND_BINOMIAL	I, R	I	Random binomial
RAND_POISSON	R	I	Random poisson
RAND_UNIFORM	R, R	R	Random uniform
RAND_IUNIFORM	I, I	I	Random integer uniform
RAND_NORMAL	R, R	R	Random normal
RANDOM	I	R	Random

A.3.4   Bit-array functions

Function	Arguments	Returns	Meaning
SIGNED	W	I	Signed value (m.s.b. of W is a sign bit)
ASHL	W, I	W	Arithmetic shift left by I, enters 0s
ASHR	W, I	W	Arithmetic shift right by I, preserves sign
LSHL	W, I	W	Logical shift left by I, enters 0s
LSHR	W, I	W	Logical shift right by I, enters 0s
BITS_OF	W1, I1, I2	W	Slice of bit-array expression; l.s.b of W1 is 0
EXPAND_BIT	B, I	W	Expand bit; creates a bit array of I bits, all equal B
MUX	W1, W2, B	W	Returns: W1 if B=0, W2 if B=1

A.3.5   String functions

Note: the index of the leftmost character in a string is 0.

Function	Arguments	Returns	Meaning
STRING_EXTRACT	S, I1, I2	S	Extracts a string of length I2 from index I1 of S
STRING_INDEX	S1, I, S2	I	Index of substring S2 within S1; -1 if not found
STRING_CONCAT	S1, S2	S	Concatenates strings
STRING_LENGTH	S	I	String length
CHAR_TO_ASCII	S	I	ASCII value of first character of S
ASCII_TO_CHAR	I	S	Returns S of one character with ASCII value I
INT_TO_STRING	I	S	Converts I to decimal string; I can be negative
STRING_TO_INT	S	I	Integer value of a decimal string

A.4 Reactions and Behavior of Activities

A.4.1 Statechart labels

A *statechart label* is one of the following:

- `trigger`, which is a single event expression; note that `[condition]` is a legal event expression.
- `reaction`, which is of the form `trigger/action`.
- `/action`.

A.4.2 State reactions and reactive mini-specs

A state reaction and a reactive mini-spec is a list of one or more reactions (i.e., of the form `trigger/action`) separated by `;;`:

```
reaction;; reaction;;
reaction;;
...
```

The `;;` is optional at the end of the list.

Restrictions on events, conditions, and actions depend on whether they are used in a state or activity. See Sec. A.2.

A.4.3 Procedure-like mini-spec

A *procedure-like mini-spec* has the syntax of an action. See Sec. A.2.4.

A.4.4 Combinational assignments

A *combinational assignment* has the following syntax:

```
CE :=EXP1 when COND1 else
     EXP2 when COND2 else
     .. .
     EXPN
```

Here, `CE` (the *combinational element*) is a primitive data-item or condition, or it is an alias data-item. `EXPi` is a data-item or condition expression. `CONDi` is a condition expression. `N` can be equal to 1 (in which case the assignment is just `CE:=EXP1`) or more.

Combinational assignments in a sequence are separated by `;`, like actions in a sequence.

A.5 Flow of Information

A.5.1 Flow labels and information-flow components

Flow labels in activity-charts and module-charts and information-flow components can be any primitive (variable) data element (event, condition, data-item) or information flow. In addition they can be components on any level of a primitive data element (array component, array slice, and record or union field). Array components can use only literal constants.

A.5.2   Actual bindings of generic parameters

Actual bindings of parameters in generic instances have the same syntax as flow labels. See Sec. A.5.1.

B

Early Warning System Example

Functional Decomposition Approach

B.1 Textual Description of the System

The early warning system (EWS) receives a signal from an external sensor. When the sensor is connected, the EWS processes the signal and checks whether the resulting value is within a specified range. If the value of the processed signal is out of range, the system issues a warning message on the operator display and posts an alarm. If the operator does not respond to this warning within a given time interval, the system prints a fault message on a printing facility and stops monitoring the signal. The range limits are set by the operator. The system becomes ready to start monitoring the signal only after the range limits are set. The limits can be redefined after an out-of-range situation has been detected or after the operator has deliberately stopped the monitoring. See Fig. 1.1.

B.2 The Model

B.2.1 The hierarchy of charts

Figure B.1 depicts the hierarchy of charts in the EWS model.

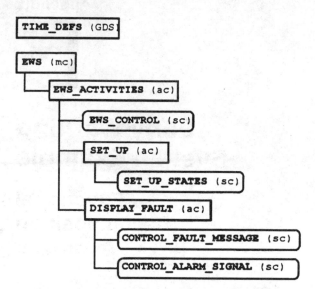

Figure B.1   Hierarchy of charts in the EWS model.

B.2.2   The charts

Figures B.2–B.8 depict the charts in the EWS model.

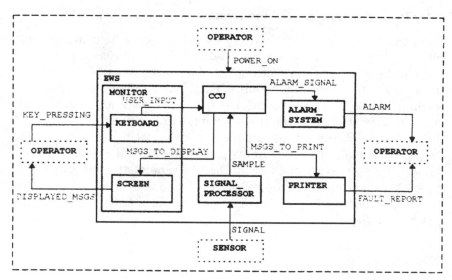

Figure B.2   Module-chart EWS model.

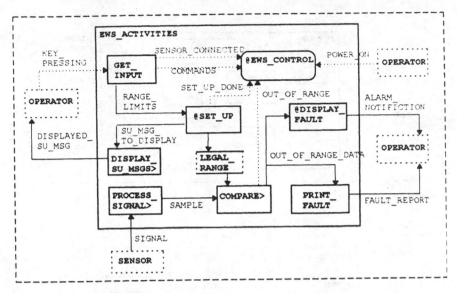

Figure B.3 Activity-chart EWS_ACTIVITIES.

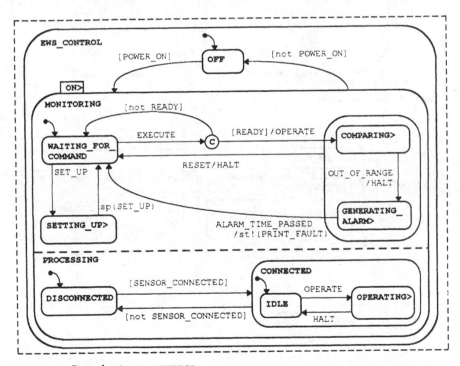

Figure B.4 Statechart EWS_CONTROL.

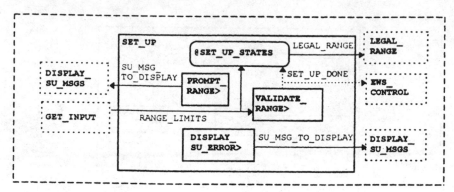

Figure B.5   Activity-chart SET_UP.

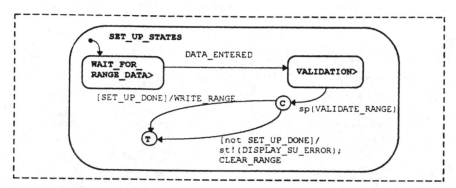

Figure B.6   Statechart SET_UP_STATES.

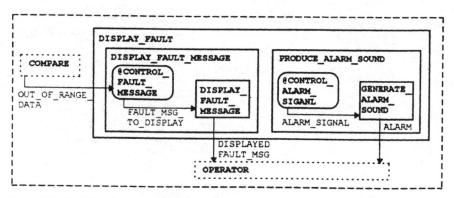

Figure B.7   Activity-chart DISPLAY_FAULT.

 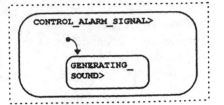

Figure B.8 Statecharts CONTROL_FAULT_MESSAGE and CONTROL_ALARM_SIGNAL.

B.2.3 The Data Dictionary

Modules

Module: EWS
Defined in Chart: EWS
Described by Activity-Chart: EWS_ACTIVITIES

Module: OPERATOR
Defined in Chart: EWS
Defined as: environment

Module: SENSOR
Defined in Chart: EWS
Defined as: environment

Activities and data-stores

Activity: COMPARE
Defined in Chart: EWS_ACTIVITIES
Termination Type: reactive controlled
Mini-spec:

```
wr(SAMPLE)/
    if ((SAMPLE < LEGAL_RANGE.LOW_LIMIT) or
        (SAMPLE > LEGAL_RANGE.HIGH_LIMIT)) then
            OUT_OF_RANGE;
            OUT_OF_RANGE_DATA.VALUE:=SAMPLE;
            OUT_OF_RANGE_DATA.LIMITS:=LEGAL_RANGE
    end if
```

Implemented by Module: CCU

Activity: CONTROL_ALARM_SIGNAL
Defined in Chart: DISPLAY_FAULT
Implemented by Module: CCU

Activity: CONTROL_FAULT_MESSAGE
Defined in Chart: DISPLAY_FAULT
Implemented by Module: CCU

Activity: DISPLAY_FAULT_MESSAGE
Defined in Chart: DISPLAY_FAULT
Implemented by Module: SCREEN

Activity: DISPLAY_SU_ERROR
Defined in Chart: SET_UP
Termination Type: procedure-like
Mini-spec:

```
SU_MSG_TO_DISPLAY:=`Range error; try again´
```

Activity: DISPLAY_SU_MSGS
Defined in Chart: EWS_ACTIVITIES
Termination Type: reactive controlled
Combinational assignments:

```
DISPLAYED_SU_MSG:=SU_MSG_TO_DISPLAY
```

Implemented by Module: SCREEN

Activity: GENERATE_ALARM_SOUND
Defined in Chart: DISPLAY_FAULT
Termination Type: reactive controlled
Implemented by Module: ALARM_SYSTEM

Activity: GET_INPUT
Defined in Chart: EWS_ACTIVITIES
Description: Transforms key pressing to data
Termination Type: reactive controlled
Implemented by Module: KEYBOARD

Data-store: LEGAL_RANGE
Defined in Chart: EWS_ACTIVITIES
Resides in Module: CCU

Activity: PRINT_FAULT
Defined in Chart: EWS_ACTIVITIES
Description: Issues fault data to the printer

Activity: PROMPT_RANGE
Defined in Chart: SET_UP
Termination Type: procedure-like
Mini-spec:

```
SU_MSG_TO_DISPLAY:=`Enter range limits´
```

Activity: PROCESS_SIGNAL
Defined in Chart: EWS_ACTIVITIES
Termination Type: reactive controlled
Mini-spec:

```
started/TICK;;
TICK/ $VALUE:=SIGNAL;
    SAMPLE:=COMPUTE($VALUE);-- ext. function
    sc!(TICK,SAMPLING_INTERVAL)
```

Implemented by Module: SIGNAL_PROCESSOR

Activity: SET_UP
Defined in Chart: EWS_ACTIVITIES
Termination Type: reactive self-terminated
Implemented by Module: CCU

Activity: VALIDATE_RANGE
Defined in Chart: SET_UP
Termination Type: procedure-like
Mini-spec:

```
fs!(SET_UP_DONE);
if RANGE_LIMITS.LOW_LIMIT<RANGE_LIMIT.HIGH_LIMIT
    then tr!(SET_UP_DONE)
end if
```

States

State: COMPARING
Defined in Chart: EWS_CONTROL
Activities in State: COMPARE (throughout)

State: CONTROL_ALARM_SIGNAL
Defined in Chart: CONTROL_ALARM_SIGNAL
Static Reactions:

```
ns/tr!(ALARM_SIGNAL);;
xs/fs!(ALARM_SIGNAL)
```

State: DISPLAYING_FAULT_MESSAGE
Defined in Chart: CONTROL_FAULT_MESSAGE
Activities in State: DISPLAY_FAULT_MESSAGE (throughout)

State: GENERATING_ALARM
Defined in Chart: EWS_CONTROL
Activities in State: DISPLAY_FAULT (throughout)

State: GENERATING_SOUND
Defined in Chart: CONTROL_ALARM_SIGNAL
Activities in State: GENERATE_ALARM_SOUND (throughout)

State: ON
Defined in Chart: EWS_CONTROL
Static Reactions: ns/fs!(SET_UP_DONE)
Activities in State: DISPLAY_SU_MSGS (throughout)

State: OPERATING
Defined in Chart: EWS_CONTROL
Activities in State: PROCESS_SIGNAL (throughout)

State: SETTING_UP
Defined in Chart: EWS_CONTROL
Static Reactions: ns/st!(SET_UP)

State: VALIDATION
Defined in Chart: SET_UP_STATES
Static Reactions: ns/st!(VALIDATE_RANGE)

State: WAIT_FOR_RANGE_DATA
Defined in Chart: SET_UP_STATES
Static Reactions: ns/st!(PROMPT_RANGE)

Events
Event: ALARM_TIME_PASSED
Defined in Chart: EWS
Definition: tm(en(GENERATING_ALARM),ALARM_DURATION)

Event: DATA_ENTERED
Defined in Chart: SET_UP_STATES
Definition: wr(RANGE_LIMITS)

Event: EXECUTE
Defined in Chart: EWS

Event: EXECUTE_KEY
Defined in Chart: EWS

Event: HALT
Defined in Chart: EWS_CONTROL

Event: OPERATE
Defined in Chart: EWS_CONTROL

Event: OUT_OF_RANGE
Defined in Chart: EWS_ACTIVITIES

Event: RESET
Defined in Chart: EWS

Event: RESET_KEY
Defined in Chart: EWS

Event: SET_UP
Defined in Chart: EWS

Event: SET_UP_KEY
Defined in Chart: EWS

Event: TICK
Defined in Chart: EWS_ACTIVITIES

Conditions
Condition: ALARM_SIGNAL
Defined in Chart: EWS

Condition: POWER_ON
Defined in Chart: EWS

Condition: READY
Defined in Chart: EWS_CONTROL
Definition: SET_UP_DONE and in(CONNECTED)

Condition: SET_UP_DONE
Defined in Chart: EWS_ACTIVITIES

Data-items
Data-Item: ALARM
Defined in Chart: EWS
Data-Type: real

Data-Item: ALARM_DURATION
Defined in Chart: EWS_CONTROL
Data-Type: real
Defined as: constant
Definition: 30.

Data-Item: DISPLAYED_FAULT_MSG
Defined in Chart: EWS
Data-Type: string

Data-Item: DISPLAYED_SU_MSG
Defined in Chart: EWS
Data-Type: string

Data-Item: FAULT_MSG_TO_DISPLAY
Defined in Chart: EWS
Data-Type: string

Data-Item: FAULT_REPORT_TO_PRINT
Defined in Chart: EWS
Data-Type: record
  Field Name: FAULT_TIME   Field Type: TIME
  Field Name: FAULT_VALUE   Field Type: integer
  Field Name: FAULT_RANGE Field Type: RANGE

Data-Item: FAULT_REPORT
Defined in Chart: EWS
Data-Type: string

Data-Item: HIGH_LIMIT_SLIDER
Defined in Chart: EWS
Data-Type: integer

Data-Item: LEGAL_RANGE
Defined in Chart: EWS_ACTIVITIES
Data-Type: RANGE

Data-Item: LOW_LIMIT_SLIDER
Defined in Chart: EWS
Data-Type: integer

Data-Item: RANGE_LIMITS
Defined in Chart: EWS
Data-Type: RANGE

Data-Item: OUT_OF_RANGE_DATA
Defined in Chart: EWS_ACTIVITIES
Data-Type: record
 Field Name: VALUE Field Type: integer
 Field Name: LIMITS Field Type: RANGE

Data-Item: SAMPLE
Defined in Chart: EWS
Data-Type: integer

Data-Item: SAMPLE_INTERVAL
Defined in Chart: EWS_ACTIVITIES
Data-Type: real
Defined as: constant
Definition: 2.

Data-Item: SIGNAL
Defined in Chart: EWS
Data-Type: bit-array 23 downto 0

Data-Item: SU_MSG_TO_DISPLAY
Defined in Chart: EWS
Data-Type: string

Actions

Action: CLEAR_RANGE
Defined in Chart: SET_UP_STATES
Definition:

```
LEGAL_RANGE.LOW_LIMIT:=0;
LEGAL_RANGE.HIGH_LIMIT:=0
```

Action: PREPARE_MESSAGE
Defined in Chart: CONTROL_FAULT_MESSAGE
Definition:

```
$VALUE_STR:=INT_TO_STRING(OUT_OF_RANGE_DATA.VALUE);
$OUT_STR:=STRING_CONCAT($VALUE_STR,' is out of range:\n');
$LOW_STR:=STRING_CONCAT(
    INT_TO_STRING(OUT_OF_RANGE_DATA.LIMITS.LOW_LIMIT),
    ` - `);
$HIGH_STR:=INT_TO_STRING(OUT_OF_RANGE_DATA.LIMITS.HIGH_LIMIT);
$RANGE_STR:=STRING_CONCAT($LOW_STR, $HIGH_STR);
FAULT_MSG_TO_DISPLAY:=STRING_CONCAT($OUT_STR,$RANGE_STR);
```

Action: WRITE_RANGE
Defined in Chart: SET_UP_STATES
Definition: LEGAL_RANGE:=RANGE_LIMITS

User-defined types

User-Defined Type: RANGE
Defined in Chart: EWS
Data-Type: record
    Field Name: LOW_LIMIT   Field Type: integer
    Field Name: HIGH_LIMIT   Field Type: integer

User-Defined Type: TIME
Defined in GDS: TIME_DEFS
Data-Type: record
    Field Name: HOURS   Field Type: integer min=0 max=23
    Field Name: MINUTES   Field Type: integer min=0 max=59
    Field Name: SECONDS   Field Type: integer min=0 max=59

Information-flows

Information-Flow: ALARM_NOTIFICATION
Defined in Chart: EWS_ACTIVITIES
Consists of:

    ALARM
    DISPLAYED_FAULT_MSG

Information-Flow: COMMANDS
Defined in Chart: EWS
Consists of:

    SET_UP
    EXECUTE
    RESET

Information-Flow: COMMAND_KEYS
Defined in Chart: EWS
Consists of:

    SET_UP_KEY
    EXECUTE_KEY
    RESET_KEY

Information-Flow: DISPLAYED_MSGS
Defined in Chart: EWS
Consists of:

    DISPLAYED_FAULT_MSG
    DISPLAYED_SU_MSG

Information-Flow: KEY_PRESSING
Defined in Chart: EWS
Consists of:

    COMMAND_KEYS
    RANGE_SLIDERS
    ENTER_KEY
    SENSOR_CONNECTED_SWITCH

Information-Flow: MSGS_TO_DISPLAY
Defined in Chart: EWS
Consists of:

SU_MSG_TO_DISPLAY
FAULT_MSG_TO_DISPLAY

Information-Flow: MSGS_TO_PRINT
Defined in Chart: EWS
Consists of:

FAULT_REPORT_TO_PRINT

Information-Flow: RANGE_SLIDERS
Defined in Chart: EWS
Consists of:

LOW_LIMIT_SLIDER
HIGH_LIMIT_SLIDER

Information-Flow: USER_INPUT
Defined in Chart: EWS
Consists of:

COMMANDS
SENSOR_CONNECTED
RANGE_LIMITS

References

M. Alford, "SREM at the Age of Eight: The Distributed Computing Design System," *Computer* (April 1985), pp. 36–46.

B. Boehm, "Software Engineering," *IEEE Transactions on Computers* (December 1976), pp. 1226–1241.

——, "A Spiral Model of Software Development and Enhancement," *Computer* (May 1988), pp. 61–72.

G. Booch, *Object-Oriented Analysis and Design with Applications,* 2d ed., Benjamin/Cummings, Redwood City, CA, 1994.

W. Bruyn, R. Jensen, D. Keskar, and P. T. Ward, "ESML: An Extended Systems Modeling Language Based on Data Flow Diagram," *ACM Software Engineering Notes* **13** (January 1988), pp. 58–67.

J. Cameron, *JSP and JSD: The Jackson Approach to Software Development,* 2d ed., IEEE Computer Society Press, Los Alamitos, CA, 1989.

A. M. Davis, *Software Requirements: Analysis and Specification,* Prentice Hall, Englewood Cliffs, NJ, 1990.

T. DeMarco, *Structured Analysis and System Specification,* Yourdon Press, New York, 1978.

M. Dorfman and R. H. Thayer, *System and Software Requirements Engineering,* IEEE Computer Society Press, Los Alamitos, CA, 1990b.

——, *Standards, Guidelines, and Examples on System and Software Requirements Engineering,* IEEE Computer Society Press, Los Alamitos, CA, 1990a.

N. Francez, *Program Verification,* Addison-Wesley, Reading, MA, 1991.

H. Gomma, "Prototypes—Keep Them or Throw Them Away?," *State of the Art Report on Prototyping,* Pergamon Infotech Ltd., 1986.

——, *Software Design Methods for Concurrent and Real-Time Systems,* Addison-Wesley, Reading, MA, 1993.

—— and D. Scott, "Prototyping as a Tool in the Specification of User Requirements," *Proceedings of the Fifth International Conference on Software Engineering,* 1981, pp. 333–342.

D. Harel, "Statecharts: A Visual Formalism for Complex Systems," *Science of Computer Programming* **8** (1987), pp. 231–274. (Preliminary version appeared as Technical Report CS84-05, The Weizmann Institute of Science, Rehovot, Israel, Feb. 1984.)

——, *Algorithmics: The Spirit of Computing,* Addison-Wesley, Reading, MA, 1987; 2d ed., 1992a.

——, "On Visual Formalisms," *Communications of the ACM* **31** (1988), pp. 514–530.

——, "Biting the Silver Bullet: Toward a Brighter Future for System Development," *Computer* (January 1992b), pp. 8–20.

—— and E. Gery, "Executable Object Modeling with Statecharts," *Computer* (July 1997), pp. 31–42. (Also in *Proceedings of the 18th International Conference on Software Engineering,* Berlin, IEEE Press, March 1996, pp. 246–257.)

——, H. Lachover, A. Naamad, A. Pnueli, M. Politi, R. Sherman, A. Shtull-Trauring, and M. Trakhtenbrot, "STATEMATE: A working Environment for the Development of Complex Reactive Systems," *IEEE Transactions on Software Engineering* **16** (1990), pp. 403–414.

—— and A. Naamad, "The STATEMATE Semantics of Statecharts," *ACM Transactions on Software Engineering and Methodology* **5** (October 1996), pp. 293–333. (Preliminary version appeared as Technical Report, I-Logix, Inc., 1989.)

—— and A. Pnueli, "On the Development of Reactive Systems," *Logics and Models of Concurrent Systems* (K. R. Apt, editor), NATO ASI Series, Vol F-13, Springer-Verlag, New York, 1985, pp. 477–498.

D. Hatley and I. Pirbhai, *Strategies for Real-Time System Specification,* Dorset House, New York, 1987.

International Telecommunication Union, *CCITT Specification and Description Language (SDL), ITU-T Recommendation Z.100,* 1995.

M. Jackson, *System Development,* Prentice-Hall, Englewood Cliffs, NJ, 1983.

I. Jacobson, M. Christerson, P. Jonsson, and G. Overgaard, *Object-Oriented Software Engineering: A Use-Case Driven Approach,* Addison-Wesley, Wokingham, UK, 1992.

J. Z. Lavi and J. Kudish, "Systematic Derivation of Operational Requirements Using the ECSAM Method," *Proceedings of the IEEE Computer Society Israel 7th Conference on Computer-Based Systems and Software Engineering,* June 1996.

J. Z. Lavi and M. Winokur, "ECSAM—A Method for the Analysis of Complex Embedded Computer Systems and their Software," *Proceedings of the 5th Structured Techniques Association Conference,* Chicago, May 1989.

J. Z. Lavi, M. Winokur, R. Gallant, and J. Kudish, *Embedded Computer Systems Specification and Design—the ECSAM Approach,* IAI Technical Report, October 1992.

J. Loeckx and K. Seiber, *The Foundations of Program Verification,* John Wiley & Sons, New York, 1984.

D. McCracken and M. Jackson, "Life Cycle Concept Considered Harmful," *ACM Software Engineering Notes,* (April 1982), pp. 29–32.

Z. Manna and A. Pnueli, *The Temporal Logic of Reactive and Concurrent Systems: Specification,* Springer-Verlag, New York, 1992.

Military Standard: Defense System Software Development, DOD-STD-2167A, U.S. Department of Defense, Washington, DC, February 1988.

Military Standard: Software Development and Documentation, MIL-STD-498, U.S. Department of Defense, Washington, DC, December 1994.

J. L. Peterson, *Petri Net Theory and Modeling of Systems,* Prentice-Hall, Englewood Cliffs, NJ, 1981.

Rational Corp., *Documents on UML (the Unified Modeling Language),* Version 1.1 (http://www.rational.com/uml/), 1997.

W. W. Royce, "Managing the development of large software systems: Concepts and techniques," *Proceedings IEEE WESCON,* August 1970, pp. 1–9.

J. Rumbaugh, M. Blaha, W. Premerlani, F. Eddy, and W. Lorensen, *Object-Oriented Modeling and Design,* Prentice-Hall, Englewood Cliffs, NJ, 1991.

B. Selic, G. Gullekson, and P. T. Ward, *Real-Time Object-Oriented Modeling,* John Wiley & Sons, New York, 1994.

D. J. Smith, *HDL Chip Design: A Practical Guide for Designing, Synthesizing and Simulating ASICs and FPGAs using VHDL or Verilog,* Doone Publications 1996 (2d 1997, with minor revisions).

R. H. Thayer and M. Dorfman, *System and Software Requirements Engineering,* IEEE Computer Society Press, 1990.

P. T. Ward, "How to Integrate Object Orientation with Structured Analysis and Design," *IEEE Software* (March 1989).

——— and S. J. Mellor, *Structured Development for Real-Time Systems,* Yourdon Press, New York, 1986.

D. P. Wood and W. G. Wood, "Comparative Evaluations of Four Specification Methods for Real-Time Systems," *Technical Report CMU/SEI-89-TR-36,* Software Engineering Institute, Carnegie-Mellon University, Pittsburgh, PA, 1989.

E. Yourdon and L. Constantine, *Structured Design,* Prentice-Hall, Englewood Cliffs, NJ, 1979.

P. Zave, "The Operational Versus the Conventional Approach to Software Development," *Communications of the ACM* (February 1984), pp. 104–118.

Index

ABOUT THE AUTHORS

David Harel is the Dean of Mathematics and Computer Science at the Weizmann Institute of Science in Rehovot, Israel. Dr. Harel is also the founder and chief scientist of I-Logix, Inc., the global firm that developed the STATEMATE system, and has been a visiting researcher and scientist at Carnegie-Mellon and Cornell Universities, as well as at Lucent Technologies, NASA, and IBM.

   Michal Politi, formerly Vice President of Development for I-Logix Israel, Ltd. was responsible for the methodology and implementation of STATEMATE. She has headed computer research and development projects for the Israeli Defense Forces.